Governing for Prosperity

EDITED BY
BRUCE BUENO DE MESQUITA AND HILTON L. ROOT

Governing for Prosperity

Yale University Press / New Haven and London

Designed by Mary Valencia. Set in Stone type by The Composing Room of Michigan,
Inc., Grand Rapids, Michigan.
Printed in the United States of America by Vail-Ballou Press, Binghamton, New York.

Library of Congress Cataloging-in-Publication Data

Governing for prosperity/edited by Bruce Bueno de Mesquita and Hilton L. Root.
    p.   cm
Includes bibliographical references and index.
ISBN 0-300-08017-4 (cloth : alk. paper)—ISBN 0-300-08018-2 (pbk : alk. paper)
1. Economic policy—Case studies. 2. Capitalism—Case studies. I. Bueno de
Mesquita, Bruce, 1946– II. Root, Hilton L.

HD87.G687 2000
338.9—dc21
99-057676

A catalogue record for this book is available from the British Library.

The paper in this book meets the guidelines for permanence and durability of the
Committee on Production Guidelines for Book Longevity of the Council on Library
Resources.

10 9 8 7 6 5 4 3 2 1

Contents

1. WHEN BAD ECONOMICS IS GOOD POLITICS

Bruce Bueno de Mesquita and Hilton L. Root

At the beginning of the twentieth century, one could reasonably argue, collective property yielded a path to prosperity and the unplanned swings of market forces could not possibly be superior to central planning. The empirical record has convincingly debunked what many wise people believed. Countries that adopted collectivist, centrally planned cheap labor experienced political and social upheaval. Market economies, by contrast, tended to experience relatively rapid economic growth, enhanced competitiveness, and relatively stable social and political orders, even as the cost of labor rose. The debate on the virtues of the socialist model as an alternative to capitalism seems settled; market economies enjoy a clear victory. Yet vast portions of humankind still live with the daily tragedy of hunger, poverty, and disease. These are preventable and are not the product of ignorance or of inevitable natural forces; rather, they are the product of reversible institutional and political failures caused by perverse incentives created by some political institutions.

Substantial variation in economic performance can no longer be attributed to ignorance about what makes an economy grow; observers must look elsewhere than at competing economic theories to explain national economic failure. Today, the key to economic success or failure—indeed, to a broad array of policy successes or failures—lies within the political institutions of sovereign states. Political arrangements create incentives for political leaders to foster growth or to steal their nation's prospects for prosperity. How to govern for prosperity is likely to be the most important policy puzzle of the twenty-first century.

The chapters on political economy in this volume attempt to provide useful solutions to this puzzle. Each chapter explores how institutional arrangements create and foster growth-oriented or growth-inhibiting incentives. The central thesis of this book is the following: given the state of knowledge about the economics of growth, the solution to poverty lies in the construction of political institutions that provide leaders with incentives to focus on the welfare of their citizens. Society does not have to wait for civic-minded leaders to improve citizen welfare, but it does have to construct institutions for growth that reflect the interest of leaders in securing political power. In too many instances, institutional arrangements turn bad public policy into good politics.

We identify two contrary impulses in politics: the impulse among politicians to fight over the distribution of goods and the impulse to coordinate the protection of future access to benefits. The choice between fighting over current distribution and coordinating on future benefits depends on the extent to which incumbents rely on allocating private goods or public goods to stay in office. That dependency, in turn, is a function of the political institutions under which they operate. Certain features of democracy promote a focus on public goods and on coordination, whereas key aspects of autocracy promote attentiveness to the allocation of private goods and, therefore, to questions of distribution.

Under normal circumstances governments allocate access to resources through taxation, regulation, and spending. Leaders can choose to allocate resources for the provision of public goods that benefit all or to provide private goods that benefit their cronies. When leaders provide privileged access to resources, they interfere with efficient distribution through the market's decentralized decision making, weakening the economy and diminishing the total resources at a leader's disposal. Why leaders would knowingly choose policies that lead to economic decline is one of the great conundrums that accounts for much of the world's poverty.

Economists typically view leaders as benign agents promoting the welfare of their society who would not knowingly precipitate an economic crisis. This book recognizes that deliberate policy failures are ubiquitous throughout history and seeks a solution to this dilemma in the incentives of leaders to stay in office. Political leaders want to stay in power. They are willing to purchase political loyalty at any cost to the economy, including providing privileged access to resources, thereby weakening the nation's economic performance. Although dispensing privilege may place the well-being of the national economy in jeopardy, leaders may disregard the economic costs until they run out of enough resources to stay in power: their focus is on political crisis, not economic crisis. A political crisis arises only when incumbents are not able to purchase sufficient loyalty to retain office. Politicians worry about an economic crisis when it becomes a political crisis.

The character of political institutions determines when an economic crisis becomes political. A society's political institutions are democratic, in part, when they require leaders to satisfy a large coalition of supporters in order to stay in office. When private goods must be divided among too many people to be of much value to most members of the winning coalition, then leaders are compelled to focus on allocating resources through the provision of public goods and, therefore, respect market decision making. By contrast, autocratic leaders generally require a much smaller winning coalition to stay in office. With a small winning coalition, autocrats can choose to use private goods as the means to stay in office, rewarding the cronies who make up their winning coalition. Thus, for autocrats, economic crises need not represent political crises and so they can attend to distribution problems without much concern for general or future prosperity. Democratic institutions deprive leaders of this choice, compelling leaders through formal, institutional constraints to provide effective public policy and avoid economic crises. This dynamic, more than elections, is the crux of the relationship between democracy and growth.

The literature on political institutions and economic growth uses the logic of democratic societies to analyze the stability of nondemocratic societies. In doing so, it attends to coordination issues as the main problem of politics and so views institutional transitions as dependent on coordination. This perspective has produced compelling explanations of how political crises lead to dramatic institutional transitions in which coordination among political rivals dominates their distributive decisions. Examples of such transformations include the French, Glorious, Russian, Tokagawan, American, and Chinese revolutions. As is evident from this list, some of the institutional transformations seem to have ensured an emphasis on coordination even after the crisis, while others have restored distributional conflicts as usual. Scholars have paid scant attention to the political rationality that underlies the persistence of regimes with poor public policy performance. Because such persistent regimes are largely overlooked, knowledge about transitions concerns important but rare events in which revolution is the product of the logic of coordination (Goldstone 1991; Moore 1966; Skocpol 1979; Tilly 1978, 1993).

Each chapter examines means of resolving or avoiding distribution and coordination problems as the way to settle or avert economic and political crises. Chapter 2, by North, Summerhill, and Weingast, highlights differences between successful and unsuccessful responses to economic crises. The authors identify the essential institutional characteristics of economic order and explain what political institutions require to sustain order. Their perspective does not explore why political authorities should be motivated to provide order. Thus, they provide one of the two conceptual frameworks in this book. The second framework, outlined in Chapter 3 by Bueno de Mesquita, Morrow, Siverson, and Smith, is concerned with the motivation of political authorities to sustain disorder or order. Many political regimes persist for long periods of time with high levels of disorder, such as in Mexico and India, both discussed in this book. In their discussion of Mexico in Chapter 5, Haber and Razo evaluate the costs and benefits of disorder and note that even revolutionary change cannot be counted on to resolve distribution issues or to alter the path of economic growth. In a complementary way, Root and Nellis show in Chapter 4 that the adoption of democratic principles of governance without the adoption of a democratic system of public administration likewise does not assure resolution of distributive problems that jeopardize economic growth. Zak's Chapter 6 focuses more generally on the impact of political instability on economic exchange, while Feng in Chapter 7 and Barro in Chapter 8 highlight the macro-effects of political institutions on economic growth rates.

Chapters 3 and 4 investigate the political incentives for leaders to promote order or to rule through disorder. These chapters deal with the range of political regimes that allow or even encourage leaders to rule by mismanaging their nation's resources. In that way, they offer a fresh perspective on how disorder can be incentive-compatible with political survival. They draw attention to divergences in private interests as a key feature of day-to-day politics and show when such divergences promote or inhibit political survival. By contrasting the focus on coordination in one set of chapters and the tensions arising from the clash of divergent interests in other chapters, this book covers the gamut of complementary insights on fundamental social change.

Typically, economists approach economic reform by assuming that decision makers and citizens have a common interest and that leaders simply need information about how best to realize those interests. We disagree. Distributional differences allow decision makers to resolve political differences through punishment strategies rather than through cooperation. Weaker parties, to be successful, must accept the status quo because they can increase their welfare only through the leader's largesse. When an economic crisis eliminates the leader's ability to distribute sufficient largesse, then the norm of political loyalty weakens, as it depended on the leader's ability to dispense private rewards. For this reason, crises provide a momentary opportunity for institutional change. The economist's approach to reform, then, is particularly well suited to designing interventions in crises, but it underestimates the strength of the conventions that sustain poor economic policies. A crisis can eliminate the ability of leaders to reward loyalty, thereby making economic change possible. However, only when crisis looms does such a perspective apply. Most of the time, societies are surrounded by economic policies that are deleterious to prosperity and social welfare. Economists provide economic policy solutions that are tried, tested, and true for promoting prosperity, but they rarely confront the political incentives that block economic reform. By identifying different institutional sources for these incentives, we attempt to provide a genuine political economy of economic reform and to bridge the gap between the solutions of economists and the political reality of obtaining and holding political power.

This book draws attention to the complementary institutional lessons to be drawn from the literature on resolving or managing distributional conflicts and the literature on shared risks and cooperation at moments of dramatic social change—moments that are often precipitated by the collapse of the existing governing apparatus. A fundamental problem in politics is that there are no clear ways simultaneously to resolve the problems of cooperation which predominate in crises and the problems of allocation or distribution (Morrow 1994), characteristic of politics as usual. The reason is straightforward. Coordination requires sharing information. Distributional motivations lead to the suppression of information. That is why governments, like democracies, that focus on coordination emphasize the transparency of laws and regulations, while autocracies emphasize the opaqueness that contributes to discretion. Crises provide a focal point for constructing new institutions because the divergent interests of elites are diminished by the lack of resources worth fighting over. When there is no crisis, rivalry over control of the society's wealth can eventually precipitate a crisis unless the elites agree to design institutions to prevent their competition from degenerating into plunder. Rare indeed are the situations in which political leaders have incentives to be so farsighted as to make substantial sacrifices in the present for the well-being of future generations.

HOW CAN GOVERNMENTS STAY IN POWER DESPITE FAILED OUTCOMES?

Something is fundamentally wrong when stealing a country's resources is a virtue. Yet, Mobutu Sese Seko, who ruled Zaire for over twenty years, provided an example—albeit extreme—of political leadership that is rapidly devastating the welfare of much of the world's population. He proclaimed: "You who have stolen money and put it into homes in Zaire and not abroad, I congratulate you."[1] Throughout much of the world, governments provide neither peace nor prosperity, and longevity of leadership inversely correlates with policy performance. Bueno de Mesquita, Morrow, Siverson, and Smith (Chapter 3) show that leaders in polities with autocratic institutions can enhance their prospects of remaining in office by over 40 percent under conditions of declining prosperity. By contrast, leaders in polities with more democratic institutions have more than a 50 percent increase in the risk of being ousted from office if they fail to produce economic growth. Policies required to produce prosperity often diminish a leader's hold on power, resulting in an inverse correlation between revenue growth and political survival. This book is designed to stimulate debate about how to alter this unfortunate correlation by identifying incentives to govern for prosperity.

Scholars commonly believe that regime type determines a government's responsiveness to the needs of its population. Cross-country comparisons do not support such a clean conclusion. India is a democracy with poor policies; Korea and Singapore undertook significant economic reforms as essentially one-party states. True, the majority of authoritarian governments failed to promote growth or to gain the business sector's confidence. However, the differences between so-called authoritarian states may be as great as what separates them from the democratic alternatives (Root 1996).

As Barro (Chapter 8) points out, democracy often leads to redistributive policies that stymie growth. Because the median voter in most democracies receives significant redistributive benefits, redistributive policy is attractive to a majority. In autocracies, leaders do not have to satisfy a majority; they have more latitude to do what they want with the economic surplus they control. Although some leaders may usurp that surplus for themselves, others are motivated to invest in successful growth policies. Because there is no median voter to consider in autocracies, the quality of their policies, including economic growth policies, would be expected to vary more than it does in democracies. In fact, the variance in economic growth rates for autocracies is about twice what it is for democracies.[2] Taiwan, Korea, Hong Kong, and Singapore were all autocratic when their leaders pursued growth-oriented policies.

Since 1974, peaceful transition to democracy has occurred in more than thirty dictatorships. The transition to successful economic policies has been less dramatic and is not the inevitable outcome of political transition. The relationship between political transitions and economic growth is complex. Political crises often provide the impetus for institutional changes that result in improved economic performance. Aaron Tornell has calculated that "between 1970 and 1995, virtually 80% of trade reforms occurred during periods of either economic crisis or drastic political change, although the probability that a reform occurs in a particular country-year is 3%, this probability [if] conditional on a crisis and a drastic political change is 60%."[3]

Yet, crises also create great uncertainty that discourages investment. The net effect of such political instability, thus, is not clear-cut. North, Summerhill, and Weingast (Chapter 2) argue that political order is critical for growth. Their argument focuses on resolving commitment problems that make investors leery. For instance, they note that without political institutions that assure the protection of property rights, it is extremely difficult to attract investment. Their analysis compares the United States and Latin America over time. Examining economic growth in seven geographic regions for the past thirty years, Feng (Chapter 7) also concludes that stability, along with political consensus and political and economic freedom, promotes growth. Zak (Chapter 6) provides carefully reasoned theoretical arguments for the importance of political stability in promoting growth. He explores how instability leads to the deflection of resources away from their most efficient application. Yet, Haber and Razo (Chapter 5) contend that, in Mexico at least, "the periods of political instability . . . had relatively minor effects on investor confidence, investments in new plant and equipment, rates of entry and exit by firms, industrial structure or productivity growth."

Table 1.1 presents the empirical record with regard to economic growth and three distinct indicators of political instability: the number of major institutional changes per year in each country examined, the number of major cabinet changes, and the number of attempted coups d'état. The table helps sort out the seeming contradiction between Haber and Razo's claim that in-

Table 1.1. Instability and Economic Growth Rates

Variables	Coefficient	Robust Std. Error	Probability
Constant	0.050	0.003	0.000
Institutional change	0.003	0.002	0.068
Cabinet change	−0.011	0.005	0.021
Coups d'état	−0.028	0.009	0.003

Note: $N = 2,141$; $F = 5.87$; $R^2 = 0.06$; $p = 0.001$.

stitutional instability is not problematic for growth and the claims by Feng, Zak, and North and colleagues that political order is essential for growth. As shown, institutional changes by themselves do not have a significant impact on growth, exactly as Haber and Razo claim. Yet fundamental changes in political leadership, such as accompany coups d'état and major cabinet changes, do significantly diminish the prospects of growth. Institutions themselves can be impediments to or assets for growth. Therefore, changing them can influence growth for the good or for the bad. If institutions are devised to protect leaders who perform poorly or if the enforcement of law is weak so that institutional constraints are easily circumvented, then change can be good for prosperity. If the existing institutions are enforced and punish poor policy performance and they are changed, then the changes can be expected to hinder growth. It is easy to erect institutions with the gloss of the rule of law. The key is to ensure that politicians are given institutional incentives to enforce the rules and govern in the spirit of the constitution. Stable institutions, by themselves, neither promote nor hinder growth. Stable institutions that constrain economic risk taking by failing to protect property rights, for instance, are harmful to economic welfare especially because they are stable.

If the knowledge of what makes markets work effectively is widely known, then we must explain why so many governments resist changing their policies and their institutions until forced to do so in order to surmount a crisis. The difficult puzzle is to explain how some can lead without regard to the welfare of their society, whereas others, who may be no more civic-minded, are compelled by institutional arrangements to govern for the good of their citizens.

A THEORY OF POLITICS

In order to understand why countries reform their policies and institutions, it is necessary first to understand the institutional context of political competition within sovereign nations. The rules by which a country determines its leadership also determine how the economy is managed and in whose interests. The key to governmental responsiveness lies in part in the relationship between the size of the selectorate, the subset of the population that chooses the country's political leadership, and the size of the winning coalition that keeps the incumbent in office.[4] The size of the governing coalition affects how different the interests of the country's political leadership are when compared to those of citizens at large. Incumbent leaders select and implement public policies that have public or private goods components. They can put everything into public policy that benefits everyone or into private goods consumed only by members of the winning coalition, or they can provide any mix of public and private benefits to their followers and to the citizens at large.

As the winning coalition grows in size, the incumbent is able to offer less in the way of benefits to particular members of the coalition. This means that to ensure a focus on public policy, the winning coalition must be so large that its members can gain very little from private allocations because those allocations would be spread too broadly to be financially attractive. To compete with challengers who offer voters alternative policies, leaders must offer the majority of the selectorate better policies. Thus, policy-based competition is characteristic of polities dominated by large winning coalitions.

Only the winning coalition enjoys private goods allocated by leadership. If members of the coalition defect, they risk forfeiting access to private goods. If the selectorate is large, defectors from the winning coalition will have limited hope of forming an alternative winning coalition that includes them. Knowing this, leaders will offer the minimum of private goods and keep the surplus for themselves (as in the case of Mobutu, Suharto, or Marcos). Thus, when the coalition is small, leadership has the option of managing the nation's resources such that the surplus is transferred to the holders of political authority.

The small coalition presents problems analogous to those posed by the ownership position of firm management in the private economy. If management does not own equity in the firm, it will be more reckless with its investment decisions, or it may underinvest in the country's future prosperity. Similarly, the size of the winning coalition can provide political leadership with incentives to devise effective policies by affecting conflicts of interest between the governing elite and the citizens who will absorb the cost of poor policies. When winning coalitions are small, two sets of conflicting interests occur: moral hazard occurs, so that leadership has no stake in controlling costs and maximizing the value of investments; and leadership may choose investments that benefit themselves rather than the welfare of the country. They will be more likely to choose investments that are not profitable or are not in the citizens' interests but from which they can gain personally.

One source of conflict is that political leaders, that is, the managers, will try to increase the size of the economy they control by increasing state intervention in allocative decisions. By increasing the size of the state, they gain opportunities for distributing and collecting rents. Management will be tempted to spend too much on perks for themselves because they enjoy the perks and bear only part of the cost. Government will design procedures to maintain independence from outside interference or citizen oversight. Investment priorities will be further distorted when governments enjoy large flows of donor money for which they are not accountable to any local constituency. A gross misalignment of incentives occurs when leaders can extract private profits from projects contracted in the name of the country. They can borrow far too much for projects that are not required to contribute to a country's social resources.

WHY DEMOCRACY IS NOT SUFFICIENT
Democracy is often valued as a mechanism that ensures competition within a country's leadership for the promotion of successful policies; it is assumed that voters will dismiss governments that produce policy failures. The president of the United States, his secretary of state, the Agency for International Development, and numerous other entities in the United States government, for instance, have declared that the promotion of democracy is one of their central goals. Democracy is generally taken, in policy declarations, to mean the free and competitive selection of government leaders and the protection and promotion of civil rights. The correlation between wealth and democracy is often confused with a causal argument in which open elections are presumed to lead directly to growth. That is not to say that democracy is antithetical to growth. After all, almost all the wealthy nations in the world are democratic. However, as the case of India, the Third World's largest and oldest democracy, indicates democratic governance does not necessarily engender effective policy performance. As discussed in Chapter 4, India's free, competitive elections can be accompanied by economic policies that foster poverty and social unrest rather than peace and prosperity. The Third World's most consistent and stable democracy offers a compelling example of the reasons that democracy—that is, elections—are not sufficient for policy accountability and that political parties that fail to enhance social welfare through successful policy processes continue to be elected. Those poor policies are generally consistent with institutional arrangements that offer incentives for leadership to compete through patronage rather than through effective policies.

Why has India's democracy not engendered accountable political organizations or the capacity for effective policy making? The primacy of patronage politics in India has led to elections that are personality driven. Political mobilization via patronage robs the government of its ability to protect rights in a rule-bound fashion. Leaders who come to office by virtue of their personal appeal are likely to rule by fiat rather than by means of rules and established procedures. Their patrimonial leadership has emasculated the state, privatized the public realm, and eroded public institutions without empowering civil society. Personalization of authority eventually ends in venality and the misuse of authority, illegitimacy, corruption, deinstitutionalization, and ungovernability. The leaders of India's Congress Party championed democracy as a way to foster public judgment, civic responsibility, and problem-solving capabilities in the population. They hoped that a strong civil society would subject the state to legal constraint and public accountability. This ideal and the reality of holding power have come apart. To consolidate political power, Congress disbursed patronage rather than policy goods. Congress leaders used their access to official positions to reward followers. Empowering local power brokers, or "big men," with access to governmental services controlled by the party, Congress created a patronage network that spanned all of India.

Because of bloc voting, India's governing coalitions represent a small subset of the selectorate, allowing the governments to rule through private goods disbursement. Real political competition does not exist in patronage systems because the incumbent dominates the resources necessary to win votes. Leaders can maximize the welfare of their followers through the distribution of patronage. Once out of power, however, they can easily be made to appear incompetent because they no longer have access to the patronage goods necessary to win electoral favor. Challengers can promise to change the distributional mix so that followers coalesce around ethnic loyalties rather than public policy issues, giving political bosses power over ethnic blocs that can be manipulated to support particular candidates. Although large numbers of citizens receive tangible benefits from the government, candidates who are committed to reforming the public sector do not succeed.

Committing resources to implement effective policies is politically unnecessary when the disbursement of private goods to winning coalitions is the key to electoral competition. Indeed, because public policies are enjoyed by all constituents, whether they have supported the would-be provider or not, there is little incentive to forgo the chance to acquire private goods by defecting from a winning coalition in order to back a challenger who promises public policy benefits instead. Unless the institutional structure changes incentives, strategically sophisticated "voters" will have no reason to back policy-oriented candidates in bloc-voting or small winning coalition systems.

Nontransparent political institutions will be preferred over transparent ones, enabling leadership to transfer public resources to constituents. When special privileges, access to graft and bribes, tax loopholes, sweetheart deals for cronies, and judicial favoritism are the basis of electoral competition, poor institutions will serve more effectively than good institutions. Private goods can be distributed to compensate supporters for poor policy performance. When electoral support does not depend on their policy performance, politicians have no incentive to invest in effective institutions or in policies that will yield broad economic benefits.

Despite gross failure, civil service reform has not been seriously undertaken in much of the Third World because political competition is based on private goods allocation. When politicians receive utility from the allocation of private goods rather than from policy performance, few opportunities in government exist for technically competent individuals. Again, South Asia serves as a useful example. India, Pakistan, Sri Lanka, and Bangladesh all export their highly trained professionals, whereas East Asian governments compete to keep theirs by paying them well (Campos and Root 1996).

In a patronage system, leaders do not have to worry about policy outcomes as much as they do about private goods. When institutional objectives are diverted from converting public assets into private ones, managerial incentive problems are purposely created. The government generates imperfect information, and to mask any government abuse of power it limits public information about the efficiency of its agents. The ability to choose policies or to change in response to new information reflects the existence of effective institutions. Instead, governments may devise systems that provide imperfect information on resource management. Mistakes are hard to see, and because the costs and benefits are borne by different individuals, there is no incentive to reveal mismanagement. Institutions are maintained to keep the consequences of policies hidden so that government can be strategically managed to produce outcomes that are not transparent and for which leaders are not held accountable.

SYSTEMIC SOURCES OF CORRUPTION

Corruption often represents the willful deviation from political outcomes that are valued by the majority when private rather than public goods keep politicians in office. Government can increase its ability to dole out corrupt rewards by exercising control over profits and competition in the marketplace. By reducing competition in the marketplace, governments create opportunities for private gain. Corruption can be such a highly valued, politically determined good that leaders will organize the economy to maximize opportunities for their followers to collect bribes. They do so by controlling, for example, import/export licenses, foreign currency allocations, and building permits.

Although bribery is the most easily detected form of corruption, it is usually just the tip of the iceberg. One of the most insidious abuses that occur when public power is used for private gain results from an inappropriate pattern of governmental expenditures. When the governing coalition is small, government can increase its share of revenue by shifting the composition of expenditures to those areas from which it can collect bribes. Governments may over-invest in big-ticket projects whose economic value is difficult to assess— bridges, dams, rockets, jets—rather than in human resource development. It should not be surprising that social spending increases with the size of the winning coalition. Over 30 percent of all variation in levels of human capital from 1961 to 1982, for instance, is accounted for by the size of the winning coalition and the size of the selectorate, as shown in Table 1.2.

Governments with small winning coalitions underinvest in human capital because the choice of government expenditures reflects kickbacks to the decision makers. This is why militarism and small governing coalitions often coalesce. Military budgets provide great opportunities for corruption among top political leaders. In the procurement of military hardware the monetary amount that constitutes a kickback to decision makers is difficult to determine. Education, by contrast, is typically underfunded because the kickbacks are not attractive. Social spending as a percentage of total government expenditure is particularly low when governing coalitions are small, because the opportunities for graft in education are dispersed too broadly to be of interest to a tightly knit leadership clique. Hence, government expenditure on education, health, and housing as a percentage of total expenditure is lowest in those countries ruled by small winning coalitions. Even when social expenditures are made, the funds will be ineffectively allocated unless government invests heavily in managing delivery systems.

DISCIPLINING THE BEHAVIOR OF THE GOVERNING COALITION
Because political parties in the developing world are often fronts for powerful private interests or individuals, a democracy must be defined as more than a

Table 1.2. Political Institutions and Average Labor Force Education

Variables	Coefficient	Robust Std. Error	Probability
Winning coalition size	6.85	1.15	0.000[a]
Selectorate size	−1.63	0.90	0.037[a]
Constant	1.85	0.63	0.004

Note: $N = 2,045$; $F = 22.33$; $R^2 = 0.31$. [a]One-tailed significance.

system of government that holds multiparty elections. Designing mechanisms to ensure that large selectorates and large winning coalitions function to impose accountability is the primary challenge. Individual citizens have little reason to monitor the government's performance or diligence. Only those with a large stake in the outcome of a particular policy or regulation are likely to do significant monitoring. The ownership share of citizens in their country's development is generally not sufficiently concentrated to ensure that management does not waste the country's resources. Only citizens with a large stake have the incentive to pay the costs of monitoring the actions of government officials. Dispersing control rights through a large selectorate makes it difficult for citizens to monitor what leaders do. Incentives for accountability are actually relaxed by the existence of a large selectorate if governance rests in the hands of a narrow clique. The problem of inadequate monitoring is a free rider problem that arises when an individual bears the bulk of the cost of the monitoring effort but shares the benefits that result from monitoring with all other citizens.

The ways leaders address the interests of key economic interest groups can have a direct and significant impact on the policies adopted. Countries that care to restrain the opportunism of government develop institutions that concentrate monitoring among those groups with an interest in the outcome. The leaders of East Asia's high-performing countries found a solution to this dilemma by concentrating large shareholders in deliberation councils to monitor the agencies and policies that matter to their sector (Campos and Root 1996). Deliberation councils give citizens with a concentrated interest in a particular government policy a role in its monitoring.

Professional ethos and institutions to safeguard professional reputations tend to be lacking in the developing world because professional associations that practice peer monitoring are typically absent. Institutions that nurture concern for professional reputation or consequent market opportunities by collectively monitoring reputations can significantly improve the trade environment. Professionals who reliably assess the quality of professional services offered by peers have played a major role in improving public sector performance in the now developed Western countries (Greif, Milgrom, and Weingast 1994).

Economic and political reform usually reflects a power struggle among the elite. This phenomenon has been observed throughout history. Because most political change emerges from crises, many countries experience uneven growth. East Asia's high-performing economies, by contrast, have experienced few boom and bust cycles because their key interest groups have consistently played a monitoring role, thereby keeping government officials focused on providing successful public policies. Political reform is a consequence of crisis because few leaders are motivated to create institutions that favor growth over the allocation of private goods to a few core constituents. Only those leaders who are unusually competent at producing public goods are inclined to change institutions to favor prosperity. However, the elite on whom incumbents depend to retain their hold on office often have incentives to modify institutions in a way that results in greater prosperity.

Members of autocratic winning coalitions have, as we intimated earlier, a norm of loyalty to the incumbent because of the private goods they are receiving. The leader, who in turn counts on the loyalty of the winning coalition, is free to skim substantial resources for his or her own use. Of course, members of the winning coalition want more of those resources to go to them. Therefore, they have an incentive to weaken the expectation of their loyalty. A key way to do so is to propose institutional changes that expand the size of the winning coalition, thereby reducing the narrow focus of existing privileges. A direct though unintended consequence of the winning coalition's interest in expanding its access to resources is that the quality of public policy improves, benefiting the greater society (Bueno de Mesquita, Morrow, Siverson, and Smith 1999).[5] This improvement in public policy arises because as the winning coalition expands, to remain in office the incumbent must provide more public goods and fewer private goods. This is one explanation of why pressure arising from competition among the elite can lead to trade liberalization and the opening of an economy.

INSTITUTIONAL CHOICE AND ECONOMIC GROWTH

Although the study of the political foundations of market economies is still in its infancy, the chapters that follow firmly support the following conclusion: the great political transition toward effective governance of the market economy occurs when abstract policy making and goal setting supplant the satisfaction of private interests as the primary purpose of government. Institutions that make leaders accountable for policy performance are the basis of this transition. Policies that are identified with market-led growth have been the products of institutions that motivated politicians to provide effective policy outcomes to their constituents.

More than two thousand cases across more than eighty countries—spanning decades and even centuries—have illustrated that when governing coalitions are a small subset of the population, they are not constrained to select investments that maximize the total value of the nation's output. Instead, these coalitions choose to invest in ways that build the private fortunes of the members of society whose support sustains those in power. The design of incentive and coordination systems to help structure and manage economies to better serve broad social interests distinguishes those countries that can sustain growth from those that fail. Social conflict, crime, and other sources of political instability are major deterrents to investment (see Chapter 6). Much of that instability reflects a control contest between citizens and the small coalitions that govern the allocation of resources. The battle over control will become violent unless a reform bargain is struck by which all social groups will benefit from growth. The designing of political institutions that allow the peaceful, cooperative settlement of such inevitable control battles is the key to long-term growth because it reduces the dramatic expressions of social instability that pose the greatest risk to continuous economic development. As Chapters 2, 5, 6, and 7 ably demonstrate, managing the threat of instability greatly facilitates prosperity. Large winning coalitions are one of the strongest factors reducing the threat of coups d'état, nonconstitutional changes in leadership, and other sources of growth-inhibiting instability.

The design issue—forging institutions to make political leaders responsible for policy outcomes—must be resolved within the confines of national sovereignty. Institutions that make politicians accountable domestically for policy outcomes will be focal points of accountability in the emergence of international capital markets. Capital will follow where the institutions of good governance have been established domestically. Nations can benefit from international capital flows by crafting institutional structures that allow all social groups to participate in and benefit from the growing sectors of the economy. The alternative is political instability and growth corruption which benefits a narrow elite stratum for short periods of time only.

How to govern for prosperity may well be the most significant policy question in the coming century. By providing answers to this dilemma, the study of political economy can help turn the twenty-first century into the first period in human history in which hunger and abject poverty are banished from the human experience. By demonstrating the link between institutional choice and economic growth, the following chapters seek to shed light on ways to solve this puzzle.

Notes

1. *The Economist,* September 28, 1996, p. 53.
2. The statistics on growth rates for autocracies versus democracies are as follows:

	Growth Rate N	Variance	Min	Max
Autocracies	1,075	0.0049	−0.370	0.360
Democracies	1,191	0.0023	−0.266	0.288

Data on regime type are from the Polity III data; growth rates are Heston-Summers's data, from Fischer (1993).

3. A. Tornell, 1998.

4. Bueno de Mesquita and colleagues examine the effect of two institutions: the size of the selectorate and the size of the winning coalition. "Rigged election" autocracies typically have a large selectorate and a small winning coalition. Democracies typically have a large selectorate and a large winning coalition. Military juntas and monarchies generally have a small selectorate and a small winning coalition. A large selectorate, coupled with a small winning coalition, induces the members of the winning coalition to be loyal to the incumbent leadership by raising the risk and cost of defection, as explained in Chapter 3.

5. Bueno de Mesquita and colleagues also show special circumstances under which the winning coalition prefers to reduce its size.

2. ORDER, DISORDER, AND ECONOMIC CHANGE
LATIN AMERICA VERSUS NORTH AMERICA

Douglass C. North, William Summerhill, and Barry R. Weingast

INTRODUCTION

Successful societies require a means for securing political order. That scholars often take order for granted in developed societies does not imply that it is unimportant. Although most economists ignore problems of disorder, creating order is a task necessary to establishing the foundations of long-term economic growth. As the turmoil in post-independence Spanish America—or today in the former Yugoslavia and the Great Lakes region of Central Africa—demonstrates, political order is not automatic. Political order is a public good that must be carefully constructed.

Because political order is a necessary condition for economic and political development, we must enquire about the conditions that provide for it. Citizens behave very differently under political disorder, that is, when they fear for their lives, their families, and their sources of livelihood. Focusing solely on market reform or the instruments of democracy is insufficient to help a developing state or one in transition move onto the path of development. We argue that the sources of political order involve state capacity concerning the creation of credible commitments.

Establishing and maintaining social order in the context of dynamic change has been an age-old dilemma of societies and continues to be a central problem in the modern world (Huntington 1968). It is one thing to establish order in societies; it is something else to maintain order in the process of economic and political change. The issue is at the core of understanding the nature of political-economic change over time.

The contrasting historical experiences of Latin America and North America provide an ideal comparative study to explore the issues. In the remainder of this introductory section we describe why the two areas are such a valuable source of comparative study, we go on to provide a brief comparison of their contrasting political/economic histories in the late eighteenth and early nineteenth centuries, and we explore the relevance of a standard factor endowments model of trade theory as an explanation for the contrasting histories. In the second section, we develop a theoretical framework to analyze those contrasting stories. The third section applies the analysis to the first fifty years of U.S. independence in British North America and the fourth section applies the framework to the first fifty years of Latin American independence. The final section evaluates the reasons underlying the different political/economic paths of British North America and Spanish America.

The modern states of Latin America and British North America began as overseas colonies of the rising hegemonic nations of Europe; the former by the Spanish and Portuguese, the latter by the English and French. Although the successful discovery of "treasure" biased early Spanish development, both areas were amply endowed with natural resources. Both the American colonies and the Spanish colonies achieved independence in the late eighteenth and early nineteenth centuries after revolutionary wars. But at this point the similarities stop.

During the late eighteenth and the first half of the nineteenth century, the United States created a stable political democracy and was well on its way to becoming the richest economy in the world. The institutional foundations were the Constitution, which replaced the Articles of Confederation, and a stable, well-specified system of economic and political rights that together provided the credible commitment that was a necessary prerequisite to efficient economic markets. In contrast, after independence most of Spain's former colonies on the mainland imploded in a costly and deadly spiral of warfare, *pronunciamientos* (organized revolts against the government), and *caudillismo* (the political phenomenon of local or regional political bosses who have a comparative advantage in the use of violence, in particular against other political groups or factions). This spiral continued through mid-century. Disorder prevailed for decades, revealing the absence of institutional arrangements capable of establishing cooperation among rival groups. Destructive conflict, rooted in the independence struggles and disputes over early republican state-building, diverted capital and labor from production and consigned the new nations to a path of stunningly poor performance in comparison to the United States. Even the nations that remained relatively orderly—Brazil and Chile—established centralized governments and economic policies that provided little incentive for economic expansion. Throughout Latin America, state monopolies previously reserved to kings persisted under independent governments.

The United States, too, experienced disorder in the mid–nineteenth century. Indeed, the American Civil War was one of the most deadly and costly wars of that century. But that war was only a brief interruption to both political democracy and economic growth; within two decades of war's end, the healing process was well under way. The former Confederate states had been reintegrated into the polity, and by then the American economy led the world in manufacturing capacity, agricultural output, and per capita income.

In turning to the toolbox of the social scientist, international trade models building on contrasting factor endowments provide a useful first step toward an explanation. Much of the early history of Latin America, the Caribbean, and part of what is now the southern United States was based on large plantation agriculture or slavery in mining. At independence this implied both huge disparities in wealth and significant racial diversity throughout the Caribbean and Latin America. In British North America, especially in New England and the middle Atlantic states, the climate favored grain agriculture. These regions were not considered particularly valuable at the beginning of the European settlement of the new world. Economic production in this region reflected few economies of scale and did not lend itself to the profitable employment of slaves. Endowments had two direct effects on the polity, both favorable to economic growth. First, the disposal of land and the size of farms resulted in a relatively equal distribution of wealth; second, the unprofitability of slavery resulted in racial homogeneity. In Latin America, huge inequalities and racial diversity translated into substantial political hurdles to the establishment of secure political foundations for economic growth.[1]

The phenomena of disorder, violence, and economic decline—pervasive throughout post-independence Spanish America—cannot be accounted for in a trade model, however. Factor endowments were constant across independence—in terms of both traditional economic factors, such as land, labor, and capital, and broader ones, such as climate, the distribution of wealth, and the racial mix. Although factor endowments were one of the important sources of the American Civil War, they do not explain America's rapid recovery from disorder and its renewal of economic growth. Indeed, nothing about the new political order in the United States was automatic. Several critical events—such as the transformation of the Articles of Confederation into the Constitution—could have easily failed, greatly hindering the rise of the United States to the richest nation in the world. Nor were the internecine wars inevitable following independence throughout Spanish America. No deus ex machina translates endowments into political outcomes. If that were so, Argentina would be as rich as the United States, and Hong Kong, Japan, and South Africa would never have become rich.

What is missing from the standard economist's approach is an understanding of the mechanisms that translate ex ante conditions—such as beliefs, institutions, and endowments—into political outcomes, including order and disorder.

A THEORY OF POLITICAL ORDER AND DISORDER

We begin our analysis by defining political order and describing its characteristics in a static environment. We next define the conditions for disorder and the conditions for the movement from order to disorder. We are then in a position to explore the process of change and the way in which it can produce either order or disorder.

Political Order

For an individual, we define *political order* as requiring three fundamental aspects of personal security: one's life, family, and source of livelihood. We say that order holds for a society when it holds for most or all individuals. For society, we define *disorder* as the opposite; a large proportion fears for its lives, families, or sources of livelihood and wealth.

Political order exists ideally—and in game theory—when the participants find it in their interest, given their expectations about the actions of others, to obey the written or unwritten rules that call for respect for one another. In sociology, conformity is usually attributed to the internalization of social norms; individuals want to behave in ways conducive to the existing social order. In this way, social control is exercised over potential deviance by others. This requires that, in equilibrium, all members of society have an incentive to obey and enforce the rules and that a sufficient number are motivated to punish potential deviants (Calvert 1995).

A system of order has the following characteristics:

1. An institutional matrix that produces a set of organizations and establishes a set of rights and privileges
2. A stable structure of exchange relationships in both political and economic markets
3. An underlying set of institutions that credibly commits the state to a set of political rules and enforcement of rights protecting the organizations and exchange relationships
4. Conformity as a result of some mixture of norm internalization and external (to the individual) enforcement

Disorder occurs when:

1. Rights and privileges of individuals and organizations are up for grabs, implying disruption of existing exchange relationships in both economic and political markets
2. Conformity disappears as a result of either disintegration of norms and/or change in enforcement

The first point of political order recognizes that the political system defines and enforces citizens' rights, including their freedom to organize and exchange. No assumption is made about the extent and scope of these rights and freedoms. Points three and four require that these rights and freedoms exist in practice, not just in theory. The third point requires that those rights and freedoms that exist in practice reflect a degree of credible commitment that makes it in the interests of political officials to observe them. Point four specifies that citizens have an incentive to conform with those social and political norms that exist. Finally, the first point under disorder implies the negation of the first three points under political order.

Let us draw out the logic of these ideas. The approach rests on the observation that individuals behave differently under political order than under political disorder. Individuals who fear for their families, livelihoods, or wealth make different choices from those who do not. Creating order is a central task in the establishment of the foundations of long-term economic growth. As the turmoil in post-independence Spanish America demonstrates, political order is not automatic.[2] As with macroeconomic stability, political order is a public good that must be carefully constructed.

To the extent that order occurs in a given society, it is provided through the political system. So, too, is the choice of the form of an economy, for example, a market economy versus a centrally regulated one. Establishing political order involves what political scientists sometimes call "state-building" (Evans et al. 1985; Skocpol 1979; Skowronek 1982)—identified here as creating the capacity to promote political order. To address questions about political order, we draw on our earlier work (North 1990; North and Weingast 1989; Weingast 1995; and Summerhill 1999) as well as that of Greif (1998), Eggertsson (1990), and Liebcap (1989).

Our answer about the sources of political order involves state capacity concerning the creation of credible commitments. Secure property rights, for example, are essential to any market economy. Yet, economists rarely think about the political assumptions necessary to maintain secure property rights. To see that economists make political assumptions, consider the *fundamental political dilemma of an economy* (Weingast 1995): any government strong enough to protect property rights, enforce contracts, and provide macroeconomic stability is also strong enough to confiscate all of its citizens' wealth. A central task for understanding long-term economic development is to discover what determines when a government does one or the other. We argue that endowments alone do not determine the outcome, though endowments may greatly influence the form of government and hence the ability of a government to provide credible commitments.

Finally, the foregoing list provides the conditions for political order, but not for economic growth. For the latter to occur, in addition, the institutional matrix would have to provide positive incentives for the organizations' entrepreneurs to engage in productive activities (North 1990; Bueno de Mesquita, Morrow, Siverson, and Smith 1998). Economic growth thus requires both political order and a range of positive incentives for productive and entrepreneurial activity.

Sources of Order and Disorder

A bare-bones description of the process of change is straightforward. The "reality" of a political/economic system is never known to anyone, but human beings do construct elaborate beliefs about the nature of that "reality"—beliefs that are both a positive model of the way the system works and a normative model of how it should work. The belief system may be broadly held within a society; alternatively, widely disparate beliefs may be held. The dominant beliefs (that is, of those political and economic entrepreneurs in a position to make policies) over time result in the accretion of an elaborate structure of institutions—both formal rules and informal norms—that determine economic and political performance. At any moment in time this institutional matrix imposes severe constraints on the choice set of entrepreneurs seeking to improve their political or economic positions. The resultant path dependence typically makes change incremental. But change is continually occurring (although the rate will depend on the degree of competition among organizations and their entrepreneurs), resulting in alterations of the institutional matrix, revisions of perceptions of reality, and therefore new efforts of entrepreneurs to improve their position in a never-ending process of change. Change can also result from non-human-induced changes in the environment, such as natural disasters; but overwhelmingly it is humans themselves who incrementally alter the human landscape.

Now we are in a position to relate the process to the foregoing analysis of sources of order and disorder. The place to begin is with the beliefs held by the members of a society, because it is the beliefs which translate into the institutions that shape performance. Shared mental models reflecting a common belief system will translate into a set of institutions broadly conceived to be legitimate (Denzau and North 1994). Diverse and conflicting beliefs usually are derived from wide disparities in the experiences of members of a society (resulting from differences in wealth, social structure, race, ethnic backgrounds) and are exacerbated by the failure to define and enforce universalistic political and economic rules that apply to all members of that society (see, e.g., Horowitz 1985).

Whether the change is incremental or revolutionary, the result is typically to produce some consequences that are unanticipated. This is so because: people's perceptions of reality are faulty; the belief system produces an "incorrect" model of the issues; and the policy instruments available to the players are very blunt instruments to achieve the desired objectives. Let us explore each of these in turn.

A complete understanding of reality would entail not only information about all relevant aspects of the society but an understanding of how it all is put together. As Hayek pointed out many times, such knowledge is beyond human capacity.

The belief systems that society develops can and sometimes do capture sufficient portions of that "reality" to provide useful and predictable results. But frequently they fail to incorporate fundamental aspects of reality, particularly involving circumstances people rarely face. The rise and demise of communism provides only the most recent illustration.

The policy instruments available to the players are changes in the formal rules (constitutions, laws, regulations), but it is the combination of formal rules, informal norms, and their enforcement that constitute the institutional matrix that shapes performance. Policy makers have no control, at least in the short run, over informal norms and only very imperfect control over enforcement of both the formal rules and the informal norms. In consequence, policies—such as privatization in Russia—often produce results different from those anticipated.

Finally, we come back to path dependence. It is a powerful phenomenon, resulting from a range of constraints imposed on the players. Because existing organizations (and their entrepreneurs) owe their survival to the existing institutional matrix, they tend to oppose fundamental institutional change. Equally important is the existing belief system that defines the perceptions of the actors with respect to avenues of legitimate change. Attempts at revolutionary action, for example, alter only the formal rules, not the informal norms, and therefore usually make such change less revolutionary than its supporters envision.

Theoretical Propositions

We offer two sets of propositions: about conditions for political order in a society, and about political disorder. Two different bases of political order exist, each with its distinctive type of politics, economics, and political institutions. We call the first the consensual basis for political order. Under this type of order, political officials observe a series of universal citizen rights. These governments tend to be democratic with a market economy. We call the second the authoritarian basis for political order. Under this type of political order, political officials cannot sustain a set of universal rights, and instead abuse the rights of a major portion (if not all) of the citizenry. These governments draw support from a limited portion of citizens, and tend to be authoritarian and unable to sustain a market economy. In reality, our ideal types set up a continuum of types between the ideals; for the purposes of this chapter, however, we discuss the ideal types. We now discuss the logic underlying the two types of political order.

Consensual political order. For political officials to adhere to a set of citizen rights under the consensual basis of order, these rights must be self-enforcing. That is, it must be in the interests of political officials to honor those rights (Ordeshook 1992; Weingast 1995). Although this proposition is easy to state, the general conditions underlying constitutional stability have proven difficult to uncover. In what follows, we provide several insights into this question.

Our first principle of political order concerns the relationship between a shared belief system about the legitimate ends of government and the extent of citizen rights.[3] All rights accorded to citizens—whether personal, economic, religious, civil, or political—imply limits on the behavior of political officials. These hardly constitute rights if political officials can violate them at will. Stable democratic constitutions, for example, require that political officials observe a set of limits regarding citizen expression, freedom of organization, and leadership succession; economic growth requires that political officials honor a series of property rights associated with markets; and secure religious freedom requires that political officials allow freedom of observance and organization.

For these rights to exist in practice, political officials must (somehow) find it in their interests to observe these rights. The key to the consensual basis of political order is the establishment of credible bounds on the behavior of political officials. Put another way, citizen rights and the implied bounds on government must be self-enforcing for political officials.

The nature of beliefs about the state—including those about various rights—determines in part whether political officials honor citizen rights (Weingast 1997). To see this, suppose that a consensus exists in society over the appropriate rights accorded citizens and the legitimate ends of the state; further, suppose that citizens are willing to react against political leaders who transgress these rights. Then political officials in this society will respect these rights. Because violation of rights under these conditions risks a leader's political future, the leader will honor them. In this case, we can say that the rights—and the implied limits on the behavior of political officials—are self-enforcing.

In contrast, the absence of consensus over rights and ends of the state implies that a leader can transgress what some citizens consider their fundamental rights while still maintaining sufficient support from other citizens to survive. In this case, the rights are not self-enforcing. The absence of a consensus and therefore of the protection of citizen rights provides the basis for authoritarian political order.

Because the experience and interests of citizens diverge markedly, most societies are characterized by a lack of consensus. They are therefore not likely to honor economic, political, and personal rights associated with liberal democracy and a market economy.

Creating a shared belief system in a society is a type of coordination problem with a vast number of potential solutions (Weingast 1997). Policing the behavior of political officials requires that citizens react in concert when officials violate their rights. The threat of withdrawal of political support, rarely needed to be made explicit in secure democracies, is part of what keeps political officials in line. The central problem facing citizens therefore concerns how citizens come to agreement about the types of actions that should trigger their reactions against the state. Because citizens' political, economic, and social positions typically differ considerably, there is no natural coordination solution to this problem.

A major factor determining whether a consensus occurs in a given society is whether political leaders have, at some point, created a focal solution to the coordination problem. Creation of focal points typically occurs at a time of crisis—a time that dislodges an old pattern or equilibrium. A focal point must have several properties. First, it must make explicit an agreement about the rules governing political decision making, the rights of citizens, and the appropriate bounds on government. Second, the agreement must (implicitly or explicitly) specify the relevant trigger strategies telling citizens when to react against political officials who attempt to violate the terms specified in the agreement. Third, because shared belief systems and consensus rarely result when a dominant political group can impose its will on others, the agreement is necessarily a compromise among opposing elites.

Agreements creating focal solutions typically come in the form of elite pacts (Higley and Gunther 1991). Examples occur throughout the history of representative government, including: the English Magna Carta in 1215 and Glorious Revolution in 1689; the United States Constitution, the Missouri Compromise of 1820, and the Compromise of 1877 (ending Reconstruction); the 1990 South African agreement to end apartheid; the 1957 Colombian pact and the 1991 El Salvadoran pact, both ending civil wars and bringing social peace and a semblance of democracy; and the various treaties underpinning the formation of the European Community. To succeed, these focal solutions must be widely accepted by citizens. Only then do they have a chance of being protected by citizen action in the face of potential violations.

Maintaining a stable democracy, a stable constitution, or a thriving economy each requires a specific type of shared belief system. Citizens must believe that these institutions are appropriate for their society; they must accept the decisions made by these institutions as legitimate; and they must believe that their rights should be protected, in the sense that they are willing to react against governments that try to deprive them of these rights.

Nothing is automatic about creating the focal point necessary for consensual order, however. As noted, because the situations of most citizens differ markedly, citizens are likely to disagree about what constitutes fundamental rights and the legitimate ends of the state. Authoritarian rulers can exploit these differences by gaining the support of some citizens while taking advantage of others. This asymmetric society cannot sustain a consensual set of rights accorded to all or most citizens. Instead, the state takes advantage of some citizens while giving better treatment to its constituents. Because of the difficulties in creating the basis for consensual rights, the authoritarian basis of political order is more natural than the consensual basis.

Our second principle suggests another aspect of the survivability of constitutions and stable democratic orders. Studied by Przeworski (1991, ch. 2) and extended by Weingast (1997), the principle holds that successful constitutions limit the stakes of politics. That is, they place bounds on the range of political choices, in part by assigning citizen rights and other limits on governmental decision making. The greater the range of issues subject to political decision making, the greater the stakes.

High stakes have several consequences. First, high stakes make it far less likely that those in power will give up that power. The reason is that they have too much to lose from the policy changes that would occur if they gave up power. Fear of losing power—whether due to losing an election, sustained unpopularity, or fiscal crises—often drives leaders to sabotage constitutional and democratic rules. Lowering the stakes—by means such as protecting particular rights—lowers the incentive for losers to sabotage the rules. Similarly, high stakes imply that those out of power are more likely to use extraconstitutional means to attain power or to resist onerous policies imposed by those holding power.

Our third principle is related to the second. An absence of well-defined and widely accepted rights combines with high stakes to produce *rent-seeking*. This is a term that has many meanings, so we define it carefully. Rent-seeking occurs when rights to a valuable political privilege, asset, or territory are absent, inadequately specified, or inadequately enforced.[4] The absence of well-defined rights to an asset implies that individuals and groups will expend resources to attempt to capture that asset. Those who capture the right or who believe they have those rights will expend resources defending their rights.

An important implication of the rent-seeking perspective is that it yields comparative statics predictions. In our context, these hold that the more valuable the asset, the more resources individuals are willing to spend to capture it. A major conclusion of this perspective is that competitors seeking the asset will, in the aggregate, spend up to the value of the prize. Under some conditions, they will spend more. Competition for the asset when rights are inadequately specified dissipates the net social value of the asset to zero. The greater the resources devoted to rent-seeking, the lower a society's wealth.

The second and third principles interact as follows. Higher political stakes imply greater levels of rent-seeking. The greater the stakes, the more resources are devoted to capturing and defending valuable rights.

Our final proposition is that reducing the stakes requires that the state create credible commitments (Greif 1998; North and Weingast 1989; Weingast 1995). All societies that provide a secure basis for citizen rights—including those fostering democracy, a stable constitutional order, and economic growth—do so by providing credible commitments for the state and public officials to honor these conditions. Because they provide protection from opportunism and expropriation, credible commitments are necessary to provide asset owners a secure environment within which to invest. They are therefore essential to economic growth. Credible commitments are also essential to the maintenance of political and democratic rights. Establishing credible commitments requires the creation of political institutions that alter the incentives of political officials so that it becomes in their interests to protect the relevant citizen rights. When this occurs, we say these rights are self-enforcing for political officials.

Our four principles have an important implication for the two types of political order. The smaller the range of credible commitments of the state, the larger the rent-seeking; that is, the smaller the range of credible commitments, the larger the value of capturing the state and the larger the risks of not holding power. Smaller degrees of credible commitment imply that citizens and groups will, in the aggregate, spend larger portions of their resources in order to capture power. Greater political stakes, in turn, imply more resources devoted to capturing the state and to protecting oneself from the state and thus fewer resources devoted to productive activity. In the limit, in a polity in which everything is up for grabs, citizens and groups will dissipate the entire social surplus trying to capture power and protecting what they have. Put another way, too few credible commitments yields a state that is at best stagnant, at worse, engaged in civil war.[5]

Our first principle relates to the maintenance of political order. Building a social consensus about individual rights creates the credible commitment to protect these many rights. To the extent that constitutions limit the stakes and lower rent-seeking, they must be self-enforcing. A critical requirement for making these limits self-enforcing is a social consensus supporting these limits. This consensus makes the limits self-enforcing by providing officials with the incentives to honor them.

These principles also have implications for the differences between the two bases of political order. Because the two bases of political order differ in the nature of social consensus about citizen rights, the relative absence of consensus in some societies implies that those bases of order are more likely to be authoritarian and less likely to be able to sustain market economies. Although citizens in these regimes are better off if they can coordinate on a set of citizen rights, the political impediments to doing so are legion.

An important basis for authoritarian political order is that citizens fear disorder. Many authoritarian regimes have emerged from disorder, developing some support among the citizenry precisely because they could provide order. Any attempt that holds the potential to improve on the authoritarian basis for order by creating rights also holds the potential of dislodging the current political system, unleashing disorder—a topic we turn to shortly. In the wake of such fear, many citizens will prefer the current regime.

We offer two principles about the often sudden emergence of political disorder. The first concerns an event that dislodges the old mechanisms that provided credible commitment in society without providing adequate substitutes. Examples of such events include disasters, but often they reflect a crisis that allows a sudden turnover in political power by groups who seek major political change. Crises often dislodge the old order in any of several ways. For example, an economic crisis may lower the resources available to the state to distribute to its constituents. The loss of political benefits may persuade some supporters of the regime to oppose it. Crises may also interact with our first principle of order in the sense that they destroy the consensus supporting the regime.

In accord with our principles of order, if, following a crisis, the new groups are able to establish a consensus about the new form of political organization, new credible commitments can be established and political order maintained. We study below how the American Revolution fits this case. Absent a new consensus, however, credible commitments are far more difficult to establish. Political disorder is more likely, as we discuss below for Spanish America.

Here we argue a comparative statics type of result: constitutions supported by a social consensus that limit the stakes of politics, that protect the rights of all citizens, and that give all citizens some stake in the status quo are less likely to experience disorder than constitutions that discriminate against particular groups who may then be tempted to use violence to disrupt the status quo.

A second principle concerns revolutionary change. A rich and multifaceted literature exists on revolutions and social movements (e.g., Moore 1966; Skocpol 1979; Tarrow 1994; and Tilly 1993), and it seems fair to say that there are many sources of revolutionary change. Below, we draw on one principle of revolutionary change. As noted above, change is typically incremental. Nonetheless, revolutions can begin with a set of incremental changes that persuade some individuals and groups that revolution is a lesser risk than a continuation of the incremental changes perceived to threaten the survival of one group. The steps in this process are as follows (de Figueiredo and Weingast 1999):

1. A set of political entrepreneurs articulates a new set of beliefs in fundamental conflict with the existing order—beliefs that are typically held, at first, only by a small minority.
2. The opponents of these entrepreneurs act in ways that make these ideas appear to be true, "confirming" (in the Bayesian sense) the revolutionary beliefs in the eyes of pivotal players. Thus events occur beyond the direct control of the proponents of the new ideas that lend some credence to this set of beliefs.
3. The result is a spread of the beliefs to some of the pivotal political decision mak-

ers. When the pivotal decision makers accept the radically new beliefs, they provide sufficient political support for radical action.

The conditions provide a set of circumstances sufficient for radical, discontinuous political change to occur. They help explain the sudden emergence of radical politics, for example, in the recent ethnic violence in Yugoslavia (de Figueiredo and Weingast 1999), the secession crisis preceding the American Civil War (Weingast 1998), and, as we discuss below, the American Revolution.

We offer two further insights about disorder. First, our perspective suggests that governments that restore order on an authoritarian basis are likely to systematically transgress the rights of their opponents. Because citizens in these regimes have no means to agree on what citizen rights should be enforced, universalistic rights cannot be policed. This allows the regime to repress some parts of society while retaining the support of others. We observe that authoritarian regimes which have restored order commonly repress their opponents, for example, in the numerous governments in Mexico following independence.

Second, our perspective suggests that a society with a consensual basis for political order is less likely to experience disorder than a society with an authoritarian basis. The reason is that consensus implies greater citizen rights and hence stricter limits on government. More secure rights and stricter limits, in turn, lower the stakes of politics, implying greater protection for individuals. The de Figueiredo and Weingast (1999) model of the emergence of disorder implies that the higher the stakes, the more quickly citizens will resort to violence to protect what they have.

We argue that there are three ideal states of political organization: the consensual basis of political order, the authoritarian basis of political order, and political disorder. Our principles regarding political order suggest that the consensual basis for order emerges in societies that lower the stakes of political action through institutions that establish credible commitments on the state. One mechanism requisite for making these commitments credible or self-enforcing is a social consensus that supports these commitments. Regarding the emergence of political disorder, we suggested how major changes—such as economic crises, disastrous foreign wars, or natural disasters—may dislodge the old, political equilibrium, and with it, the mechanisms protecting citizens' rights. We also specified conditions under which radical changes in beliefs may occur, thus causing sudden shifts in the policies citizens support.

POLITICAL ORDER IN POST-INDEPENDENCE BRITISH NORTH AMERICA

The theoretical principles discussed above provide considerable insights into the reasons for stability in the British empire prior to the revolutionary crisis, the outbreak of the revolution, and the re-emergence of political order and sustained economic growth in the post-revolutionary era.

Political Order in the British Empire

The mechanisms of credible commitments to property rights within the British empire were based on federalism.[6] Although eighteenth-century contemporaries did not use the label "federal," the empire's structure clearly fits the definition of federalism (Weingast 1995). First, the empire had multiple levels of government, each with its relatively well-defined sphere of authority. Until the end of the Seven Years' War in 1763, the British role in America was limited to empire-wide public goods, notably, security and international trade. Colonial assemblies, working with a British governor, held broad authority over local public goods, property rights, religious freedom, and contract enforcement, subject to some constraints of British law. Second, the institutions of the empire placed considerable constraints on the British role within the individual American colonies. Third, British institutions created a common market within the empire, preventing individual colonies from raising trade barriers.

The pervasive French threat bound together both sides of the Atlantic in a relationship based on common interests. Because both sides needed each other, they were able to create and adhere to a system of political and economic autonomy inherent in the empire's federal structure. Although either side might be tempted to cheat, both sides found the empire's federal structure convenient. Indeed, the strict line between the system-wide issues of trade and security and all other domestic issues within the colonies (such as religious freedom, taxation, property, and social regulation) created a "bright-line" credible commitment mechanism. In this system, deviations by either side were easy to detect. In terms of our propositions for consensual political order, the empire's federal structure created a natural focal solution, making actions by either side easy to police.

Over the 100 years prior to 1763, the British came to accept local political freedom in exchange for the colonists' acceptance of British control over the empire, including trading restrictions on the colonists. The institutions of the empire combined with the shared belief system supporting these institutions to underpin cooperation from both sides of the Atlantic.

In the late seventeenth and early eighteenth century, the British colonies were lonely outposts, far from the British metropolis. They faced strong competition with one another for scarce capital and labor and for product markets in Britain and Europe. Economic theories of federalism predict that any colony which fails to promote and protect markets simply fails to gain economic resources and grow. Successful colonies adapted local institutions to suit local needs. Failing to provide for efficient exploitation of economic opportunity spelled economic doom. Several British colonies failed for this reason. The result was a system within the empire—and, as Weingast (1995) argues, within England itself—of market-preserving federalism, with strong institutional commitments protecting the structure and hence markets.

Legislatures—colonial assemblies—became central to providing liberty for Americans (Reid 1995; see also Greene 1986). In our terms, legislatures, working within the structure of the empire, provided a series of credible commitments to a range of economic, political, and religious rights. Over the 100 years prior to the Seven Years' War (1756–1763), incremental change and precedent within the British system gradually gave these assemblies greater political autonomy and freedom, which they used to underpin essential political, personal, religious, and economic rights.

In the British constitutional system of precedent, long-standing practice had enshrined these arrangements with constitutional authority (Greene 1986; Reid 1995)—or so the Americans thought, until the years of controversy between the end of the Seven Years' War and the outbreak of the Revolution. For the century before the end of the Seven Years' War, harmony and political stability reigned, all within the federal system of the empire. A strong system of property rights protected both economic assets and freedom of religion. Both sides of the Atlantic supported these arrangements.

In sum, the theoretical principles articulated above help explain the system of order within the British empire. Order was based on a shared belief system supporting the empire's federal structure and a range of local powers accorded to colonial assemblies. The relatively low political stakes limited both the range of political controversy within each colony and the degree of rent-seeking.

The Emergence of Disorder and Revolution

In the dozen years following the close of the Seven Years' War, controversy and crisis emerged, ending in revolution. The principles discussed above provide considerable insight into the emerging disorder.

After 1763, various changes in British policy toward the empire threatened this system (Greene 1986; Rakove, Rutten, and Weingast 1999; Tucker and Hendrickson 1982). Three were critical for imperial policy. First, although the war removed the French threat, it did so at a huge financial price, leaving Britain with the largest debt ever. The British naturally turned to the colonies to finance a portion of the debt. Second, the French defeat greatly changed the empire. Prior to the defeat, the American colonies represented a major portion of the empire. Anything that hurt the Americans hurt the empire. After the Seven Years' War, this was no longer necessarily true. In the new and much larger empire, the British might reasonably design empire-wide policies to govern the system that might harm one part. Third, following the French defeat, Americans had much less need for the British security umbrella and, therefore, less reason to conform to British interests (Tucker and Hendrickson 1982).

These changes helped dislodge the old system. The demise of the French threat simultaneously lowered the cost each side was willing to bear to retain the relationship. At exactly this moment, the British had a much larger empire with a considerable range of new problems.

Britain's large financial burden and the new structure of the empire produced considerable anxiety in the American colonies. These changes led many Americans to conclude that Britain would no longer observe the principles of federalism within the empire. This view was especially strong among the emerging radical group. This group argued that the precedent of the British directly intervening in colonial affairs through taxes meant the end of liberty, including the end of autonomy for colonial assemblies, and hence all that Americans held dear. With this precedent established, the British could alter other policies at their discretion. Put another way, this precedent would destroy the bright-line commitment mechanism protecting federalism and local political freedom within the empire.

In the beginning, most Americans paid little attention to the radicals—their noise about liberty did not ring true. The British had yet to provide much cause for believing that they intended major policy changes. Further, moderates and opponents both feared that the alternative to British rule was worse.

In a series of halting steps, the British sought various forms of financial support from the colonies. In 1766, they asked the Americans to provide for the quartering of British troops within the colonies. Americans believed the troops unnecessary—after all, if they were not needed while the French remained a viable threat, why were they needed after the French defeat? Worse, many Americans believed that the British insistence on setting domestic colonial policy would set an undesirable precedent. The New York colonial assembly refused to pass legislation supporting all the troops in the colony. The British reacted strongly, in part believing that a strong response would discourage further action and help isolate their opponents. As punishment, the British suspended all acts of the New York Assembly until the colony complied with the Quartering Act.

Several years later, the British passed the Tea Act (1773) effectively granting the East India Company a monopoly on importing tea. A group of Massachusetts Patriots protested the act by dumping tea in the Boston harbor. Here, too, the British acted quickly, believing they could isolate the radicals through a harsh response designed to discourage the other colonies from supporting the radicals. Specifically, the British passed the Coercive Acts, including four laws. The first closed the port of Boston, and a second virtually annulled the charter of the Massachusetts colony, including disbanding the Massachusetts Assembly. The additional acts also aimed to punish Massachusetts: the Administration of Justice Act, which provided that colonial officials would be tried outside of the colony, and the Quartering Act, which applied to all colonies and allowed the imperial officials to seize property to support troops if the colonial assembly did not allocate the necessary funds.

The British actions backfired. Instead of isolating the radicals, the Coercive Acts provided striking evidence supporting the radicals' contentions. To many Americans, the British reaction seemed out of proportion to the events. Because colonial assemblies were central to liberty and the preservation of all colonial rights, the British willingness to suspend colonial legislatures turned many moderates against the British. As the radicals suggested from the beginning, the new British policies threatened American liberty. The British reactions seemed to provide the proof.

Rakove (1979) suggests further evidence concerning the political swing of the moderates from opposing to supporting the radicals. Rakove argues that as late as 1775, American moderates would have accepted a credible compromise—had only the British offered one. The unwillingness of the British to provide a credible compromise provided further evidence that the radicals were correct. What else could explain the pattern of British behavior, including the direct threats to American liberty? The unwillingness of the British to compromise and their seeming willingness to punish all Americans, not just radical upstarts, helped drive the moderates' swing in political support.

American radicals in the 1760s and early 1770s faced another problem. As noted, opponents thought that even if the radicals were right about the British, the alternative to British rule would be worse. Hence, many radicals came to see that part of their task involved articulating a new shared belief system about constitutionalism to place limits on the behavior of an independent American regime, were Americans to choose independence. Historians of the Revolution have spent much of the post–World War II era characterizing the evolution of these beliefs, their basis in the previous 100 years, and especially how they came to predominate the beliefs of Americans on the eve of the Revolution.[7] The revolutionaries' theory of the constitution, of how liberty is established and preserved, and of how a new national government might be created that would preserve liberty among the states all helped to adapt the earlier system of credible commitment to the new circumstances.

In short, the sudden emergence of disorder in America reflected the principles articulated above. The defeat of the French helped dislodge the old system, leading to changes in British behavior and policy within the empire. In reaction, American radicals articulated a new idea, one at first on the fringe of American beliefs, namely, that the British actions represented the end of liberty. Early on in the controversy with Britain, the politically pivotal moderates disagreed with the radicals. Yet British actions provided evidence (in the sense of Bayesian updating) in favor of these ideas, causing them to gain support among the pivotal moderates. If the radicals' claims about the British threats to liberty seemed false in the mid-1760s, they seemed far more plausible following the British reaction to New York in 1770 and Massachusetts in 1773. By 1775, moderates had switched sides to support the radicals in revolution against the British. The failure of the British to provide a credible alternative not only drove them to the British opponents but also provided further evidence that the radicals' views were correct. A majority of Americans were thus willing to support revolutionary action rather than maintain the status quo.

The Re-emergence of Order in the Post-revolutionary Era·

The principal problem facing British North Americans during the revolutionary war and the immediate post-independence period concerned how to create a cooperative system among the colonies, with new national political entities capable of respecting citizen rights and state and local political autonomy. Consistent with the first principle of political order presented above, the emergence of a shared belief system during the revolutionary debates helped establish political order after the defeat of the British. Critical elements of these shared beliefs included the central importance of liberty, the role of colonial—now state—legislatures in protecting liberty, the appropriate limits on national and state governments, and the appropriate forms of constitutional protections against tyranny. In particular, proponents of revolution adapted their theory of credible commitment in the empire, based on federalism, to the new circumstances of independence. States—already adapted to preserving liberty and providing public goods to promote public welfare and the protection of critical rights—remained equally central in the new circumstances.

Under the Articles of Confederation in the early 1780s, states retained considerable political autonomy. The national government was charged with providing national public goods, such as defense. But, in deference to protection of liberty and state autonomy, it was not given the powers or financial means to enforce its decisions.

Under these circumstances, the great problem facing those who became known as the Federalists was to grant the national government the power to provide national public goods (security, a common market, and monetary stability) while credibly committing this government to abide by these limits. As the Antifederalists came to emphasize, the danger posed by the new national government was encroachment on state autonomy and citizen rights, paralleling the previous British tyranny. The challenge facing the Federalists became how to grant national powers to provide a few critical public goods, such as national security, while preventing the national government from growing beyond those powers. In the end, the Federalists solved this problem by creating a system of market-preserving federalism and thus providing for long-term economic growth.

The principles of political order discussed above help show how the United States Constitution resolved many of these problems. The Constitution lowered the stakes of national political action in a variety of ways, including a complex system of enumerated powers, a separation of powers system, and a system of federalism placing striking limits on the national government. The debates during the revolutionary and constitutional controversies served to provide a new shared belief system about the bounds on the national government and the importance of citizen rights and state autonomy.

The Constitution's success was based in large part on the shared belief system among Americans that emerged during the revolutionary and constitutional debates.[8] As the principles above suggest, the shared belief system about liberty and the appropriate limits on the national government helped maintain limits on the national government. Indeed, when Federalists seemed to overstep these bounds in the late 1790s, many former federalists came to support Jefferson, the Federalists' chief opponent. These events ushered Jefferson into the presidency in 1800 and provided for his party's hegemonic dominance of national politics.

Americans in the United States, however, had the luxury of being able to worry about the problem caused by national government in part because they had already solved the problem of protecting the liberty and wealth of citizens, colony by colony. Within each colony, citizens did not have to worry about their rights, wealth, or religious freedom, in part because the system inherited from the British and adjusted during and after the Revolution (e.g., changing meanings of sovereignty and liberty) provided an ongoing, seasoned, and credible system of limited government based on the full separation of powers.

In the new United States, no contradiction emerged between the mechanisms establishing and protecting rights maintained under the empire and liberal and republican principles underlying the new government. These principles were already embodied in the status quo constitutional system. Thus, British North America faced no contradiction between maintaining rights to economic assets and new constitutional principles.

The United States were thus able to create a strong system of market-preserving federalism, including a common market based on private rights protected by (relatively) neutral third parties. This provided the basis for long-term growth.

Credible Commitment in the United States

The institutions inherited from the British combined with the new ideas that emerged during the revolutionary debates to yield a new view of American constitutionalism, providing for the mechanisms of commitment in the new United States. For example, colonial assemblies were central to American "liberty" (Greene 1986; Reid 1995; Wood 1969), providing for political security, religious freedom, order, and (along with the judiciary) the enforcement of property rights. After independence, colonial assemblies became state legislatures and were equally central in providing the same public goods. Just as the British role in domestic colonial affairs was limited prior to 1763, so too was the new United States government. The national government under the Articles of Confederation was greatly constrained from threatening individuals, in part because it had little power to do so. National power was focused on the provision of a few national public goods such as defense, the common market, and a stable monetary system. Even in these areas, it was greatly constrained by its inability to tax and hence to provide these goods.

With the advent of the Constitution in 1789, the United States emerged with a new national government, capable of providing national public goods. The Constitution also constrained the national government through a series of institutional mechanisms, limiting its ability to expand its powers beyond these domains. Important mechanisms included the separation of powers system, a system of implicit sectional vetoes (to the free and slave states, soon to be balanced in 1796, thus providing each region with a veto over national power), and federalism. Following the debates of the founding, a shared system of beliefs emerged about the limits on government (see, e.g., Hartz 1955; Lipset 1963; and Wood 1991). The direct import of this system was that it helped define widely shared views about the limits on government, in turn helping to police political officials that might overstep the bounds.[9] Indeed, this appears to be precisely what happened to the Federalists at the close of the eighteenth century. Federalist attempts to enhance national power, including harassing their political opponents under the Alien and Sedition Acts, helped galvanize political support for their Jeffersonian opponents.

We conclude our discussion of British North America by suggesting how the matrix of new American institutions provided the political foundation for long-term economic growth. Following the fundamental political dilemma of an economic system noted above, how did the United States protect the rights and freedoms necessary to underpin long-term growth?

Our answer begins with the British heritage, which emphasized individual economic and political rights, including local political representation. Within the British empire, Americans experienced and believed in individual initiative, private property rights, limited government, and political liberty. All this was held together by systems of local political representation and the colonial assemblies, the principal bastions of economic, political, and religious liberty. These values were widely held throughout the colonies, constituting a shared belief system.

Yet these beliefs alone were insufficient to support a limited government fostering market growth. In addition, the constitution helped create a system of market-preserving federalism (Weingast 1995). Much as market-preserving federalism prescribes, the Constitution limited the national government's powers largely to truly national public goods, such as national security, preservation of the common market, and monetary stability. In particular, the Constitution reserved most powers of economic and social regulation to the states, subject to the constraint enforced by the national government that they could not erect internal trade barriers.

Market-preserving federalism drastically reduced the stakes of national politics. Reserving most powers over everyday economic and social life to the states greatly reduced the scope of decisions made by the national government. This had two immediate effects. First, it greatly reduced the scope of rent-seeking at the national level. Second, it allowed states and regions with very different preferences to choose very different laws.

Two features of market-preserving federalism limited the stakes and rent-seeking at the state level. First, competition among the states in the face of a large common market gave states the incentives to foster a favorable economic climate. States that failed to do so lost scarce capital and labor to other states.[10] Second, the presence of hard budget constraints greatly limited the states' abilities to subsidize local economic agents.[11]

Significantly, citizens overwhelmingly supported the Constitution along with the central features of market-preserving federalism.[12] Citizens in the early American republic favored freedom for state and local governments and therefore strong limits on the national government. This shared belief system combined with political institutions, property rights, and laws to produce a system highly favorable to decentralized, competitive markets.

Factors of production were undoubtedly relevant for economic progress in the United States and for the stability of the American democracy and Constitution. As Engerman and Sokoloff (1997) observe, the lack of economies of scale and hence lack of slavery in agriculture throughout the northern United States contributed to the greater emphasis in the North on egalitarianism. Of course, the South exhibited both economies of scale and slavery, thus creating a puzzle from the factors of production perspective as to why this region supported democracy and the Constitution. Nor does this perspective answer other questions. For example, why—and how—did the North and South cooperate within one nation despite their economic differences? Second, the focus on endowments argues that the United States should have experienced economic growth. But it fails to explain why the United States evolved to become the richest nation in the world.

Our institutional perspective helps address these questions. Endowments affect economic opportunities, but they alone do not determine long-term economic performance. The institutions created by the United States Constitution implied strong protection for property rights. Its system of market-preserving federalism implied significant barriers to harmful political intervention, characteristic of developing nations, that hobbles development. This included protection for slavery where it existed. Federalism also helped underpin the system of cooperation among the North and South (Weingast 1998). Federalism implied that the most important decisions over which the Northerners and Southerners differed—notably, slavery—could be devolved to the two sections via the states and thus prevent national politics from becoming explosive. Nothing in the perspective on endowments implies a system of federalism with these qualities.

Returning to the problem of political order: security of property rights combined with strong limits on the stakes of national politics to imply that Americans faced a relatively low risk of adverse political action. As a consequence, most people could focus on productive activity rather than on investing resources to protect themselves and their families. This situation would have differed markedly if the United States had had a more centralized political system. To see this, consider Southerners' property rights to slaves, an issue on which Americans did not agree. Because a centralized system would have made rights to slaves subject to national decision making rather than decentralized to the states where it was secure, centralization implied greater insecurity for the Southern slave system of agriculture. Centralization would have therefore greatly raised the stakes over slavery, putting Northerners and Southerners at loggerheads from the beginning. Indeed, the lack of security for slavery under such a system may well have precluded their cooperation within a single country.[13] Thus, the fact that federalism limited the stakes of national politics not only fostered political cooperation, it helped underpin the system of regional specialization that helped propel economic growth over the coming decades (see North 1961).

POLITICAL DISORDER IN POST-INDEPENDENCE LATIN AMERICA

Latin America fell badly behind the advanced, industrializing economies of the North Atlantic during the nineteenth century (Haber 1997). While the United States forged ahead with a steadily growing national economy, increasingly efficient markets, and an array of national institutions that provided for lengthy, uninterrupted periods of political stability, the newly independent Latin American nations languished in relative backwardness and, in most cases, political turmoil.

The contrast between the two regions is especially striking given their respective histories. Both areas were colonies of expanding European powers in the sixteenth and seventeenth centuries. Both were rich in terms of land and natural resources. Both saw the rise of thriving commercial cities and the growth of overseas trade, albeit constrained by colonial mercantilism. Both achieved political independence from their mother countries within forty years of each other. Nonetheless, the costs of the "lost" nineteenth century, specific to Latin America, remain apparent. For much of Latin America, the twentieth century was one of quite successful economic performance. The lag in levels of per capita GDP that persists in Latin America today is attributable in large part to events in the nineteenth century.[14]

In the half century following independence, the presence of widespread political instability and violence distinguished much of Latin America, especially Spanish America, from the United States. While the United States enjoyed an enduring set of political arrangements that both provided for stability and protected markets from predation, most of Spanish America erupted in internecine war. This instability imposed several types of costs. It diverted resources from economic activity and channeled them into *caudillo* ("strongman") armies and a variety of praetorian efforts (Gootenberg 1989; Stevens 1991). Importantly, instability also made it impossible to establish institutions that could bring the expected private returns from investment closer in line with social returns. The results were disastrous. Mexico, by way of example, plunged into a serious depression that endured until after mid-century (Coatsworth 1990). The new Andean republics experienced similar turmoil and likely brooked similar costs.

Historians have long examined the failures of Spanish America's tumultuous post-independence period as disruptions inherent in the process of "state-building" in Spain's former colonies. For example, Safford (1987) holds that: "the most important theme in the political history of Spanish America in this period is the difficulty encountered in establishing viable new states. . . . Most Spanish American states were unable fully to re-establish the legitimacy of authority enjoyed by the Spanish crown before 1808" (p. 50). Safford continues: "A deep and abiding problem faced by Spanish American elites was that of constructing political systems that could command effective and enduring authority. . . . The first, and most enduring problem was that of reconstructing legitimate authority in the absence of the king"(p. 56). Those historians have, however, neglected to examine the types of political institutions that constrain groups from attacking each other. Such institutions play a central role in establishing political order through political organization, which raises the costs both to the state for expropriating particular groups and to one group for attacking another. By making it sufficiently costly for any one group to capture the state and employ its resources (organizational and material) against other groups, particular institutional arrangements help prevent strategic "miscalculations" of the type that may lead a group to be preemptively aggressive against another because it fears victimization (de Figueiredo and Weingast 1999).

Throughout Spanish America, independence did not result in stability. The Crown had long provided an important enforcement mechanism, which in turn provided the basis for authoritarian political order. Corporate groups obtained a series of rights that limited the ability of any colonial group to expropriate or attack another. Although this system provided for political order, it did not provide incentives for long-term economic growth.

In the vacuum created by independence, third-party enforcement of rights and exchange vanished, and no institutions emerged that made aggression by one group against others in society sufficiently costly to prevent internal war. The result was widespread turmoil, violence, and political instability. Without stabilizing institutions, there was little hope of achieving efficient economic organization. Most groups scrambled to preserve the protections and privileges formerly accorded by the Crown, or to secure new powers via control of the state. The result was severe economic contraction.

Brazil and Chile represent variations on these themes and reveal the importance of the types of institutional arrangements adopted in the new independent nations. These new nations successfully constructed institutions that promoted political stability after independence. Neither did so, however, by means of political organization that promoted economic competition and cooperation among subnational administrative entities. Instead, both states were heavily centralized. They thus failed to capitalize on their accomplishments in securing stability in the political realm. Any trappings of federalism were in fact contingent entirely on the central government's willingness to grant limited regional autonomy in administration and policy. As such, central government could abrogate this "top down" federalism at its convenience, and did so whenever necessary. Market-sustaining federalism was virtually absent in these cases. Instead of competing for mobile factors of production, provincial elites competed for pork and protection within national legislatures. By creating institutions that protected groups from aggression and expropriation, these nations avoided the turmoil of Peru and Mexico, and saved themselves from a sharp economic downturn. But they did not promote material progress in the way that the United States did. The result was relatively flat economic growth, which improved only when they reorganized their polities in ways that happened to emulate the United States.

Our investigation of Spanish America proceeds as follows. We first study the political foundations of the empire and then examine the imperial mercantile system. We conclude with a focus on the emergence of disorder following independence.

Political Foundations of Order in the Spanish Empire

To understand the emergence of disorder in the independence period, we must first understand the political foundations of stability under the empire. Within the context of the Spanish empire, colonial administrative institutions provided the political basis of stability. Credible commitments took a specific form. In addition to the geographic organization of colonial administration, the Spanish Crown relied heavily on a corporate organization of society and politics, notably the army, the Church, and the nobility and landed elites (Coatsworth 1990). Each group possessed a series of juridical privileges and thus a degree of protection from the Crown and its agents. Because Spain needed the long-term cooperation of these corporate groups, it developed a complex set of rules, practices, and norms across the empire that sought to promote mutual dependency and cooperation between the Crown and the corporate groups, and among the corporate groups themselves.

Under the Spanish empire, valuable economic rights (for example, to exploit labor, land, and investments) and valuable political rights (for example, the privileges of the military and the Church) were protected by a system of centralized power based on political loyalty to an absolutist Crown. Rights to land originated with grants from the Spanish Crown. Protection of these rights rested on a system of privilege based on personal and corporate connection to the Crown.

The foundation of this system was political exchange, whereby elites' rights and privileges were held by virtue of sustained loyalty toward and support for the Crown. Given the powers of and constraints on the absolutist Crown, the political exchange of rights for political support ensured the Crown's long-term survival. In contrast, a system of rights based on legal title enforced by neutral third parties, such as courts, would not serve the Crown's interest in long-term survival. Once rights were created, holders of those rights based on legal title enforced by an independent judiciary would no longer depend on the Crown. This mechanism could not sustain long-term loyalty toward the Crown. Although Spain is labeled an "absolutist" state, this did not mean that the Crown could act arbitrarily; many privileges were protected by institutions and customs, including the nobles' representation in the Cortes.

The Spanish empire encompassed a system of rights and exchange, thus providing for authoritarian political order. It did not, however, provide incentives for long-term economic growth.

Commitment to rights and privileges in the imperial system was created and maintained across the system. The Crown sought empire-wide cooperation of corporate groups in its competition with other European powers. Even if the Crown or its agents might benefit from mistreatment of a corporate group in any one colony, this action would jeopardize cooperation of that group across the system. The Crown's inclinations toward expropriation would be counterbalanced by the potential loss of cooperation of that group in other colonies.

Each corporate group provided important services to the Crown throughout the empire. In exchange, the Crown gave each a series of rights and privileges. Together, the Crown and the corporate groups created an effective imperial system that competed for resources in the new world and for influence in Europe.

Imperial Mercantile Regulation
Although the Spanish mercantile system provided the basis for authoritarian political order, it heavily constrained trade and hence economic development

in the colonies. Trade regulation worked against the development of intercolonial trade, the development of a dense network of ports, and a common market among the colonies. This regulation thus limited the incentives for colonists to capture the gains from specialization and economic exchange throughout Spanish America. Before returning to the problem of order following independence, it is worth considering Spanish mercantile regulation in some detail.

Spain's need to police both its monopoly system and its system for extracting precious metal led to a series of striking economic constraints. First, it concentrated trade in a tiny number of ports to serve its entire empire across two continents, one in Spain and three in America. Instead of developing hundreds of ports across thousands of miles of coastline, allowing each to compete for trade and develop a supporting surrounding economy—paralleling the economic development in British North America—Spain tightly constrained economic development. Second, it created the so-called fleet system governing all transatlantic trade.[15] The fleet system restricted intercolonial trade, forcing most trade between colonies to go through Spain and Portugal. Only with special license could trading ships engage legally in intercolonial commerce, and it was not until 1789 that all of Spanish America was finally freed from these restrictions (Lockhart and Schwartz 1983, p. 364).

In combination, these economic restrictions prevented the development of a dense commercial network in Spanish America. Products from Río de la Plata could not be shipped from its natural port (present-day Buenos Aires), but instead had to travel thousands of miles overland to Peru. In parallel with the political intervention of modern developing countries, these regulations highly constrained economic development, including the development of a stronger system of specialization and exchange across colonies. The monopoly power of the *consulado* merchants prevented free markets, setting prices artificially high and imposing deadweight losses on colonial economies.[16]

The wide range of endowments across Spanish America should have led to the same type of dense economic development along many South American coasts as observed on the east coast of North America. Yet the Spanish mercantile system explicitly prohibited this. The monopoly system also transferred profits from producers to "merchants and speculators, thus eliminating incentives to investment in new technology or to hire additional labor" (Burkholder and Johnson 1990, p. 139). In contrast to the view of Engerman and Sokoloff (1997), nothing about factor endowments dictated this regulatory system.

The Crown had its motives, however. Spanish regulations worked to keep the bullion flowing to Spain but did not promote the economic development of the new world. As North (1981, 1990) suggests, the Spanish system was geared to maximizing short-term rents for Spain, not long-term economic growth for the imperial system. The system of monopolies was in part designed to capture rents today for the monarchy and for Spain. Attempts to trade outside the system were to be prevented so as to maximize the bullion available for Spain (the lucrative trade between the Spanish American colonies and Asia drained away bullion).

The Spanish mercantile system rested on short-term fiscal rationality (North 1981, ch. 11). Allowing free trade and free economic development would have sabotaged this system. Over the long haul, freer economic exchange would have created a richer system. But in the short run, dismantling the mercantile restrictions would have meant less revenue for the Spanish Crown.

One facet of Spanish revenue extraction concerned the arbitrary expropriations under Spanish absolutism. Consider the expulsion of the Jesuits in 1767 from Spanish America. This case illustrates how Spanish absolutism failed to provide complete credible commitments to its supporters. In this case, Spain expropriated the property and revoked the rights and privileges of a once critical but no longer needed set of constituents. After the Glorious Revolution in 1689, nothing comparable could occur in England or British North America. As the Jesuits were among the largest wealth holders in Latin America, this led to huge expropriations. According to Skidmore and Smith (1992), "The best properties of the Jesuits' were auctioned off and the proceeds, of course, went to the crown" (p. 28).

In sum, the Spanish mercantile system had downstream consequences. Forcing the colonies to trade with Spain implied less development of local products for self-sufficiency, including far less intercolonial trade. By means of smuggling, many got around these rules. But this was costly, in no way offsetting the losses imposed by the imperial restrictions.

The late Spanish imperial policy had some negative effects on domestic production in the new world (Lynch 1986). For example, in Mexico, in the twenty years prior to independence, Spain undid much of the Mexican system of local monopolies, destroying considerable local production. Over the long run, this policy might have helped the colonies increase their specialization and exchange. But in a relatively short period, these benefits did not materialize. The Latin American economies were thus far less integrated economically than were the economies of the North American colonies. Of course, geography was a bigger factor.

In sum, Spanish mercantilism appears designed to maximize the Crown's extraction from the new world, at considerable cost to economic development of the empire. In contrast, the British empire's federal structure seems close to a system designed to maximize economic development within the empire. Spain bore large costs throughout the entire system to increase the Crown's share.

The Emergence of Disorder in Spanish America

Post-independence turmoil in Mexico, Peru, and the Río de la Plata extended from the wars of independence. Events both overseas and at home sparked those conflicts. Dissatisfaction among the native-born (Criollo) classes with absolutist policies stemmed from the disruptions and changes of Spain's Bourbon reforms (and Portugal's analogous Pombaline reforms) that unfolded throughout the eighteenth century. In an attempt to generate new revenues for the Crown while preserving peninsular interests in the American colonies, the Bourbon Kings pursued a series of measures designed to increase economic activity with an eye specifically toward generating tax revenue. These policies simultaneously created new opportunities for some colonials, and reduced the opportunities for sectors such as domestic woolens production, while tightening the squeeze on all from the royal fisc. Compounding the economic pressure of the Bourbons' administrative changes was worsening economic performance in the late eighteenth-century economy of New Spain (Coatsworth 1990, pp. 57–80, passim), and perhaps Peru as well.

In the environment of growing tensions in the Americas at the end of the eighteenth century, events in Europe sparked the first dose of autonomy for these colonies. Napoleon's imprisonment of the Spanish King in 1807 created a breach between the King's loyal subjects overseas and the French-controlled government in Spain. This quickly evolved into conflict about the redefinition of the colonies' relationship with the metropolis, leading to outright independence struggles between criollo forces and the Spanish Army.

The outbreak of Independence movements in Spanish America was indeed a lagging indicator of the problems that Bourbon absolutism confronted. Initiated in the absence of authority from Spain, local juntas emerged, in many cases to rule in the name of the jailed king. The questionable legitimacy of the French-imposed rulers and the collapse of the Spanish Bourbons left Spanish Americans poised to break away. A final insult from the Spanish Liberals, seeking to maintain trade restrictions on the colonies while simultaneously denying the criollos equal representation in the incipient Parliament, confirmed some of the worst fears of Spanish Americans regarding the true nature of reforms promised by Spain (Lynch 1986, p. 36). Independence wars unfolded in distinct waves; one, beginning in the Río de la Plata, moved over the Andes, while another moved from Venezuela through Colombia, and a third insurgency ebbed and flowed in New Spain. Together, the three main swaths of warfare left the Spanish with too much terrain to control, and too many resisters to dominate.

The defeat of Spanish forces in the 1820s throughout Spanish America resulted in the fragmentation of Spain's former colonies into new republics. These in turn virtually collapsed under the weight of the challenges of what historians refer to as "state building." They lacked self-enforcing institutions that constrained predatory action. In the face of widespread violence, political organization disintegrated into smaller units, typically organized around a *caudillo* for protection.

The dimensions of potential and actual conflict were numerous, and at once centrifugal and centripetal. In the archetypal cases, Mexico and Peru, the Church and the regular army struggled to maintain their preeminence among society's corporate entities. That preeminence was rooted in wealth, juridically defined privilege, and authority over the affairs of the nation. Working against that centralizing tendency, regional groups with disparate interests sought local political autonomy. Disagreements over trade policies and uncertainty over the intentions of central governments led them to seek to escape the central government's heavy hand. These forces promoted the formation of competing militias. The phenomenon of *caudillismo*—which occurred when regional strongmen vied militarily for the control of the state, exemplified in the extreme by Mexico's Antonio López de Santa Anna—became pervasive. Incessant warfare made rapid turnover of the national officeholders endemic (Stevens 1991). *Caudillos* attained national power in both Peru and Mexico, sapping the economy by leveraging forced loans from merchants. State indebtedness mounted, foreign debt obligations went unpaid, and domestic expropriation grew increasingly common (Tenenbaum 1986). All this fueled economic stagnation and outright contraction. The political turmoil that proved so costly persisted in Mexico through much of the 1860s; a semblance of stability appeared in Peru only in the 1870s, and Argentina remained subject to *caudillo* uprisings, in diminishing degree, until the early 1870s as well.

In most of Spanish America, it was not until a half century later that one of these competing groups emerged victorious. As the opportunity costs of continued conflict grew ever larger, the survivors constructed institutions that created stability. Establishing order became a goal in itself, as widespread elite support grew for institutions that would promote order. And this occurred at the expense of economic growth and individual liberty. The order that emerged in no way constrained the state.

Underpinning this pattern of instability was a complete lack of experience in autonomous decision making and government. For Spanish America, up to independence, autonomous institutions of self-government existed only at the most local level, and possessed heavily circumscribed authorities. Unlike the English colonies in North America, where some limited self-rule served as an institutional precedent for the new nation, state-building in Spanish America required that such institutions be created from scratch in an environment of dramatic change and uncertainty. In the absence of any institutions from the colonial era that would either dampen that uncertainty about the intentions of competing groups or constrain the attempts of groups that might aggress against others, open warfare became the norm.

Theoretical Factors Underpinning Political Disorder and the Failure to Reestablish Political Order and Republican Governments

The theoretical principles developed above shed considerable light on the emergence of disorder and the failure to reestablish order after independence throughout Spanish America.

In contrast to British North America, the break with the metropolis destroyed many of the institutions that provided credible commitments to rights and property within the Spanish empire. Each colony had a centralized political system headed by a governor who answered to the Crown, without an independent legislature and judiciary. Although the governor might be tempted to expropriate a privileged group, the fact that he would have to answer to Spain for his actions dramatically altered his incentives. Unless the Crown valued the expropriation, expropriation risked punishment.

Creoles gaining political power after independence inherited a centralized political system without inheriting critical elements of the formal and informal constraints protecting corporate groups and other elites. Those newly in power did not have to worry about the effects of their decisions across the empire; nor did they have to answer to the Crown for their decisions. The absence of constraints meant a potentially unconstrained executive and administrative apparatus. According to Safford (1987), "organization of the power in the [colonial] system ultimately depended upon the king. Without the presence of the king, the system shattered. 'In the absence of developed and interacting economic interest groups having a stake in constitutional process, the new countries were plunged into alternative regimes of anarchy and personalist tyranny. The contest to seize a patrimonial state apparatus, fragmented from the original imperial one, became the driving force of public life in each new country.'"(p. 116; quotation from Morse 1964, p. 157).

At the same time, independence set in motion contradictory impulses. Most corporate elites wanted to maintain their privileges, rights, and assets that depended on the old system. Countervailing this impulse was the nascent republicanism, exemplified by the adoption of American-like constitutions. Unfortunately, republican and liberal principles conflicted with the system of maintaining corporate privileges, for example, landed elites' right to labor, and the independence and power of the Church and the military (Safford 1987, p. 117).

The conflict implied a tradeoff: stronger rights and privileges for corporate groups weakened republicanism. Because corporate rights placed important policies, privileges, and public benefits outside of the political purview, they directly conflicted with the Republican principles that elected officials should control public policy. This conflict placed at stake political control over a major portion—perhaps the majority—of social resources, including: the army; huge landholdings and related production and commercial activities; various monopoly rights and privileges associated with productive and commercial activities; rights to a considerable portion of the labor force; and the property of the Church, including its productive and commercial activities. The greater political control demanded by republicanism compromised these privileges, juridically protected under the imperial system. To the extent that any group felt its rights, privileges, or property would be compromised—for example, expropriated by government action—they would undoubtedly fight rather than submit. In many newly independent states, the new political elites threatened to abolish these rights and privileges.

Two further problems emerged at this time. First, major groups at independence typically disagreed about who should make up the citizenry. One conflict concerned the *peninsulares,* who held a privileged position under the empire. Should they be accorded equal rights as the much larger group of criollos? As much of this group's property and special rights was due to the royal system that privileged them, many in the newly independent states felt the new states should abandon this group's privileges. Doing so would effectively expropriate much of this group's wealth, property, and special access to revenue. Some felt, further, that this formerly privileged group should be excluded from political citizenship. A second conflict emerged in other states, particularly Mexico. Native Americans, nearly enslaved under the imperial system, played a significant role in the struggle for independence in some states. Some felt that these groups should be rewarded for their efforts with citizenship and equality. Others disagreed, seeking to maintain the repressive regime that defined and enforced their rights. Second, the new regimes exacerbated problems of uncertainty over rights and privilege by failing to conform to the new constitutional principles.

The principles of political order and disorder discussed above bear directly on the conflicts that emerged. First, in contrast to the inhabitants of British North America, Americans in the former Spanish empire did not come to share a belief system about the role of government, the state, corporate privilege, and citizenship. The conflicts noted above imply a deep division over the definition of society (who should comprise the citizenry) and over the principal ideas along which society should be organized. This division reflected the absence of consensus over the legitimate ends of government and hence over the nature of government transgressions. Our first principle of political order suggests that these deep divisions implied the failure of the shared belief system necessary to police limits on the state.

Second, constitutional adherence requires that the constitution limit the stakes of political power and controversy. The absence of agreement about the basic elements of political structure and public decision making combined with the absence of a shared belief system to imply an absence of credible commitments by the new states. This absence had several consequences. First, it indicated an inability to create the appropriate political institutions defining citizen rights, limiting the stakes of political power, and creating incentives for economic growth. Indeed, the inability to agree on and create basic political institutions led directly to political instability in both the rights established under the old system and the new rights that the new regimes attempted to create.

Under these conditions, our theory shows, citizens in the new societies were unlikely to be able to police adherence to limits on political power. Instead, these conditions fostered the development of an authoritarian system. The absence of widespread support for constitutional principles made adherence to them unlikely. The principles of rent-seeking and limiting the stakes combine with the absence of consensus to produce the following implications. Because the basic disagreements covered such a large portion of social resources, the stakes were high. Because basic issues were not settled, the rewards to capturing power and the costs of being out of power were both large.

The absence of the first two conditions indicates that the third principle of rent-seeking comes in to play. The absence of credible limits on the state implied rational anxiety on the part of corporate groups and other elites. Their rights, privileges and wealth, often representing the lion's share of productive assets in these societies, were at stake. Those seeking to uphold what they view as their rights are willing to fight to protect them. Those in power have incentives to oppose these groups, either because they want to implement republican principles or because they want access to these groups' wealth. The absence of credible limits implies an absence of political institutions that would prevent this. The result is political turmoil and disorder. The main consequence was civil war.

The internecine wars following independence reflected the standard problem of an absence of credible commitment, high stakes, and rampant rent-seeking. Additional factors helped perpetuate political struggle based on an unconstrained political system and the resulting civil war. The wars for independence and the subsequent civil wars left debts—sometimes quite large. These debts, in combination with an economy that had contracted, implied that the new governments had substantial financial difficulties. Financial problems, in turn, indicated a short time horizon and thus an absence of thinking about long-term economic development. This combined with the absence of credible limits on their power to seek additional sources of revenue. Political survival depended on financial survival. That reinforced the tendencies to threaten corporate groups and other elites.

This behavior by the government induced local groups to seek protection, and hence the emergence of *caudillismo,* further contracting the economy. Groups outside of the ruling group would act to insulate themselves, implying limits on the reach and authority of those in power. In combination with the

economic contraction, this indicated growing political autonomy across regions within each new state. In this climate, repressed groups sought greater
freedoms, often using violence to create local independence. All this activity
sowed the seeds of spiraling disorder and a contracting economy. When order
reemerged, it took the form of authoritarian coercion.

Safford (1987) provides some support for this perspective: "Formal constitutional systems were enacted, most of which provided for the transfer of
power through elections and guaranteed individual liberties. But these formal
constitutional provisions frequently proved a dead letter. No political group
believed its adversaries would abide by them. Those who held power bent constitutional principles and often harshly repressed those in opposition in order
to retain the government. Those out of power believed, generally correctly,
that they could not gain possession of the state by means formally prescribed
by the constitution, because those who held the government controlled the
elections. Opposition politicians, both military and civilian, therefore waited
for, and took advantage of, moments of government weakness in order to over-
throw the ruling group" (pp. 50–51). Safford also provides evidence for the
rent-seeking account: "Many, if not most, of the political conflicts in Spanish
America in the period after independence were fought simply to determine
who would control the state and its resources" (p. 84).

In the end, reestablishment of political stability required a return to many
of the traditional forms of Spanish society. According to Wiarda and Kline
(1990):

Precisely because [the first thirty years of independence] were so chaotic
and governments so prone to breakdown, this period gave rise to a number
of what would become the historic drives of Latin American development
policy. These may be identified as the quest, given the prevailing instability, to secure and maintain order at all costs; to populate and thus to fill the
area's vast empty spaces; to control and civilize the Indian and African elements so as to prevent future social upheavals; to strengthen the oligarchy
through immigration and a general Hispanicizing of the population; to
maintain and strengthen existing structures such as the army and, in many
areas, the church; to fill the organizational void and correct the historic *falta
de organización* (absence of organization); and to develop a political model
that would reflect the area's earlier glory and its hope for the future. That
model was frequently the authoritarian-autocratic model of 16th century
Spain and Latin America. (p. 33)

Sustained political disorder emerged in the struggles for independence
throughout Spanish America and continued well beyond independence. Although some areas managed a degree of stability, such as Chile, the more common pattern was that of internecine wars, such as Mexico and Peru.

Our theoretical perspective helps explain this disorder. On independence, people throughout Spanish America disagreed about the fundamental basis of political, economic, and social organization. They therefore disagreed about the basic form of rights and privileges, of political institutions, and the legitimate ends of the states. Further, they often disagreed about who should be citizens.

These factors combined to imply that the first two conditions of our theory of political order fail to hold: an absence of a shared belief system and an absence of political institutions that limit the stakes of political conflict. The absence of these conditions implied that nothing was immune from political controversy. Because the stakes were enormous, virulent and violent rent-seeking ensued and a vast portion of social resources was subsequently dissipated. The result was warfare and economic contraction.

CONCLUSIONS

Too often, economists and political scientists take political order for granted. When studying the everyday politics and economics of taxation, legislative voting, or economic regulation in the developed world, scholars can safely abstract from concerns about political order. For many developing societies, however, political order is a more central concern. And the history of every developed country is replete with moments of disorder, demonstrating that political order is not always a given.

To prosper, societies require a means for securing political order. Because political order is a necessary condition for economic and political development, we must enquire about the conditions that provide for it. Citizens behave very differently when they fear for their lives, their families, and their sources of livelihood.

Our chapter provides a series of propositions about the establishment and maintenance of political order and about its breakdown. In brief, we argue that political order can emerge in one of two ways: an authoritarian society where order is based on coercion, and a consensual society where order is based on social cooperation. Consensual order requires that the state provide a degree of credible commitment to political institutions and citizen rights. The first proposition about consensual political order concerns citizens and embodies three conditions for consensual political order: there must be sufficient agreement among the citizenry that their political institutions are desirable; citizens must be willing to live under the decisions made by these institutions; and citizens must be willing to defend these institutions against abuse by political officials (Weingast 1997). When citizens disagree about desirable political institutions or the legitimate ends of the state, they cannot police limits on political officials, which leads to an authoritarian society.

The second proposition about consensual political order is that successful societies must limit the stakes of political decision making. Citizens must have sufficient rights—whether de facto or de jure—ensuring that substantial aspects of social, economic, and political life are beyond the reach of the state. The absence of sufficient rights implies that high stakes attend normal politics. This, in turn, has two major consequences. First, those in power will be less likely to give up that power when they lose elections. Second, those out of power are more likely to resort to extralegal means of political transformation.

The third proposition highlights an implication of the second. When rights to valuable assets (whether physical capital, land, or technology) are absent, incompletely specified, or inadequately enforced, individuals will compete for those rights, often expending in the aggregate up to or more than the asset's value. Resources devoted to competing for the right—as opposed to its use—are unproductive and therefore dissipate the net social value of establishing the right, possibly to zero. The greater the uncertainty over citizen rights, the greater the social resources devoted to competition for them. In the limit, everything is at stake in a society without basic agreement about rights or the rules governing economic and political choice. Citizens in such a society devote most of their resources to fighting one another, and the society is characterized by conflict, turmoil, political disorder, and economic contraction.

The final proposition is that providing political order requires that the state credibly commit itself to establish and maintain a variety of citizen rights, ensuring that citizens possess a sufficient degree of political security from political opportunism. Without this protection, rights are insecure. Furthermore, without it, citizens will insufficiently invest in economically productive activities, investing instead in means of protecting themselves from undesirable action from one another and from the state. Credible commitments also tie together the principles of political order just noted. The willingness of the citizenry to defend their rights and their institutions helps make these institutions and rights credible.

Force plays an important role in the emergence and maintenance of authoritarian order. First, it lowers the degree of support necessary to remain in power. Second, because many authoritarian regimes emerge from political disorder, many citizens are willing to submit to the regime if it establishes order. The threat of a return to disorder drives many to support the regime, if somewhat reluctantly.

Authoritarian states typically fail to establish any form of consensus over citizen rights. This has two consequences. First, citizens cannot police limits on government; therefore, universalistic rights are difficult to enforce. Second, the absence of consensus indicates that the regime draws support from some segment of the population, and often tramples the rights of the rest.

Revolutionary America

We apply our approach to a comparison of economic and political development in the Americas. Specifically, we study the years before and after independence in British North America and Latin America. Both regions began as colonies of major European states. Independence in both began with revolutions to throw off the metropole. Yet independence brought on stark contrasts in political and economic behavior. Fifty years after independence, the United States was well on its way to being the richest nation in the world. Fifty years after independence, most of Spanish America was emerging from decades of internecine warfare and economic contraction.

The Spanish (North 1987) and British carried their governance systems for political and economic systems across the Atlantic. In both systems, rights to land in the new world began with grants from the Crown. Yet there the similarities ended. The Spanish empire lodged these rights in a system of privilege based on personal and corporate connection to the Crown. In contrast, the British system lodged rights in what became a system of transferable titles enforced by the judiciary.

The foundation of the Spanish system was political exchange, whereby elites gained rights and privileges by virtue of sustained loyalty and support for the Crown. Given the powers of and constraints on the absolutist Crown, the political exchange of rights for political support helped ensure its long-term survival. In contrast to the English monarchy, the Spanish Crown was never forced to create a more decentralized and less personalistic system of rights.

A second aspect of the Spanish system was that the Crown was financially constrained, forcing numerous bankruptcies. Because this resulted in a short-time horizon for the Crown, many critical economic and political decisions were made for short-term financial expediency rather than long-term gain.

The English system of rights depended directly not on political loyalty, but on legally enforced rights. Although the English experienced considerable conflict over rights, their enforcement, and royal power during the seventeenth century, these controversies were decisively settled in the Glorious Revolution of 1689. A representative system emerged as central to enforcing rights and other systematic limits on the Crown. In contrast to the Spanish Crown, the British Crown was not financially constrained after the Glorious Revolution, reducing the scope of political decisions made for short-term financial expediency.

These two systems had direct consequences for economic development in the Spanish empire. The economy throughout the empire resembled more of a modern undeveloped country than a thriving market system. In contrast, after the Glorious Revolution, the British empire represented one of the largest common markets in the world, with a relative absence of government intervention.

The Spanish Crown governed the empire in large part to raise revenue, often sacrificing long-term economic growth. Static deadweight losses from trade restrictions and customs fees in New Spain were considerably larger than those estimated for British North America. Sundry royal monopolies and monopsonies, the most famous example of which was tobacco, created further disincentives to invest and undertake productive activity in Spanish America. Economists and historians have not precisely determined the dynamic consequences for long-term growth of colonial economic distortions intended to benefit the king's coffers. But there can be little doubt they were considerable. The set of trade restrictions greatly increased transportation costs. Huge land grants absent a system of titling often prevented land from being traded to its highest valued user. The fleet system, as economically inefficient as it was, generally served its purpose of moving bullion safely to Spain (Burkholder and Johnson 1990, p. 139). Finally, the Crown's short-time horizon implied that it preferred the immediate revenue to a more competitive system that would foster greater development, and perhaps greater revenues later.

Prior to the revolutionary struggles, the British mercantile system was comparatively lax. It allowed the development of seemingly endless numbers of ports across British North America, did not constrain intercolonial trade, and did not impose a range of monopolies on critical economic activities. The British did constrain aspects of trade within the empire (some products could be shipped only to England), but these constraints were considerably weaker than those of the Spanish system.

British colonies were governed locally through representative assemblies, an independent judiciary, with a British-appointed governor. This system provided a systematic rule of law protecting individual rights and governing local production.

The federal structure of the British empire combined with a decentralized investment and a common market (with an absence of local trade barriers) to develop a flourishing system of specialization and exchange within the empire.

Our principles of political order help explain the differences between British North America and Spanish America that emerged after independence. In British North America, the revolutionary struggles helped produce a new shared belief system concerning the Constitution, liberty, federalism, and the role of the national government in the society. These ideas and institutions represented natural adaptations of those preceding the revolutionary struggles. A new constitution—encompassing strong systems of separation of powers and federalism—combined with the new shared belief system to provide credible limits on the national government. A range of rights, protected under the British system by colonial assemblies and limits on the degree of British intervention, came to be protected by the new states and by limits on the degree of national intervention. Secured rights included property, contracts, and religious freedom. In particular, asset holders felt secure in their property rights; citizens felt secure in their political rights (including, it must be noted, slaveholders who felt secure in their right to own human chattel). The constitution and market-preserving federalism greatly limited the stakes of politics and helped provide the secure political foundations for markets. Complementing these formal institutions was the shared belief system that these institutions should be protected and that elected officials that sought to violate them should be punished.

Our perspective thus emphasizes the importance of path dependence, and we have sought to explicate the mechanisms underlying this phenomenon. The political interests of most British colonists led them to seek protection for their rights held under the old system. Colonists were able to adapt the rules of the political and economic game, including citizens' rights, to the new environment. In particular, the new rules of the game preserved the means of defining rights, of making political decisions, and of underpinning economic production and exchange. Self-governing colonies became self-governing states. One of the main changes concerned the substitution of the national government for the British. The new United States also retained most of the British rules of the economic game, from property rights to free trade across colonies/states.

Agreement over rights and the rules of the game kept the costs of rent-seeking to a minimum. Although some problems emerged with respect to security and the common market under the Articles of Confederation, these were largely resolved by the new Constitution. In short, British colonists had experienced considerable political and economic freedoms under the empire, and these were maintained after independence.

In Spanish America, by contrast, the demise of the old system raised new conflicts that the nascent states proved unable to resolve. Throughout this region, attempts to create new republican institutions came into conflict with the old order. Under the royal system, rights were granted to individuals and groups based on personal ties to the Crown. The result was huge land grants to wealthy individuals and the church; rights and privileges for the military; and a large series of local monopolies ranging from production, to commerce, to long-distance trade. Self-government occurred nowhere in the Spanish system.

Unfortunately, the new republican constitutions, typically modeled on that of the United States, threatened the old system of corporate rights and privilege. The political interests of those holding rights and privileges led many if not most to fight to keep them. In contrast to the United States, no set of political mechanisms from the Spanish empire could be easily adapted to fit the new political environment.

The contradiction between the republican principles and corporate rights had several implications. Upon independence no shared belief system emerged in any state within Spanish America. Deep political conflicts emerged instead. Many favoring corporate privileges demanded political restrictions that threatened central aspects of the liberal republican aspects of the constitution, while the political institutions favored by those favoring republican institutions threatened critical aspects of the system of corporate privilege. Moreover, economic and political rights were deeply intertwined. By and large, those holding monopoly rights sought to preserve them.

The structure of the Spanish empire, therefore, created in every colony a wide range of politically powerful groups that demanded restrictions on economic activity. These groups also played a role in dooming attempts to create a common market across the former colonies. An understanding of the political interests created under the empire thus helps explain the continuity between the Spanish system and that after independence of the strong limits on economic activity. The result was—and remains—a significant burden on economic development.

Political clashes among the various groups within most newly independent states inevitably led to political conflict, which was often violent. The inability to resolve the contradictions indicated considerable uncertainty regarding economic and political rights, the structure of economic production, and everyday life. The absence of a shared belief system implied that political officials did not face a population willing and able to police limits on their behavior. Thus, rather than limit the stakes of political conflict, the new constitutions exacerbated political conflicts. Put simply, the lack of agreement on the basic rights and political structure implied that virtually everything was at stake.

Under these circumstances, the principles of rent-seeking yield the familiar implication: when citizens' lives, families, and sources of livelihood are at stake, they are willing to divert huge amounts of resources from productive activities to defend their families and possessions. Within the Spanish empire, the result was political disorder throughout most of the region. This framework thus helps explain the emergence of internecine warfare, the local *caudillo* organization of politics, and the spiraling economic contraction.

Our perspective complements that of neoclassical economics. As Engerman and Sokoloff (1997) argue, factor endowments played critical roles in the development of the Americas. Endowments were clearly the driving force underlying the pattern of European colonization. But endowments alone are insufficient to explain the variation of behavior after independence, even when we expand the notion of endowments to include a society's racial diversity and inequality. These endowments were constant across independence, so they alone cannot explain the divergence among the United States, Spanish America, and Brazil. In particular, nothing in the neoclassical perspective shows why the United States took the path toward becoming the richest nation in the world—instead of remaining a well-to-do state on the European periphery. The neoclassical perspective also fails to explain the violence and economic contraction in Spanish America, as opposed to the relative stability in Brazil.

Endowments are critical in explaining the economic and political behavior after independence, but no deus ex machina translates these endowments into political order and political choice. We emphasize instead the principal political mechanisms translating endowments and other aspects of political interest into political behavior and economic performance. Political interests at independence were not solely a function of endowments, but included a range of economic and political factors in the Spanish empire.

Our approach emphasizes the political mechanisms of path dependence as a critical feature of the political and economic landscape in the Americas following independence. British colonists held considerable political and economic freedoms. On independence, their political interests led them to seek to preserve their system of political, economic, and religious freedom, and these interests were largely in harmony. Spanish colonists faced considerable restrictions on their political and economic freedom. These colonists inevitably clashed over how to create a new political order out of the older royal system of central administration.

In closing, we observe that aspects of the patterns we study remain with us at the turn of the twenty-first century. The United States retains a robust system of federalism, democracy, limited government, and thriving markets. Much of Latin America retains incompletely secure democracy and a questionable foundation for citizen rights and markets. Indeed, important aspects of the impediments to economic growth under two centuries of empire remain today. Central aspects of conflicts over land rights, for example, have never been completely resolved. As recent events in Chiapas, Mexico, suggest, these struggles are still capable of yielding violence.

Notes

Douglass C. North is a senior fellow at the Hoover Institution, Stanford University, and Luce Professor of Law and Liberty at Washington University, St. Louis; William Summerhill is associate professor of history, UCLA; and Barry Weingast is senior fellow at the Hoover Institution, and the Ward C. Krebs Family Professor and chair, department of political science, Stanford University. The authors wish to thank Norma Alvarez, Delia Boylan, Bruce Bueno de Mesquita, Maite Careaga, John Carey, Stanley Engerman, Stephen Haber, Francisco Monaldi, Jack Rakove, Armando Razo, Andrew Rutten, Kenneth Sokoloff, and Alan Taylor for helpful conversations.

1. Engerman and Sokoloff (1997) and Engerman, Haber, and Sokoloff (1997)explore this view.
2. A long list of works in political science emphasize this point. See the literature on ethnic conflict (Horowitz 1985), Consociationalism (Lijphart 1975) and democratization (Diamond 1999; O'Donnell and Schmitter 1986).
3. This proposition draws on the model in Weingast (1997), in turn drawing on a long tradition in political science, including Almond and Verba (1963), Lipset (1960), and Putnam (1993).
4. We use this term in the sense of Barzel (1989), Frank and Cook (1995), Krueger (1974), Milgrom and Roberts (1990), Tollison (1981) and Tullock (1975).
5. As Migdal (1988) suggests, these are "strong societies, weak states."
6. The following material on the British empire, the revolutionary crisis, and the eruption of revolution draws on Rakove, Rutten, and Weingast (1999).
7. On the emergence of a predominant idea, see Wood (1969). General works include Bailyn (1967) and Morgan (1992); more recent works, Greene (1986) and Reid (1995).
8. Also significant was the large exodus of the loyalists after the revolution, removing the most extreme opponents of the newly independent states from the polity.
9. Weingast (1997) explores the mechanisms by which widely shared belief systems help police limits on the behavior of public officials.
10. See, e.g., Davis (1963) on banking and Romano (1985) on corporate charters.
11. Hard budget constraints limit a government's ability to sustain endless losses. Under the Constitution, states faced a hard budget constraint because of two conditions: the inability of the federal government to bail out states from their financial losses and the inability of the states to borrow endlessly. In contrast, a government whose financial losses are subsidized by the national government does not face a hard budget constraint.
12. Although there was some debate in the 1790s about the role of the national government in economic development (Hamilton's position), the opposition led by Jefferson decisively defeated the Federalists in 1800 (see Wood 1991).
13. Historians agree that throughout the Constitutional Convention, Southerners demanded institutional protections for their peculiar institutions. See, e.g., Banning (1995), Finkelman (1996), North and Rutten (1987), Rakove (1995).
14. Like all generalizations, this one ignores some important differences across the former Spanish colonies. For example, around the turn of the century, Argentina became one of the richest nations in the world. Argentina's failure to sustain this level of development is thus a twentieth-century phenomenon.
15. The fleet system was highly inefficient, and became less regular over time. Only twenty-five sailed from New Spain from 1650 to 1699; and only sixteen to Panama. If this system had large economic costs, "[n]onetheless, in meeting its primary responsibility—getting American bullion safely to Spain—the fleet system was remarkably effective" (Burkholder and Johnson 1990, p. 139).

16. According to Skidmore and Smith (1992, p. 30) prior to the proclamation of 1778, commerce from Río de la Plata was required to make the "long torturous route overland to Panama and finally across the Atlantic" (p. 30) After the removal of restrictions, Río de la Plata grew. In 1776, the port of Buenos Aires was a "small and lackluster town" but it grew to "a city of 50,000 by the year 1800" (p. 28).

3. POLITICAL INSTITUTIONS, POLITICAL SURVIVAL, AND POLICY SUCCESS

Bruce Bueno de Mesquita, James D. Morrow,
Randolph M. Siverson, and Alastair Smith

Policies that promote peace and prosperity are, by almost any observer's yard-stick, successful policies. Politicians are ever eager to gain high office. It stands to reason, then, that politicians in office must also be eager to enhance their nation's welfare in order to enhance their own chances for continuing in office. Presumably, politicians who provide peace and prosperity for their citizens are more likely to stay in office and reap the benefits of power than those who perform badly. In particular, on the surface it seems obvious that leaders who ruin their country's economy, lead their country into disastrous military defeat, or otherwise fail to provide for the welfare of their citizens must have poor prospects of staying in power.

Only one impediment stands in the way of these seemingly obvious claims: they are not always true. The institutional context in which the leader holds power drives his or her attention to the welfare of the citizens of his state, and so the truth of these claims depends on the political system that chooses a nation's leader. In some instances even small failures of policy lead to the removal of a leader, while in others, seemingly endless blunders have little or no effect on a leader's ability to remain in office.

Compare two leaders often paired in the public mind: George Bush and Saddam Hussein. The economic and foreign policies of George Bush's administration were certainly better for the American people than the economic and foreign policies of Saddam Hussein have been for the people of Iraq. Yet the American people removed George Bush from office, while Saddam Hussein stayed in command in Baghdad. Why do leaders who follow poor policies survive? The traditional explanation is that repression maintains these leaders in office. However, we argue that deep-seated institutional features of a political system, not the oppressive nature of a regime, allow these leaders to retain office despite their failed policies. Indeed, those institutional features may well be essential to such repressive regimes and explain why they can get away with repression.

Variations in just two political institutions not only help explain the puzzling fact that leaders continue in office despite policy failure but also provide powerful insights into the political economy of peace and prosperity.

These two institutions are the size of the selectorate and the size of the winning coalition. By the *selectorate,* we mean those people in a country who have an institutionally granted right or norm that gives them a say in choosing the government.[1] By the *winning coalition,* we mean those members of the selectorate whose support is essential to keep the incumbent leadership in office. These concepts are explained more fully in the section entitled "The Theory."

Our theory implies that from a leader's point of view the optimal set of institutions for retaining power and the optimal institutions for promoting effective public policy may be quite different from each other. In demonstrating this, we point to a fundamental reason some leaders do not adopt policies that create economic growth. Such policies are not politically feasible in certain institutional settings, while these same policies are imperative for political success in others. In this way we highlight the critical role that political choices, and the institutions that shape those choices, play in promoting or retarding peace and prosperity. We further emphasize that these institutions—aside from whether leaders are enlightened or not—are the key to policy success. Civic-mindedness is neither necessary nor sufficient for the selection of effective public policies. The absence of civic-minded leaders does not preclude successful policies.

Three closely related questions are at the center of our inquiry. First, and most generally, how do political institutions influence longevity in political office? Second, and following from this, why do some political systems seem more prone to policy failure than others? Finally, why do some autocratic leaders, that is, those leaders in systems with a small winning coalition, deliberately create a large selectorate?

Our analysis of these questions is presented in six parts. First, we broadly illustrate our central claims with historical examples. We then construct an institutional theory of politics that provides resolutions of the three puzzles posed above. We explain the implications of the theory and extract testable hypotheses. The measurement procedures for testing the hypotheses are then explained, following which we provide preliminary empirical evidence for our claims. In the final section we draw together our answers to the questions posed above with some surprising, even disturbing, conclusions.

ILLUSTRATIVE EXAMPLES OF THE THREE PUZZLES OF POLITICAL SURVIVAL

In 1917, the Bolshevik revolutionaries in Russia, having helped defeat the czar and having then toppled the Kerensky government, launched a staggeringly large social experiment, which implemented an entirely new form of nonmarket economy based on the labor theory of value. Rather than permitting and protecting private property, the new principle stated that almost all property belonged to everyone, at least nominally. As contemporary economic theory and the Soviet experience suggest, the determination to reduce (even the ill-protected) property rights of the czarist regime resulted in few Russians placing real value on the property they were responsible for exploiting "in the general interest." The economic experiment implemented the tragedy of the commons on a vastly dramatic scale. Because all property was public, no one had an incentive to protect or enhance the value of Soviet property, and all had an incentive to exploit such public property for personal gain.

The Bolsheviks wrought profound political changes to accompany the social and economic changes. Lenin substituted democratic centralism for the sweeping powers of the czar. The label was different, but the mode of leadership seemed similar to czarist rule. Once a decision was taken, all members of the new winning coalition—the party elite—were expected to adhere to that decision; there was little room for dissent. Such a principle required that the winning coalition be kept rather small, as it had been during the reign of Czar Nicholas. Had it been large, controlling it would have been difficult, and dissent would have been possible. Lenin's principle of democratic centralism left no room for democratic competition of the sort known in the so-called bourgeois democracies at the time.

While keeping the reins of real power in the hands of a small winning coalition, the Bolsheviks pursued an innovative experiment in the design of their political system. They expanded the size of the population eligible to participate in politics, the group we term the *selectorate*. Most generously conceived, the Russian Revolution produced a selectorate based on universal adult suffrage, one of the first such voting systems in history. Even if, as seems more realistic, we count only members of the Communist Party as members of the selectorate, this privilege still extended to about forty million people by the end of the Soviet Union, a vast expansion of the selectorate from the days of the czar.

Other authoritarian regimes followed the Soviet lead. The Chinese Revolution under Mao, like the Russian Revolution before it, yielded a very large selectorate as part of a political system with virtually meaningless elections. Even conceived narrowly as simply members of the Communist Party, China's selectorate under Mao numbered at least sixty million.

Today people can look back upon the Russian Revolution and the Chinese Revolution as economic experiments that failed on a huge scale. In the Soviet case, the political experiment has failed as well. The Russian Revolution and the political system it created led, under Stalin, to mass famine in Ukraine, the murder of loyal Soviet citizens who were executed by Stalin's government as alleged "enemies of the people," and disastrous economic policies that stymied growth and led (after some initial success) the Soviet Union to fall further behind its western European and even eastern European neighbors. Mao's social experiment produced mass starvation during the "Great Leap Forward," the relocation, imprisonment, and death of millions during the Cultural Revolution, and an economic program that left China impoverished before the rise of Deng Xiaoping.

The impoverishment of a nation by a dictator is not unique to communist states like the Soviet Union and China. Saddam Hussein has done the same in Iraq while remaining in office since 1979. He too has established a system with a tiny winning coalition, drawn almost exclusively from the Tankriti clan, of which he is a member, and a large selectorate that participates in obviously rigged elections. In the 1995 presidential election, for instance, Hussein gained the approval of 99.96 percent of those who voted—turnout was 99.47 percent, leaving only about 3,300 unaccounted voters among the 8.4 million who participated. Hussein has combined the impoverishment of his country with a long term in office, with no end in sight. Numerous other examples of leadership longevity combined with policy failure can be offered.

During the same century in which Russia, China, Iraq, Zaire, Cuba, Haiti, India, and many other countries engaged in disastrous economic and social policies, the United States, western Europe, Japan (especially after World War II), and many others engaged in policies that were successful in stimulating economic growth. Millions of people in countries pursuing collectivist policies sought to vote with their feet by migrating to countries pursuing a different approach to politics and economics. The latter set of countries were all characterized by the fact that they had, relative to their total population, large winning coalitions and large selectorates. The former set of countries all had small winning coalitions while also often having large selectorates. We demonstrate theoretically and statistically that this is no coincidence.

Why do authoritarian states go through the motions of erecting universal adult suffrage electoral systems? It is inadequate to explain this fact by saying that these are only for show, to suggest governmental legitimacy. Such an explanation relies on the assumption that people are easy to fool repeatedly, but as Abraham Lincoln observed, "You can't fool all of the people all of the time." We show that even when everyone knows elections are not close to free and fair, everyone in the system—leaders, members of the winning coalition, and the citizenry—can derive tangible benefits from such a system of governance compared to the predecessor regime. In the discussion of the implications of our theory we show that the Leninist model is optimal from the perspective of leaders who want to stay in office even when their policies are ruinous for the nation. The Leninist political structure embodies the combination of institutions that mitigates the hazards politicians inevitably face and thus most enhances leadership survival.

Leaders in political systems that have small winning coalitions relative to the size of the selectorate, like the Soviet, Chinese, or Iraqi system, tend to enjoy great longevity in office. Lenin remained in charge of Russia from 1918 until his death. Stalin then remained in control for thirty years until his death. Following a brief power struggle, Khrushchev emerged as the Russian leader, keeping his power for over a decade, until his ouster in a bloodless coup in 1964. His successor, Leonid Brezhnev, died in office almost twenty years after taking control. In China the pattern was much the same. Mao Zedong and Zhou Enlai held power for over thirty years before their respective natural deaths. Deng Xiaoping, too, enjoyed remarkable longevity in office as well as in life. To put the general longevity of these leaders in perspective, consider that between 1949, the year the Chinese Revolution succeeded, and 1999, the time of this writing, China has had only three major changes in its topmost leadership (from Mao Zedong to Hua Guofeng to Deng Xiaoping, and now to Jiang Zemin, still in power). During that same period, the United States had ten different presidents and Britain had eleven prime ministers. We contend that longevity in office is promoted by political systems with large selectorates and small winning coalitions; next best for leaders are small winning coalitions and small selectorates; and least survivable are political systems with large selectorates and large winning coalitions, such as characterize democracies. Consequently, the latter systems produce the greatest incentive for leaders to adopt policies that produce economic growth for all, and the former systems the least incentive.

THE THEORY

This section presents a brief description of a model of politics that addresses the puzzles we posed earlier. A technical development of the game-theoretic reasoning behind this model is to be found elsewhere.[2] Here we focus on the basic logic and intuition behind our model.

The population of a state falls into a series of nested groups. The largest group is the set of all citizens. A subset of the citizenry has an institutionally legitimate right to participate in choosing the country's political leadership. This subset is the selectorate. The size of the selectorate is a political choice that represents one of the fundamental institutional decisions in a sovereign state. In modern, universal adult suffrage systems, the selectorate consists of all adult citizens. In King John's England of 1199, the selectorate was made up of 197 barons who alone had an institutional say in deciding who would be king. The selectorate, then, can be very small, very large, or anywhere in between.

Citizens (and noncitizen residents) who are not in the selectorate are disenfranchised. For most of history, the disenfranchised group of people constituted the overwhelming majority of the world's population. Since the Renaissance, and especially in the twentieth century, the proportion of the population that falls within this disenfranchised set has decreased dramatically.

Any incumbent leader relies on a subset of the selectorate to maintain his or her position in office. If any member of this group, which we call the winning coalition, defects to a rival leader, then the incumbent leadership is deposed. In majoritarian systems, like most modern democracies, the size of the winning coalition is functionally tied to the size of the selectorate through electoral rules. For simplicity's sake, we can say that the winning coalition in modern democracies is about equal to half the selectorate plus one additional voter, that is, the number of voters needed to win an election. In typical autocracies, the size of the winning coalition is not tied to the size of the selectorate except for the restriction that it cannot be larger than the selectorate. Autocrats then may be able to control the size of their winning coalition as well as who exactly falls into that coalition. For most of our discussion, we take the size of the selectorate and winning coalition as fixed and given, though when we talk about optimal institutional arrangements we hint at strategic decisions over the size of these institutions.

Politicians attract a winning coalition and retain its support by distributing things of value. These valued goods take two forms. Some are distributed in the form of private goods, such as special privileges, access to graft and bribes, favorable tax terms, favorable contracts, judicial favoritism, and the like. These private goods are allocated only to the members of the winning coalition whose continued support is essential for the incumbent to remain in office.[3] Other goods take the form of public policies that effect the welfare of everyone in the state. The provision of national security, general economic growth policies that increase the size of the resource pool in the state, and the like are examples of such public policies that affect citizens of the state.[4]

The total income of a society can be divided into three pools of resources. One pool is the untaxed resources that remain in the hands and at the discretion of each citizen. These resources include at a minimum the amounts required for food, clothing, shelter, and other individual necessities. The government takes the remainder of the national income as direct and indirect taxes and divides the taxed portion into two further pools. One pool is distributed as private goods to members of the winning coalition; the other pool is used to advance public policy. All citizens retain some resources for their own discretionary use, and everyone values a mix of private and public goods over receiving all benefits solely in the form of private benefits. All care about public policy, at least to the extent that the government must provide at least some minimal security to protect the opportunity of citizens to enjoy the benefits associated with whatever private goods they receive and whatever income they retain. A society cannot persist in a completely lawless state.[5]

Leaders face two problems: one of distribution and one of credible commitment. The distributional problem concerns how to divide the haul from taxes into private goods and public policy in order to reward the winning coalition. The credible commitment problem concerns the credibility of promises of goods and policy. Candidates for leadership can promise anything to gain power, but the selectorate need not believe such promises. In this chapter we focus on the distributional problem while including the effect of the credible commitment problem. To hold on to power, a leader must provide sufficient benefits to the winning coalition so that the least satisfied member still prefers to support the incumbent rather than defect to a rival. Rivals, who are assumed to exist at all times, can also promise anything. For the promises of incumbents and rivals to be credible, however, they must be related to the available pool of resources and to one another. Competition for office ensures that fully informed incumbents equal or surpass the deals promised by their challengers. Competition also ensures that leaders or rivals who do not make credible promises are ousted from office. A more detailed examination of one aspect of the commitment problem in terms of coordination issues (but not distribution issues) among citizens can be found in Chapters 2 and 4 in this book, as well as in other studies. Of course, both the coordination and distributional aspects of credible commitment are important to a fuller understanding of how institutions shape political choices.

Rivals for leadership have an incentive to offer a better mix of valued goods than the incumbent is currently providing. By doing so they can gain office. They face a problem, however. The incumbent has an incentive to provide a mix of goods that is as attractive to his or her supporters as an offer made by a rival. Such an offer does not require the incumbent to pay out as much as the rival promises to those who support the rival. Because private goods get divided among the members of the winning coalition, the rival cannot credibly promise such goods to more than the minimal number who would constitute the new winning coalition. Each potential defector from the current winning coalition then faces the risk that he or she will not be essential to the new coalition and so might be excluded from receiving any of its private goods. For the sake of simplicity, we assume that the probability of being essential to the successor winning coalition increases as the size of the winning coalition increases and decreases as the size of the selectorate increases. The more people whose support is required to form a winning coalition, all else being equal, the better the chances of being in the winning coalition, but the more people who form the pool available to be in the winning coalition, the worse any one individual's chances are. Put simply, the chance of making it into the successor winning coalition is equal to the size of the winning coalition divided by the size of the selectorate (W/S). Because challengers cannot guarantee private goods when they are trying to build a coalition, they are at a disadvantage against incumbents.

An incumbent who wants to stay in office only has to offer its winning coalition enough to hold its loyalty. Because any member of the winning coalition who considers defecting to a rival cannot be certain that he or she will be included in the rival's winning coalition, the incumbent need not offer as much in private goods as the rival does. Members of the current winning coalition then expect to receive more under the current regime than under the rival, considering the risk that a member of the current winning coalition may be left out of a new winning coalition. Any resources left over that could have been allocated to members of the winning coalition become the private, discretionary funds of the incumbent. These rents can be the basis for funding Swiss bank accounts and lavish lifestyles, or they can be used to promote pet projects. The size of the rents can readily be shown to depend on the institutional arrangements, but we do not pursue this point here.

Our central interest, instead, lies in how much of the available resources is allocated to private goods and how much to public policy and what consequences this has for peace and prosperity. We show that the distribution of goods depends on the size of the winning coalition and the size of the selectorate. In the process of explaining this dependence, we resolve the three puzzles with which we began.

LINK BETWEEN POLITICAL INSTITUTIONS AND POLICY SUCCESS: THE THEORY'S IMPLICATIONS AND HYPOTHESES

The larger the winning coalition in a country, the thinner must be spread the private goods available to purchase political loyalty. The more slices of pie that must be cut, the less each mouth gets. For a fixed quantity of resources devoted to private goods, then, it becomes harder to buy loyalty with those goods as the size of the winning coalition increases. At the same time, the value of putting government resources into public policy does not change with the size of the winning coalition. As the winning coalition increases in size, incumbents have more incentive to pour resources into public policy pursuits rather than private goods. If the institutionally mandated size of the winning coalition is large enough, then there is no incentive at all for incumbents to provide private goods. Of course, such a large winning coalition may never arise in reality, but it can be approached.

Universal suffrage democracies provide for large winning coalitions. Because the coalition is large, the amount of private goods any individual member of the winning coalition receives is relatively small on average. Consequently, in such systems incumbency is not easily protected by doling out private goods to one's backers. Furthermore, the selectorate is also large in democracies because all adults are members. The proportion of the selectorate in a winning coalition (W/S) in majoritarian systems is large (being greater than half). In other systems, the chance that a member of the current winning coalition will be excluded from a new winning coalition is high because the proportion of the selectorate needed to sustain a winning coalition is small.

The proportion of the winning coalition to the selectorate motivates the members of that coalition to support a rival, consequently focusing the leader's attention on the success of public policy. Supporters of a leader under universal suffrage democracy are relatively likely to defect to a challenger. Their chance of receiving private goods under a rival government is high. They are free to defect to a rival if the incumbent fails to produce successful policy. In other systems, current supporters are very likely to lose the private goods the leader provides if the leader is replaced by a rival, increasing their loyalty to the current leader regardless of the success of his or her policies. Majoritarian systems induce a norm of disloyalty from supporters when the incumbent fails to produce successful policy. Their loyalty is not easily purchased with private goods because those must be spread too thinly. They face a relatively low risk of losing the private goods they receive as members of the winning coalition if they defect to the challenger. Consequently, they are not much inhibited on that front. If they do not obtain public policies to their liking, they abandon the incumbent.

Majoritarian systems, then, create a stronger push for leaders to provide good policies than do other systems with smaller winning coalitions. In majoritarian systems, challengers to the leadership will also focus their promises on public policy rather than private goods. To the extent that peace and prosperity are widely valued, leaders of systems with large winning coalitions and a large selectorate have incentives to succeed at providing these goods. Their rivals strive to bid up the quality of policy at the margin to enhance their own chances of gaining power within the existing institutional framework. Poor policy performance is an invitation to be overthrown in democratic systems.

We equate good policies with those that satisfy essential constituents more than do the policies promised by their rivals. Policies that promote peace and prosperity need not be satisfactory to constituents. Barro convincingly demonstrates in Chapter 8 of this book that open electoral systems may foster redistributive policies that inhibit growth, though usually only after a substantial level of national wealth has been attained. After all, on average, there are more voters below the mean national income than there are above it. Yet this inhibition to growth is a matter of degree. No one should lose sight of the fact, demonstrated by Barro, Feng, and others throughout this book, that policies that protect property rights, foster competition, and protect access to markets tend to be policies that satisfy large numbers of citizens and foster economic success. These are good policies that lead to overall growth. In the model presented here, one layer of competition has been added as an important institutional feature: there are always rivals for political leadership. Their existence alone, however, is not sufficient to turn the competition into a rivalry over the quality of public policy. In order to understand the incentives to produce effective policy, it is necessary to understand the effects of both winning coalition size and selectorate size.

Vladimir Ilyich Lenin appears to have invented institutional arrangements that protect incumbents even when their decisions produce policy disasters, including impoverishing their countries or pursuing disastrous foreign policies. Before Lenin, in Romanov Russia, the selectorate consisted primarily of the small percentage of the population who were members of the aristocracy. Even military command depended on ties of blood more than on demonstrated military skill. The winning coalition was drawn from within the circle of aristocrats.

Lenin seems to have understood that small winning coalitions are especially attractive from an incumbent's point of view. He seems also to have understood that a small selectorate waters down the survivability of incumbents. Lenin introduced an authoritarian structure characterized by a small winning coalition and a large selectorate. One problem all leaders face, no matter how well-intentioned they may be, is that their policies do not always succeed. Democratic arrangements put leaders at risk of being ousted if they falter on the policy dimension. Whether consciously or not, Lenin devised a solution to this problem that is ideal for leaders, though not for the citizenry at large. His solution explains why authoritarian leaders can afford to perform poorly in terms of providing peace and prosperity.

Even if leaders pursue "good" policies, they may see those policies fail as a result of circumstances they cannot control. The timing of the business cycle may conspire against them, for example, so that they are victimized by a general economic downturn in the world economy even though their economic policies are relatively good ones. Agriculturally dependent economies may be adversely affected by drought, flood, or other weather-related conditions beyond the control or foresight of leaders. Well-intentioned social programs may backfire, leading to increased poverty, unemployment, social dislocation, crime, and so forth. Here the leader's policies have genuinely failed, but not because the leader was not paying attention to the quality of his or her policies. Sometimes leaders simply do not know what will or will not work until they try. That was probably true for the early Soviet leadership, although they stuck with their experiment long after its failure was apparent. The Soviet system made it hard for rivals for leadership to compete on policy grounds because the policy performance was irrelevant to how leaders were selected. In a world in which leaders are concerned with maximizing the welfare of the citizens, the continuation of failed economic policies is difficult to explain. In a world in which leaders are concerned with maximizing their own political welfare, it is less surprising that poor policies can endure.

Losing office is more likely following policy failure than after policy success, but how likely it is varies with institutional arrangements. What, from a leader's point of view, is the institutional combination that best protects longevity in office in the presence of policy failure?

It is clear that as the winning coalition decreases in size, more resources are devoted to private goods. Holding the size of the selectorate constant, a decrease in the size of the winning coalition increases the loyalty of members of a leader's winning coalition because the chance that a defector will be left out of the rival's winning coalition is greater. Smaller winning coalitions, then, help leaders hold office. Further, the challenger has a harder time attracting defectors from the winning coalition as the selectorate increases in size. Holding the size of the winning coalition constant, an increase in the selectorate reduces the chance that a defector will be accepted into the rival's winning coalition. Again, members of the current leader's winning coalition will be more loyal as the size of the selectorate increases. Combining both effects, the safest system for a leader has a large selectorate and a small winning coalition, the system that Lenin created in the Soviet Union. Consequently, Leninist-style systems induce a norm of loyalty from supporters to the leadership even when policy performance is not very good. It simply becomes easier to stay in power when the pool of possible supporters—the selectorate—is large and the number of supporters needed to maintain power—the winning coalition—is small. Both of these changes direct the competition over office away from policy and toward the provision of private goods to the winning coalition. In such circumstances, there is no need to commit many resources to the search for and implementation of effective policies. Private goods, not public policies, are crucial for political survival in such systems.

Political systems with small winning coalitions and small selectorates, like monarchies or military juntas, derive only one side of the loyalty benefits that Leninist-style authoritarian regimes enjoy. It is easier to compensate for policy failures with private goods in monarchies and juntas than in democratic systems because the coalition is small. At the same time, the selectorate is also small, which makes the chance of receiving private goods after defection from the winning coalition greater than is true in Soviet-style systems. From a leader's point of view, the Bolsheviks clearly had improved upon monarchy. Monarchies, juntas, and other regimes with similar institutional characteristics do not induce nearly as strong a norm of loyalty following policy failure as does an authoritarian structure that has a small winning coalition and a large selectorate.

Evidently, a Soviet-style political system is beneficial for leaders. It helps them keep their jobs and their access to private benefits even when they perform poorly in the policy arena. It also induces loyalty on the part of their key backers. That is a solution to our first puzzle. The endogenous norm of loyalty also helps explain our third puzzle, namely, why authoritarian leaders enjoy such longevity in office. Policy failure is not the dimension on which leaders are measured in systems with small winning coalitions, especially when the selectorate is large. It is also clear that systems with small coalitions provide substantial personal benefits for the essential supporters of the incumbent, at least according to our theory.

Keeping the winning coalition small makes monarchy and authoritarian systems attractive to the privileged few who are essential players in the political survival game. Making the selectorate large may benefit the members of the winning coalition as well, by increasing the likelihood that no one will defect, all else being equal. The norm of loyalty that large selectorates help induce protects not only the supporters of the incumbent but also the incumbent.

Even the masses can derive a benefit from the presence of a large selectorate in an otherwise authoritarian system. In monarchies, despotisms, or military juntas, only a privileged few have any chance of gaining access to private goods. Most citizens are in the disenfranchised group and can do nothing to improve their situation. But in an authoritarian system with a large selectorate, the disenfranchised group is small. Everyone has a chance, albeit a very small chance (W/S), of becoming a recipient of valuable private goods. Of course, the access to private benefits for the masses is not nearly as great as the comparable prospect of benefits in a democratic system, but for the lucky few the value of those benefits is much larger. Authoritarian systems offer a long shot at big gains, much as buying a lottery ticket offers a small chance to win millions. In that way, authoritarian structures offer a promise of upward mobility similar to a lottery, with similar limitations and attractions. The odds are long, but the rewards are great.

The Soviet system exemplified this benefit. Figures like Stalin, Khrushchev, and Brezhnev would have had essentially no chance to gain high office or private benefits during the czarist period. These men rose from common origins to positions of great power and privilege. They are exemplars of how the system Lenin invented provided a small chance—but greater than the chance under the monarchy—for anyone to gain valuable benefits. This makes the Leninist-style system initially attractive compared to monarchy or petty despotism even to the masses and even though the elections, per se, are meaningless.

Compared to political systems with large selectorates and large winning coalitions, the Leninist system looks unattractive to the previously disenfranchised. This is true for two reasons. First, the previously disenfranchised have a better chance of being enfranchised, becoming members of the winning coalition and gaining access to private goods in systems with large winning coalitions. Second, they also have a better chance of receiving good public policy in such systems, allowing them to benefit even if they are not members of the winning coalition. If the previously disenfranchised are allowed to shape political institutions, there is a good chance that they will select a system with both a large winning coalition and a large selectorate. That is an attractive structure from their point of view because it promotes high-quality public policy and it gives them reasonable access to the private goods that members of the winning coalition receive. In other systems, they have little chance of gaining access to private goods and they can expect poor public policy. For leaders, however, Leninist systems are ideal because they protect against being deposed even when policies fail. This is the answer to our second puzzle. Leaders in systems with small winning coalitions and large selectorates do not need to be as attentive to policy as a means of holding power and therefore policy failure is more likely than would otherwise be the case.

The norms of conduct toward leaders are radically different in democracies and autocracies. Autocracies induce a norm of loyalty, while democracies induce disloyalty from supporters when policies fail. Put differently, retrospective voting makes sense in democracies but is likely to be a minor factor in autocracies. All else equal, democratic leaders facing policy failure can expect to survive in office for a shorter time than authoritarian heads of systems with small winning coalitions and large selectorates faced with a similar crisis in policy. Furthermore, when the size of the winning coalition is small, private goods more easily compensate supporters for utility losses derived from the incumbent's poor policy performance. Because leaders of systems with small winning coalitions reward their supporters primarily with private goods, which induces loyalty in their supporters, they need not be especially attentive to their policy choices. So, leaders in political systems with small winning coalitions are unlikely to invest heavily in advisors and bureaucrats responsible for evaluating and choosing policies with an eye to satisfying key constituents. Being less attentive or informed about policy matters, authoritarians are likely to perform rather poorly compared to their counterparts in systems with large winning coalitions and large selectorates. These implications derived from our theory provide an explanation for the three puzzles with which we began. We restate the implications now as the hypotheses to be tested here:

Hypothesis 1: Given poor policy performance, the risk that a leader will be deposed increases as the size of the winning coalition increases.

Hypothesis 2: Given poor policy performance, the risk that a leader will be deposed decreases as the size of the selectorate increases.

Hypothesis 3: The larger the size of the winning coalition, the greater the commitment of resources by the government to the pursuit of good policy.

Hypothesis 4: The larger the size of the selectorate, the smaller the commitment of resources by the government to the pursuit of good policy.

Hypothesis 5: The larger the size of the winning coalition, all else being equal, the better the policy performance of the polity.

Hypothesis 6: The larger the size of the selectorate, all else being equal, the worse the policy performance of the polity.

THE DATA AND MEASUREMENTS

To test these hypotheses, we draw on the Polity III data set (Jaggers and Gurr 1996) and, as appropriate, militarized interstate disputes data from the Correlates of War project (Gochman and Maoz 1984). We have added to these data our assemblage of leadership information, including the name and date of entry and exit for each head of government in each country, as available, for the years between 1794 and 1993. These data were derived primarily from Spuler, Allen, and Saunders's *Rulers and Governments of the World* (1977) and checked against the historical chronology given in Langer's (1972) *Encyclopedia of World History*, Bienen and Van de Walle's *Of Time and Power* (1991), and *The Cambridge Encyclopedia* (Crystal 1990, pp. RR 42–67). Post-1965 data were also checked against *Facts on File*. The leadership data, which have been merged with the other two data sets, include information on the terms of 2,700 leaders from every continent and for every sovereign country during its period of independence over the past two centuries.

We begin by constructing indicators of winning coalition size (W) and selectorate size (S) as well as of policy failure, our core independent variables. Of course, the indicators are only crude approximations, so none of our tests can be viewed as definitive. Still, we do not believe there are any inherent biases in the measures we use that would systematically distort the results in favor of our theory. The polity data include a number of institutional variables, of which four provide a reasonable basis for constructing an index of the size of W. A fifth variable, legislative openness, seems to be a good indicator for S. We discuss the latter first.

The variable Legislative Openness measures the selective breadth of the members of each country's legislature. In Polity III this variable is coded as a trichotomy, with 0 meaning that there is no legislature. A code of 1 means that the legislature is chosen by heredity or by ascription or is simply chosen by the effective executive. A code of 2, the highest category, indicates that members of the legislature are directly or indirectly selected by popular election. It is evident that the larger the value of Legislative Openness, the more likely it is that S is large. We add 1 to this indicator, so that it varies between 1 and 3, and refer to this variable as S.

To estimate the size of W, we construct a composite index based on the variables Regtype, Xrcomp, Xropen, and Parcomp in Polity III. When Regtype is not missing data and is not equal to code 2 or 3 in the polity data set, so that the regime type was not a military or military/civilian regime, we award one point to W. When Xrcomp—that is, the competitiveness of executive recruitment—is larger than or equal to 2, then another point is assigned to W. An Xrcomp code of 1 means that the chief executive was selected by heredity or in rigged, unopposed elections. Code values of 2 and 3 refer to greater degrees of responsiveness to supporters, indicating a larger winning coalition.

Xropen—the openness of executive recruitment—contributes an additional point to W if the executive is recruited in a more open setting than heredity (that is, the variable's value is greater than 2). Finally, one more point can be contributed to the index of W if Parcomp—competitiveness of participation—is coded as a 5, meaning that "there are relatively stable and enduring political groups which regularly compete for political influence at the national level" (Polity III, p. 18). Once again, we add 1 to the indicator so that it varies between 1 and 5. The values on the index are distributed such that 5.1 percent of cases equal 1, 31.7 percent equal 2, 21.4 percent equal 3, 25.0 percent equal 4, and 16.8 percent equal 5 (based on 13,667 leadership-years as observations in the data set we used). The result is that the correlation between W and S is 0.42 ($N = 9,520$ cases without missing data), so with an R^2 of 0.18 we can be confident that W and S are measuring different characteristics of political systems.[6]

For the purposes of evaluating policy performance, we examine two dimensions: domestic economic growth and foreign policy. In the case of foreign policy, we judge it a failure if the state was engaged in a militarized interstate dispute in the year in question and it lost. In the case of domestic policy, we evaluate relative economic growth. Specifically, if the change in national accounts over the latest three years increased less or decreased more than over the period from one year before to four years before, then we judge current policy to have failed. That is, we assess failure as an inability to sustain or increase the rate of growth achieved in the recent past. Using the domestic and foreign policy indicators, we construct a variable called Poor Policy, which is coded as 1 if either policy failure condition obtains. Poor Policy is then multiplied by W and by S, yielding the indicators of interest here: PoorW and PoorS. We also construct a variable called Growth, which is the average annual change in government revenue during the term of each of the 2,700 leaders in our data set.

In order to test hypotheses about the size of government resource allocations, we add two institutional indicators. We construct two indicators, called Spop and Wpop, which are the product of S and the population of the country in question and W and the population of the country, respectively. We use the Correlates of War population data (Small and Singer 1982) and denominate total population in tens of millions, carrying the data to three decimal places (that is, ten thousand people). Because our institutional variables are likely to fluctuate in size as a function of both the inclusiveness of the country's political process (S, W) and the scale of the polity (population), we include these indicators in order to reflect the second important source of variance in the size of S and W, namely, the scale of the polity. In cases where it is appropriate to examine the effects of Wpop and Spop, we also show the effects for W and S.

TESTING THE PREDICTED INSTITUTIONAL EFFECTS

To test the theory, we begin with Figure 3.1. This figure shows the regression lines that estimate the effect of winning coalition size on longevity in office and on the average annual change in government revenue, a proxy for general economic growth. As the figure indicates and as the theory implies, political systems with larger winning coalitions produce significantly shorter longevity in office for leaders and higher annual growth for the nation. The difference in longevity is dramatic. The most democratic systems (with the largest winning coalitions) yield an average tenure in office for their leaders of only about four years. More authoritarian regimes have leaders who remain in office for between twelve and fourteen years, on average. Thus, there are around three turnovers in leadership in democratic systems for each turnover in authoritarian states.

The growth rate difference between systems with the smallest winning coalitions and those with the largest is also dramatic. On average, the difference is about 2 percent per year between systems with authoritarian winning coalitions and those with larger coalitions. Compounded over a decade, this is equivalent to a difference of nearly 22 percent in growth. Over fifty years, the span of the Cold War era, it is equivalent to a difference of nearly 270 percent in growth. To put this in perspective, the results suggest that the institutional differences between East Germany and West Germany could have been sufficient to account for the large difference in their respective wealth at the end of the Cold War, though they began in 1945 in fairly comparable circumstances.

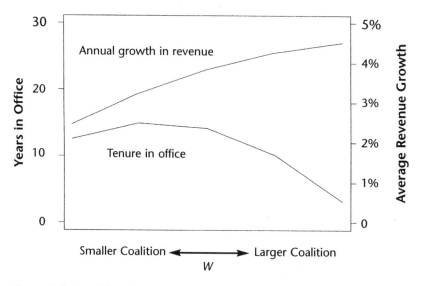

Figure 3.1. Coalition size, economic growth, and political survival

Our argument suggests that given poor policy performance, large winning coalitions are detrimental to political survival, but large selectorates are an asset from the leader's point of view. That, we contend, is why Leninist-style political systems are optimal from an incumbent's perspective. The small winning coalition of such a system helps to protect leaders from being deposed following poor policy performance, and the large selectorate further helps protect incumbents. Figure 3.2 shows that this is, in fact, the historical pattern among political leaders spanning the past two centuries and every continent. The regression line for the separate effect of winning coalitions on longevity in office is negative, indicating that poor policy performance is increasingly detrimental to office holders as their winning coalition gets larger. The regression line for the selectorate size shows a strong positive slope, indicating that larger selectorates enhance leaders' survival in office even after policy failure.

An alternative way to look at political survival is to ask by how much the risk of being deposed changes as a function of policy performance and the institutional setting. To test the theory's predictions, we evaluated statistically the likelihood that a leader will be deposed as a function of the size of the winning coalition and the quality of policy performance. The dependent variable

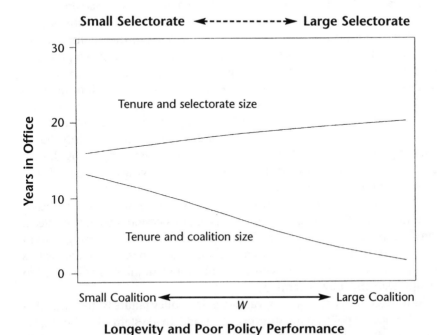

Longevity and Poor Policy Performance

Figure 3.2. Political institutions and political survival
Note: W = *coalition size.*

is simply a 1 or a 0, indicating that the leader was deposed (1) or retained (0) in the year in question.

The details behind the maximum likelihood estimation of leadership retention are of no concern here. Rather, the focus is on the substantive interpretation of the results, which are contained in Table 3.1. The evidence strongly supports the expectation that increasing winning coalition size increases a leader's risk of being deposed. We do not report the effects of selectorate size though they are consistent with the theoretical expectations. As the theory implies, the effect of selectorate size is opposite that of winning coalition size but is not statistically significant. A leader's poor policy performance, for instance, when coupled with the largest category of winning coalition, yields as much as four to thirty times the risk of being deposed when compared to the same rate of policy failure and the smallest category of winning coalition, depending on the specific mix of control variables included in the analysis.

Earlier, we asked why leaders who ruin their country's economy or lead their country during a disastrous military campaign manage to survive in office for a long time after their failure is manifest. Now we can answer that question directly. How, for instance, does the risk in a democratic system differ from the risk for an autocratic leader or dictator in a system such as Lenin introduced into Russia? Leaders like the Soviets had or much of Africa has had during the past four decades, in political systems with very small winning coalitions, essentially face almost no risk of being deposed because of their failure to produce peace and prosperity. The probability of being removed, given poor economic and/or military performance in such societies, is as low as 1 to 5 percent, depending on the control variables. American presidents, British prime ministers, and other leaders of systems with large winning coalitions, by comparison, have faced a 20 to 30 percent risk of being deposed for the same policy failures that barely affect their autocratic counterparts. Lenin certainly did introduce a political structure that protected leaders against being deposed. And, we should note, the risk to personal survival upon leaving office was, if anything, lower for Soviet (or Chinese) heads of government during this period than it was for American presidents and British prime ministers. All the heads of the Soviet and Chinese governments during this period died in their sleep. Even Khrushchev, hounded from office by a coup, lived his remaining years in quiet solitude in his state-provided dacha. One American president during this same period was assassinated while in office, and numerous assassination attempts were made against others.

The difference in political survivability given policy failure is the product of the differences in political institutions. The leader in a system with the "right" political institutions can gain long-term insurance against removal despite failure at domestic or foreign policy. Big winning coalitions pressure leaders to perform especially well on policy. These are the leaders who have the greatest in-

Table 3.1. Maximum Likelihood of Leader Removal as a Function of Winning Coalition Size and Policy Performance

Leader is removed from office	Coefficient	Standard Error	Probability	Coefficient	Standard Error	Probability
(Poor economy) × (Winning coalition size)	0.062	0.026	0.008	0.049	0.027	0.033
(Military victory) × (Winning coalition size)	-0.263	0.115	0.011	-0.240	0.114	0.018
Current tenure				-0.061	0.011	0.000
	$N = 2,336$	$\chi^2 = 12.61$	$p < 0.002$	$N = 2,245$	$\chi^2 = 55.93$	$p < 0.000$

centive to provide peace and prosperity for all citizens. Small winning coalitions coupled with large selectorates reward leaders who provide private goods to core constituents, not public policy to benefit the masses. These leaders are rewarded for fostering corruption and uncertainty (much as are those described in Chapter 4 of this volume). They have little incentive to attend to the general welfare of their citizenry, because doing so takes resources away from their critical need to provide private benefits to the essential few.

It remains for us to show that leaders who operate in systems that provide incentives to perform well on the public policy front do, in fact, perform well. We provide several different tests of this claim. As we argued earlier, political leaders who need to provide successful public policy have incentives to invest in information pertinent to policy performance. Consequently, they are likely to spend more on government and to surround themselves with advisors by appointing a large cabinet and many supporting government agents charged with acquiring information and implementing policy. There is little reason to waste government resources on a large bureaucracy if political rewards come in the form of private goods. Similarly, large cabinets make sense if leaders are concerned with the quality of their policies; otherwise, cabinet offices represent a drain on resources that could be spent keeping key constituents happy with their private benefits.

In testing the hypotheses with regression analysis, we control for prior economic performance by using a variable measured as the percentage change in the current year's national accounts relative to the national accounts three years earlier. Presumably, high expenditures are more likely to produce successful policies such as economic growth, which, in turn, provide the resources with which to spend more on government. We control for this consideration, therefore, to demonstrate the independent influence that political institutions have on government resource allocations in pursuit of political survival. We also control for total population to ensure that the effects of our institutional variables are not merely reflecting differences in the scale of various polities.

The data support the expectations regarding political institutions and government resource allocations. There is a statistically strong relationship between the size of a polity's winning coalition, its selectorate, and the size of the executive's cabinet or the magnitude of government expenditures, as shown in Tables 3.2–3.3.

Our investigation reveals that there is a standard deviation difference of approximately 3 in the expenditures of a most democratic government and a most autocratic/Leninist-style government. Taking country size into account along with Wpop and Spop, the difference that institutions make expands to an astonishing 19 standard deviations. That is, there is virtually no likelihood that the difference has arisen merely by chance.

The effects of W and S (or Wpop and Spop) are similar with respect to cabi-

Table 3.2. Government Expenditures and Political Institutions

Government Expenditures	Beta	t-Statistic	Probability[a]	Beta	t-Statistic	Probability[a]
W	0.098	4.650	0.000			
S	−0.039	−1.836	0.033			
Wpop				0.836	9.064	0.000
Spop				−0.999	−7.225	0.000
Growth	0.156	7.990	0.000	0.156	8.149	0.000
Population	0.151	7.734	0.000	0.328	2.425	0.015
	$N = 2{,}490$	$F = 37.21$	$p = 0.000$	$N = 2{,}490$	$F = 57.83$	$p = 0.000$

Note: [a]One-tailed for W, S, Wpop, Spop.

Table 3.3. Cabinet Size and Political Institutions

Cabinet Size	Beta	t-Statistic	Probability[a]	Beta	t-Statistic	Probability[a]
W	0.120	5.755	0.000			
S	−0.056	−2.700	0.004			
Wpop				0.321	3.496	0.000
Spop				−0.874	−6.255	0.000
Growth	0.022	1.139	0.255	0.025	1.290	0.197
Population	0.094	4.837	0.000	0.650	4.746	0.000
	$N = 2{,}632$	$F = 15.29$	$p = 0.000$	$N = 2{,}632$	$F = 17.18$	$p = 0.000$

Note: [a]One-tailed for W, S, Wpop, Spop.

net size. The most democratic polities have cabinets, on average, that are 2.8 standard deviations larger than those of the most autocratic/Leninist-style polities. Taking population size into account, the difference between the most democratic and the most autocratic cabinets expands to more than 7 standard deviations.

When a country's political institutions require a large winning coalition, then it is difficult for incumbents to compensate for policy failures. This is so because the average value of the private benefits received by any essential constituents is small, all else being equal. This means that leaders of such political systems must, perforce, be more attentive to the quality of their policies than are their autocratic or monarchic counterparts. No wonder they have larger cabinets and spend more on government; their survival depends on selecting "good" policies. The quality of public policy is, indeed, a function of the size of the winning coalition and the size of the selectorate. A big winning coalition makes good policy more important, while a large selectorate undermines that effect.

To evaluate the hypotheses that link policy success to institutional variables, we focus on annual economic growth rates and per capita wealth of countries as a function of the size of *W* and the size of *S*. Figure 3.3 displays the average three-year change in national wealth and the average annual per capita wealth as a function of *W* for the 2,683 nation-years for which we have complete data.

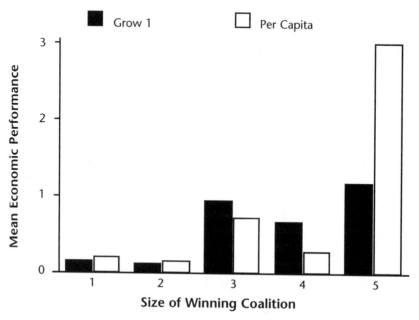

Figure 3.3. Winning coalition size, and economic performance

Figure 3.4 shows the relationship between the same indicators of economic performance and our measure of the size of the selectorate.

Both figures graphically demonstrate the effects stated in hypotheses 5 and 6. The size of W (Wpop) at the beginning of the period over which growth is measured is strongly associated with the subsequent rate of growth and per capita wealth. The effect of S (Spop) is always weaker than the effect of W (Wpop) on domestic policy performance, and its effect is either in the opposite direction or insignificantly different from no effect.[7] In a world in which information about the prospective effects of alternative policies is particularly costly, as in the preindustrial world, there is little reason to expect leaders to have developed political systems in which their own survival would be adversely influenced by the quality of their policy performance.

CONCLUSIONS

We began this chapter with three puzzles: why design a political system that has a small winning coalition and a large selectorate; how do political institutions influence longevity in office; and why do some political systems seem more prone to policy failure than others? We have provided initial answers to each of these puzzles. The answer to each one is intertwined with the solution to the other two.

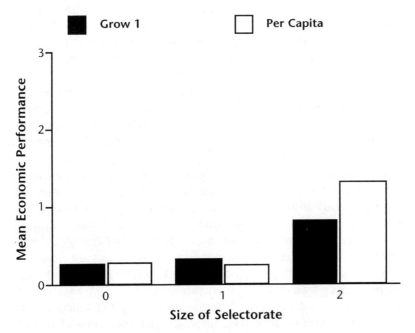

Figure 3.4. Selectorate size and economic performance

Some political systems are more prone to policy failure than others because in some systems policy failure does not represent a major threat to the political survival of the leadership. In others it does. Systems with a small winning coalition and a large selectorate are especially well designed from a leader's point of view. These systems induce a norm of loyalty among members of the winning coalition toward their leaders, even when essential supporters are confronted with policy failure. That endogenous norm of loyalty allows such leaders to be relatively inattentive to their policy performance and to have a high probability of survival following policy failure. At the same time, these systems provide ample private benefits to key supporters. These private rewards make such systems attractive from the perspective of members of the winning coalition. Even members of the masses can find such systems relatively attractive if their alternative is to live in a system in which they are disenfranchised. At least autocratic governments with large selectorates hold out a nonzero chance that any citizen will someday gain access to private benefits. Few citizens in such systems can hope to rise to the level of prominence of Joseph Stalin or Nikita Khrushchev, but a small chance is better than none at all. Under a monarchy, citizens have no hope of rising to prominence.

Political systems with large winning coalitions and, therefore, with large selectorates, do not encourage political loyalty. Quite the contrary. They encourage a norm of punishment toward leaders whose policies fail. Essential backers of the government are relatively quick to defect when policies fail. They have a high probability of joining the successor government and, in any event, they derive a relatively large portion of their utility from the government's policy performance rather than its allocation of private goods. This means that leaders in such systems have great personal incentives to be attentive to their policy performance. Poor policy performance heightens their risk of being ousted, creating an incentive to work hard to avoid policy failure. Such a system is certainly not optimal from a leader's point of view, but it is from the perspective of the citizenry. They may derive little utility from private rewards, but they are likely to be well rewarded as a consequence of the system's imperative to seek out good policies. And when the policies fail, they can expect that the rascals will be thrown out. Monarchy is a tenuous compromise between large S, small W autocracy and large S, large W democracy. In a monarchy, the norm of loyalty toward leaders among their key supporters is stronger than in a democracy, but weaker than in an autocracy. For average citizens, monarchy is the least attractive political system. Most citizens are disenfranchised, with essentially no hope of gaining access to private goods. Most, it appears, are best served by a democracy, and are better served by a large selectorate style of autocracy than they are by a monarchy or a military dictatorship. Leaders are best off with Leninist-style autocracy and worst off with democracy. Consequently, the type of political system chosen is likely to depend on who gets to do the choosing, and the evolution of systems is likely to depend on strategic decisions about modifying institutions to benefit leaders, essential backers, or average citizens.

We have demonstrated that the best institutional arrangements for leaders do not help promote good policy. Economic policy advice that does not address this fact is poor advice. Politicians cannot be expected to act contrary to their personal well-being. Consequently, leaders who promote successful policies that yield peace and prosperity must explore how to make such choices politically feasible and must be sensitive to the institutional constraints imposed by the polity's structure. Research has already begun to resolve the feasibility problem, though this is an area in which much remains to be done (Bueno de Mesquita, Newman, and Rabushka 1985, 1996; Campos and Root 1996).

Notes

This research was partially supported by National Science Foundation grant SBR-9709454.

1. Our usage is broadly consistent with the notion of "selectorate" developed by Susan Shirk in her analysis of economic reform in the People's Republic of China (Shirk 1993, p. 71), except that we assert that all political systems may be understood as having this group—not only communist states. It is also consistent with Karl Deutsch's (1961) analysis of social mobilization.

2. Bruce Bueno de Mesquita, James D. Morrow, Randolf Siverson, and Alastair Smith, "Endogenous Political Institutions and the Survival of Leaders," Hoover Working Paper, 1999.

3. In reality, of course, some private goods may be obtained by nonessential supporters of the incumbent leadership. For simplicity's sake, we assume here that such goods go only to essential supporters as a reward for their support.

4. We treat these as pure public goods, lumping their divisible and excludable components into the private goods portion of utility calculations.

5. We define the utility functions of all members of the selectorate as Cobb-Douglas functions.

6. We evaluated how beneficial S and W are as surrogates for the size of the selectorate and the size of the winning coalition, respectively, by constructing three dummy variables, called Large, Small, and Mixed. Large is coded as 1 if the index for W is greater than 2 and Legislative Openness is equal to 2. Small is coded as 1 if the index for W is less than or equal to 2 and Legislative Openness is less than 2. Finally, Mixed is coded as 1 if the index for W is less than or equal to 2 and Legislative Openness is equal to 2. We could also have created a fourth dummy variable in which $W > 2$ and Legislative Openness < 2. However, in our initial tests of the more than 1,100 cases in our data set, only 20 meet these conditions and it did not seem fruit-

ful to use them. To evaluate the reliability of the index for W and Legislative Openness as surrogate indicators for W and S, we correlated Large, Small, and Mixed with Polity III's coding of "democraticness" (Demo) and "autocraticness" (Auto), each on an eleven-point scale. The Polity III data also identify states as monarchies or not monarchies. We correlated Large, Small, and Mixed on a dummy variable coded as 1 if the state was described in the Polity III data as a monarchy. If our indicators are good surrogates, then Demo should have its highest positive correlation with Large, Auto with Mixed, and Monarch with Small. The results (too lengthy to report here) strongly support our expectations and are available in detail upon request.

7. Although we have not demonstrated this point here, the theory implies that the effects of S should generally be weaker than the effects of W.

4. THE COMPULSION OF PATRONAGE
POLITICAL SOURCES OF INFORMATION ASYMMETRY AND RISK IN DEVELOPING COUNTRY ECONOMIES

Hilton L. Root and Nahalel Nellis

Adam Smith used the notion of an invisible hand to describe how self-interest leads to social welfare.[1] Smith's classic metaphor motivated formal models by Kenneth Arrow in 1951 and Gérard Debreu in 1959. The Arrow-Debreu model proved that, given certain significant assumptions, competition leads to efficient resource allocation. The salience of the model's assumptions concerning information has attracted considerable attention in the subsequent literature of economics. In particular, Arnott, Greenwald, and Stiglitz (1994) and Greenwald and Stiglitz (1986) question the model's utility by showing that markets are not Pareto efficient when the Arrow-Debreu information assumptions are violated.[2]

This chapter demonstrates the existence of conditions that violate Arrow and Debreu's assumptions of perfect information. It is politically advantageous and rational for governments in developing countries to create information asymmetries that shape the performance of firms and markets. This insight extends the critique of Stiglitz and colleagues that the standard neoclassical assumptions are unrealistic. They also argue that government can hypothetically intervene in markets to correct information asymmetry and increase market efficiency. We demonstrate that governments that create information asymmetries cannot be expected to intervene to make markets more efficient. Therefore, in order to provide policy guidance to improve market allocation, economics must take political rationality into account.

This chapter is composed of six sections. In the first section, we present an overview of the assumptions related to information in the Arrow-Debreu model. In the second section, we use Max Weber's analysis on patrimonial authority to identify a political system that produces policies which increase information imperfections. We call that system "patronage."[3] Section three analyzes how patronage politics motivates policies that increase information imperfections. In section four, we demonstrate how these imperfections affect firms by inhibiting the formation of risk markets. The fifth section demonstrates how economic decision making in a patronage system departs from the assumptions of the fundamental theorems of welfare economics. In the conclusion, we argue that the prevalence of political patronage challenges the relevance of the standard neoclassical model in prescribing policies to improve the efficiency of market allocations in developing countries.

ARROW AND DEBREU'S ASSUMPTIONS CONCERNING INFORMATION

To define what is meant by (im)perfect information and risk markets, the information cost literature of economics—specifically that of Joseph Stiglitz (1994)—examines the two critical assumptions of the Arrow-Debreu model. The first of the two fundamental theorems argues that "competitive economies are Pareto efficient" (p. 27). In relation to the second theorem of welfare economics, which states that "every Pareto efficient allocation of resources could be attained through the use of market mechanisms" (p. 45), Stiglitz and colleagues argue the case for market-enabling government interventions.[4] Although patronage is ubiquitous, its role in distorting government performance is not accounted for.

Assumptions of the First Theorem

The first fundamental theorem, "competitive economies are Pareto efficient," assumes the following about the role of information in economic calculation:

1. Information is perfect, meaning that information is "fixed" or "unaffected by any action taken by any individual, any price, or any variable affected by collective action of individuals in a market" (Stiglitz 1994, p. 29).[5]
2. Information in markets is complete (a subset of assumption 1). Incomplete markets arise because of transactions costs, an important component of which is information costs. Without transactions costs, individuals can transfer, share, and pool risks on their own without institutions for these purposes. The existence of a full set of risk markets (see assumption 5), however, ensures that the market can efficiently transfer, share, and pool risks (Stiglitz 1994, p. 209).
3. Competition is perfect (every firm is a price taker). Markets, themselves, do not impose costs when distributing information about goods (prices) (i.e., firms do not face fixed costs when acquiring information about production or overhead costs for operation (Stiglitz 1994, pp. 28–29, 39).
4. Market economies can "solve" information problems efficiently (Stiglitz 1994, pp. 33–43). In other words, economic actors will not use information in opposition to market mechanisms or clear price signals. In economics terminology, the theorem assumes that economic actors will not create search costs or "noise."
5. A complete set of risk markets, such as credit markets, stock markets, and futures markets, are necessary because "in the absence of futures markets the price system cannot coordinate future-oriented activities, such as investments" (Stiglitz 1994, pp. 19, 29).[6] Risk markets decrease penalties to economic actors by trans-

ferring, transforming, and sharing the risks involved in economic exchange. For example, firms can raise capital by debt or by equity.

In sum, economic models in the Arrow-Debreu tradition assume perfect information and a complete set of risk markets. (Assumptions 2 through 4 are fulfilled by assumption 1.) Stigilitz's challenge of the assumption about information in the first theorem of welfare economics has resulted in the expansion of the standard considerations of "market failure" in the economic literature, which refers primarily to production externalities and public goods.[7] We posit the existence of an additional set of constraints to governance or decision-making structures used to operate the economy.

Political Patronage and the Economy

The example of contemporary India illustrates how political constraints created by patronage systems generate information asymmetries which interfere with economic calculation. In Max Weber's definition of patrimonialism, he recognized that the exercise of patrimonial control over the economy by political actors created incentives for imperfect information. Weber also anticipated that patrimonial authority would intervene excessively in the economy and impose fiscal arbitrariness. Imperfect information results from governments' discretionary application, which, in turn, inhibits risk markets.

Patrimonialism thus inhibits government intervention from accomplishing two of the goals ascribed to it by economists: lump-sum redistributions, to promote the efficiency of market mechanisms (as assumed in the second fundamental theorem of welfare economics); and the subsidy of Pareto-improving complements and taxation of Pareto-diminishing substitutes (which Stiglitz and colleagues offer as a means to reduce the externalities caused by imperfect information and incomplete risk markets). Stiglitz believes that government has instruments to alleviate moral hazard as well as the information required to use those instruments effectively. However, patronage politics makes access to such information unlikely and constrains the government's powers for Pareto-improving interventions. The government cannot do better than the market because the market is itself a reflection of information distortions generated by government policy. Government cannot reduce risk when it is one of the primary sources of risk.

PATRIMONIAL DOMINATION AND THE ECONOMY

Max Weber's linkage of political domination with economic regulation of the economy has great predictive power for explaining the new forms of patrimonial domination that emerged in developing countries following independence in the twentieth century. Using Weber's definition, we list those characteristics that apply to developing countries in general; in a later section, we specify their application to India.

Weber writes: "In the pure type, patrimonial domination regards all governing powers and the corresponding economic rights as privately appropriated economic advantages" (Weber 1978, p. 236). Patronage-based regimes will regulate economic activity as a means to expand patronage networks. This serves to undermine the formal rationality of the technical legal order, making economic calculations difficult.

Political or administrative regulations offer opportunities for strategic interventions, allowing those who exercise patrimonial political control to shape the structure and performance of the economy in ways that are inconsistent with efficient economic behavior. Regulatory discretion enables political leaders to make market participation dependent upon political contracts. The difference between distribution and production narrows, and both become politically allocated rights. These practices limit the independent status of property rights, subordinating them to political imperatives. Property rights must then be enforced through political power rather than through neutral legal mechanisms. Once the opportunities for profit are subject to administrative discretion, the outcomes of economic competition can no longer be predicted by neoclassical models.

Numerous are the instruments of administrative discretion that offer patronage opportunities to governments. The most important is a discretionary tax apparatus, highly valued by patronage-driven political masters because it can be used to control citizens' acquisitive activities. Discretionary tax levies interfere with ordinary business calculation and are the single most important motive for firms to shelter their production by cooking their books, exchanging goods in the black market, and contracting informally with trading partners. Thus, discretion in governmental decision making distorts information flows needed for the private sector to calculate the risks and rewards of economic exchange and investment.

Tax policy in most developing countries, India included, was created without formal consultation with the business sector. This is in sharp contrast with the economically successful countries of early modern Western Europe and contemporary East Asia where policies governing the economy, especially fiscal policies, have been developed through consultation. The urban commune, upon which the patrimonial leaders of western Europe depended for financial support, participated in the formulation of fiscal policy. In East Asia, corporate organization of the business community allowed for direct input into policy making and gave business veto power over potentially injurious policies (Campos and Root 1996; Root 1996). In contrast, in South Asia, as in most of the developing world, business did not have bargaining power over the formulation of fiscal policy.

The Indian economy before liberalization illustrates many of the ways political and institutional arrangements are employed by both government and economic actors for personal economic advantage. Patronage motivates politicians and their clients to deliberately fashion imperfect information in markets in order to profit from them.

PATRIMONIALISM AND THE BUREAUCRACY

Patrimonial government reproduces similar patterns of behavior in a wide range of social settings. The resulting patterns of patron/client relations produce outcomes that depend on the specific institutional configuration in a given polity. Patronage is too general to be studied outside the particular institutional setting which determines who exercises decision-making rights and the terms of exchange between patrons and clients.

Patronage influences the production of goods and services by making the right to participate in the market system depend upon the discretion of political sponsors. Instead of universal, rule-bound methods for conducting public business, patronage ensures that schools and clinics are built for supporters, not for those truly in need. Appointments are distributed to support relatives or to repay debts. Social status results from ostentatious wealth acquired by those who subvert or circumvent the government. Nevertheless, development economists typically ignore these costs as distributional.

Maintaining the loyalty of clients requires the constant flow of redistribution goods, motivating government actors to intervene in the economy and favor policies that enhance discretion over rules. Even more insidious, government does not respond to general interests when favoritism and personal preferences replace precedents and rules. Hence policies and the institutions responsible for their formulation cannot be easily disentangled. Critical economic information can be restricted only to economic agents whose interests are tied directly with the political decision makers.

INDIA'S PATRONAGE-DRIVEN POLITICS

At independence in 1947, India's colonial leaders bequeathed a formally rational system of public administration staffed by persons with legal training whose source of authority was constitutionally distinct from that of the nation's political authorities. The rules of the system were designed to protect bureaucratic decision making from political opportunism. However, this inheritance did not adequately protect the bureaucracy from succumbing to the compulsion of patronage that motivated the political system.

Patron-client relationships linked the Indian population to the national party system and to the system of rewards. These ties changed over time, in part because of political competition. At independence, tradition helped define the expectations and rewards that linked hierarchically, vertically differentiated parties. The traditional power brokers acted as both agents of the center in the locality and agents of the locality in the center.

The first group of postindependence leaders were separated from their clients by unbridgeable differences in education and wealth. These leaders did not speak the same language as their clients or share moral bonds. As the public's democratic aspirations were ignited, they sought leaders from their own caste or subcaste—people more like themselves—rather than from categorically different groups. Political competition encouraged the rise of a new set of leaders as eventually the traditional power brokers were unable to distribute patronage broadly enough to prevent others from rising to serve more particular networks. Thus, spoils-based politics led to factionalism and political fragmentation, making it impossible for India's Congress party to integrate the nation politically (Bueno de Mesquita 1978).[8]

India's Thick, Liquid Market for Corruption: The Postings Merry-Go-Round

The failure of India's bureaucracy to effectively deliver public services was not anticipated in its postindependence constitution. India's administrative institutions were designed to ensure sovereign commitment to democratically determined policy alternatives. The accountability of elected officials was flawed, despite the existence of a civil service commission grounded in the constitution: the prime minister can choose the civil service commissioner without legislative oversight.[9] Laws prevent politically motivated promotions or dismissals but do not protect civil servants from being posted arbitrarily, a major flaw. Where departments allocate licenses, subsidize goods, or raise money by black-market sales (e.g., transport, public health, civil supplies, the development authority for land and projects), posts can command a good price.[10] Power over postings, therefore, is a key to understanding corruption, which is at the core of distorted information flows.

The valuation of posts poses a significant barrier for politicians to maximize their profits by controlling posts. To surmount this barrier, an implicit auction system has evolved, allowing bureaucrats to bid for the most desirable "wet posts" from which the rupees pour. The price offered by the seeker reveals the value of the post.[11] Because posts vary significantly in terms of how much private benefit can be extracted, there is considerable competition among managers of public bureaus. The most corrupt managers have the money to compete for the most lucrative posts. To maximize the amount of revenue collected, these auctions are held frequently, hence transfers occur frequently.[12]

Efficient managers earn more than inefficient managers, but not in the production of public goods. The system fosters innovation to improve the private yield on posts because ambitious bureaucrats must recoup their investment to acquire additional resources for subsequent auctions. There is little incentive to produce public output efficiently because job performance does not influence promotions; those are decided by seniority.

One great conundrum of India's political evolution is the existence of a highly elitist and centralized civil service that is maintained in sharp contrast to the nation's democratic aspirations. India's neighbors have modified the practice and in some cases have eliminated the elite character of service. The answer is that a highly concentrated, liquid market for the sale of posts throughout India exists in the centralized administrative service. Concentrating the bidders further maximizes the amount politicians can earn when they sell the posts. For example, if an Indian Administrative Services (IAS) post arises in a particular state, it can be bid on by any member of the state administrative cadre, and posts in the central government can be bid on by any IAS cadre from any cadre in India, so that the price will increase over bids that are strictly local.[13] As in any auction market, the larger the number of buyers, the higher the asking price. An increase in the concentration of bidders heightens the value of the posts, especially when the bidders are insiders who know the value of the positions.

The evolution of the Indian civil service demonstrates how institutions can be diverted from their intended usage by subtle shifts in the rules that govern them.[14] Although merit recruitment and seniority promotions cannot be altered, discretion over postings allows politicians to circumvent the intent of the original design. Bureaucrats are shifted from post to post much more frequently than efficient job performance would justify.[15] Excessive mobility adversely affects the capacity of the bureaucracy to provide leadership: continuity of expertise is disrupted, and motivation shifts from public to private goods production.

Highly placed politicians rarely discuss the motives for transfers. Doing special favors for key constituencies can be kept secret; no mechanism exists to ensure that reasons are given. No one knows whose interests are being served or why a particular posting has been made, so that civil servants are prevented from influencing particular postings decisions in an organized manner.[16]

Competition over rewards and posts is intense, and the wrong kinds of outputs are maximized. Because a successful post holder is one who acquires funds to move to a more lucrative post, the individual must distribute goods and services for the purpose of maximizing kickbacks and bribes. Thus, bureaucrats become specialists at mismanagement, working at cross-purposes with the laws and institutions they oversee.[17]

Defenders of the postings system view it as a way to punish incompetent subordinates. The mobility of bureaucrats is not by itself a bad practice, only when it is conducted without any reference to serving the needs of constituents. Transfers have little meaning in the absence of real performance ratings and accountability for outputs. Creation of watchdog panels composed of representatives of citizen and government interests would correct the arbitrary character of the present system. When the charge is to eliminate corrupt officials, remedies other than sending the problem to another locale are likely to be more effective.

The system is competitive: to gain special advantage in the contest for better posts, officeholders must outbid their peers. The posting's competition resembles a market, but one that does not follow the ideal of Adam Smith's invisible hand. In this case, self-interest and competition do not contribute to social good or to gains from trade. To obtain the resources necessary for the acquisition of posts, individuals find themselves at variance with the goals their organizations are intended to achieve as well as the moral virtues they are expected to manifest as an example to the public. Thus, legitimacy is violated and public morality erodes.

A Double Auction: The Wrong Kind of Competition

To illustrate how bureaucratic posts may be allocated to maximize wealth extraction, we have modeled postings allocation as a game-theoretic case of a double auction. In a double auction trading game, a buyer and seller each have private information about the value of the good up for bid. In our scenario, the good is a bureaucratic post. This trading game is modeled as a static (simultaneous) game with incomplete information. The game is adapted from Robert Gibbons's model of a double auction (1992, pp. 158–56).

The seller, a politician, names an asking price, p_s, and the buyer, the potential bureaucrat and coalition supporter, simultaneously names an offer price, p_b. If $p_b \geq p_s$, then trade occurs at price $p = (p_b + p_s)/2$; if $p_b < p_s$, then no trade occurs.

The potential bureaucrat's valuation of the post is v_b. This is the value of wealth that the bureaucrat expects he can extract in his post; in other words, it is the bureaucrat's value for how "wet" the post is. The seller's, the politician's, valuation of the post is v_s. The potential bureaucrat's and politician's valuations are private information and drawn from independent uniform distributions of [0,1].

Price, p_b, denotes the potential bureaucrat's bid, the amount of wealth he offers the politician, if he should get the post. If the bureaucrat gets the post for price p, then the bureaucrat's utility is $v_b - p$; if there is no trade, then the bureaucrat's utility is zero. If there is a trade, the politician's utility is price p; if there is no trade, the politician's utility is v_s.

In the static Bayesian game, a strategy for the potential bureaucrat is a function $p_b (v_b)$ specifying the price the bureaucrat will offer for each of the bureaucrat's possible valuations. Likewise, a strategy for the politician is a function $p_s (v_s)$ specifying the price the politician will demand for each of the politician's valuations. A pair of strategies $\{p_b(v_b), p_s(v_s)\}$ is a Bayesian Nash equilibrium (E) if the following two conditions hold: for the potential bureaucrat, for each v_b in $[0,1]$, $p_b(v_b)$ solves

$$\max p_b \ [v_b - (p_b + E[p_s(v_s) \mid p_b(p_s(v_s))])/2] \ \text{Prob} \ \{p_b \geq p_s(v_s)\}$$

The expected price that the politician will demand, $E[p_s(v_s) \mid p_b \geq p_s(v_s)]$, is conditional on the demand being less than the bureaucrat's offer of p_b.

For the politician, for each v_s in $[0,1]$, $p_s(v_s)$ solves

$$\max p_s \ [(p_s + E[p_b(v_b) \mid p_b(v_b)(p_s)])/2 - v_s] \ \text{Prob} \ \{p_b(v_b) \geq p_s\}$$

The expected price (bid) the bureaucrat will offer the politician, $E[p_b(v_b) \mid p_b(v_b) \geq (p_s)]$, is conditional on the offer being greater than the politician's demand of p_s.

Many, many Bayesian Nash equilibria exist for this game. For example, consider the following one-price equilibrium, in which trade occurs at a single price if it occurs at all: for any value x in $[0,1]$, let the bureaucrat's strategy be to offer x if $v_b \geq x$, and to offer 0 otherwise. Let the politician's strategy be to demand x if $v_s \leq x$, and to demand 1 otherwise. (If the politician's demand is 1, then of course the trade will not occur.) Given the bureaucrat's strategy, the politician's choices amount to trading at x or not trading; thus the politician's strategy is a best response to the bureaucrat's, because the types of politicians who prefer trading at x to not trading do so, and vice versa. This analogous argument shows that the bureaucrat's strategy is a best response to the politician's, so the strategies are indeed a Bayesian Nash equilibrium.

In this equilibrium, trade occurs for the (v_s, v_b) pairs indicated in Figure 4.1. Trade would be efficient for all (v_s, v_b) pairs, such that $v_b \geq v_s$. But trade does not occur in the two shaded regions of the figure, as neither party would benefit. This simplistic model of a postings auction does not show that the politician extracts the highest price from the bureaucrat. That is, the politician may not derive the full value of the post. The model does show, however, that a number of possible exchanges can exist, at all x's for which $v_b \geq v_s$.

Hypothetically, in a situation where competition occurs among bureaucrats, bureaucrats' profits would be driven closer to zero, x approaches v_b, and the politician would have extracted closer to the actual value of the post. This hypothetical situation illustrates that the more perfect the competition among bureaucrats, the greater the value to the politician (i.e., competition may increase if more bureaucrats bid for posts, or if a system promotes competition in post bidding). Similarly, if bureaucrats are able to collude, they may be able to increase their returns (profits) from posts, relative to politicians. Bureaucrats may be able to offer x closer to 1, on the v_b axis.

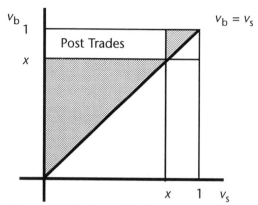

Figure 4.1. Trade equilibrium
Note: v_b = potential bureaucrat's valuation of the post; v_s = seller's (politician's) valuation of the post.

How Bureaucrats Reap Benefits through Posts

After a bureaucrat receives a post, India's institutional incentives motivate leaders to pursue patronage rents over policy performance. Bureaucratic superiors compete by providing kickbacks to the patrons or political superiors who appointed them in order to maximize their wealth and preserve their positions. Taxes and regulation are among the many means used for wealth extraction in order to provide kickbacks to superiors and income to bureaucrats, and to minimize risk of post turnover. In standard economic models, taxes and regulation are means for increasing overall economic performance (e.g., through investment-promoting redistribution or through preventing diseconomies, such as monopolies). In India, incentives exist for bureaucrats to maximize their wealth by increasing (both regular and irregular) taxes and regulation and by increasing the opaqueness or complexity of the tax-regulatory schedules. Increased complexity or opaqueness of schedules increases the discretion of the bureaucrat for both timing and quantity of bribes. The political leaders (who purportedly act as "monitors") view discretionary practices favorably because they receive kickbacks.

Political leaders have incentives to increase regulation, as it expands bureaucrats' discretion and, hence, leaders' income and kickbacks. Likewise, political leaders experience disincentives to overhaul and simplify regulation for both financial and political purposes. Deals struck with effective regulatory officials are an important source of funds for political campaigns and enhance private wealth.

How Firms Adapt to Governmental Information Asymmetry

The economic formulation of perfect information or no information asymmetries in standard economic models has four weaknesses when applied to India. We emphasize information asymmetry rather than property rights because India is generally characterized as a developing country with clearly defined property rights in the Anglo-Saxon legal tradition enforced by an independent judiciary.

Assumption 1: Fixed information.   As noted, the first theorem of welfare economics assumes that information is fixed. In India, sources of fixed information available to firms are difficult to identify. The quality of information depends on the bureaucratic or government post that supplies it and thus on the competitiveness of the bureaucratic post. For example, an import tax schedule may not be transparent; taxes may vary according to the needs of the bureaucrat enforcing the regulation. If the post is insecure, a bureaucrat is motivated to maximize short-term income; he or she will need larger kickbacks to provide funds to bid for another post when post turnover becomes arbitrary and frequent.

Assumption 2: Competition is perfect—firms are price takers (costless distribution of information).   The first fundamental theorem assumes that competition is perfect (every firm is a price taker). In addition to fixed information and a complete set of risk markets, the theorem assumes that markets distribute information about goods (prices) at no cost (Stiglitz 1994, p. 39). Even in advanced industrialized economies, this is not the case. Once the postulate of perfect information is dropped, competitive firms do not face an infinitely elastic (horizontal) demand curve (Breton and Wintrobe 1982, p. 109; Stiglitz 1994, p. 38). Because customers pay a cost to learn the prices charged by different firms, entrepreneurship can play a role in advertising or disseminating information about prices. Likewise, if the assumption of perfect homogeneity of products is dropped, entrepreneurship can stimulate quality competition and selection of product lines. Last, if the technology of production and organization is not fixed and/or known, entrepreneurship can be expanded to include innovation.

In India, the patronage system makes distribution of goods within markets more costly by distorting the effectiveness of the price system, which, in turn, weakens incentives for entrepreneurship. Overhead cost and production cost information is further inhibited in India by the suppression and unreliability of product and factor information. Variable costs to firms also increase: costs per transaction to support patronage vary unpredictably according to officials' discretionary enforcement of regulations. Because officials are not motivated to produce the necessary quantity and quality of public goods, public goods such as roads, port facilities, and airports are likely to be inadequate.[18] Public good creation will more likely be motivated by the possibility of kickbacks or political rents from would-be voters than by society's needs. Education and health facilities in rural areas are likely to be neglected most because they yield in aggregate fewer kickbacks to central leadership as compared to large military contracts or infrastructure.

Assumption 3: No "noise."   The first fundamental theorem assumes that market economies can "solve" information problems efficiently (Stiglitz 1994, p. 41). In other words, economic actors will not use information in opposition to market mechanisms. In economic terminology, the theorem assumes that economic actors will not create search costs, or "noise." Because information is rarely fixed and because information costs exist, economic actors may view information costs as entrepreneurial opportunities. For example, temporary price reductions ("sales") provide information to consumers in a competitive manner. However, because of the patronage system, *government officials* have incentives to create information asymmetries in markets to maximize their wealth extraction for purposes of patronage rather than to facilitate low-cost solutions to overcome information asymmetry. Thus, the assumption that markets in India solve information problems efficiently is nonrobust.

Assumption 4: Risk-neutral actors—a complete set of risk markets.   The first fundamental theorem assumes that a complete set of risk markets exists (Stiglitz 1994, p. 29). Risk markets decrease penalties to economic actors by transferring, transforming, and sharing the risks involved in economic exchange. For example, firms can raise capital publicly by selling debt, stock, or shares; issuing bonds; taking loans; or using equity.

However, a patronage system that creates perverse incentives inhibits risk markets. Full information of a firm's assets and liabilities opens the firm to the uncertain prospect of bureaucratic plunder. Firms suppress information about their assets and liabilities to protect themselves from political turnover or from opportunistic changes of policy. As a result, they cannot reduce risk by issuing bonds, accessing credit markets, or issuing stock or shares. Capital must be raised by opaque means, promoting informal banking. When financial markets will not diversify risk, owners will seek patronage connections instead of reducing risk by making assets liabilities transparent. Small and medium-sized firms (without political connections) will be unable to participate in financial markets on the merits of their balance sheet or the potential market for their products.

Firms must reduce the business risks they face by means other than financial markets. Firms can reduce their risks by obtaining capital or sharing risk through black or informal capital markets. This can result in an informal banking system that cannot monitor or ensure repayment, thus incurring high costs relative to the formal sector. A most efficient way to reduce risk is through a patronage relationship with government officials.

However, patronage relationships impose a new set of risks on firms, arising from probabilities of political security. Private firms in India must survive in an environment in which irregular governmental interventions—that is, corruption—creates information imperfections that produce investment risk and uncertainty. Revenue may be expropriated in any transaction; fixed and variable costs may increase by uncertain amounts, subject to bureaucratic or political discretion. A patronage relationship reduces uncertainty to firms. The patron insures predictable costs, and takes a rent for his "services." However, patronage relationships introduce a new set of uncertainties to firms and do not minimize costs. First, patronage relationships financed at a high level of government may not necessarily extend to lower-level administration or decentralized or federal governments. Patronage relationships must be formed and maintained at each of these levels, costing both capital and time (opportunity costs for capital investment) with additional uncertainty. Second, the patronage relationship may substitute political risks for market risks. Political actors may renege on commitments in response to political changes, such as loss of power by the political patron, or to policy change by the political hierarchy. Patronage relationships may be broken, however, for more strategic reasons: in any project, a political superior may receive an offer of more lucrative patronage from a competing firm, bypassing his or her subordinate's patronage relationship. Although political leaders may stage a competition among firms for contracts, unless the political hierarchy is clearly articulated, a competing or nullifying deal can be struck at competing levels in the hierarchy. It is not always easy for firms to identify and to offer appropriate benefits to the highest political leaders. Firms often discover after project commencement that they are still not safe from bids by competing firms that offer greater political kickbacks, or that additional unpredictable costs must be incurred with federal administrators.

The ideal economic formulation of the shifting of risks through competitive markets is constrained by patronage politics (Arrow 1964).[19] Instead, nonmarket relations—that is, political deals—are necessary to overcome the information asymmetries that prevent risks from being shifted through markets. These nonmarket, risk-shifting transactions are inefficient because they limit the transmission of information to politically empowered representatives of the regime. Insurance from governmental risk is then restricted to a tiny subset of the population, those possessing political contacts, instead of being shifted to the economy as a whole. Moreover, nonmarket, risk-shifting arrangements are often the source of the risks.

PATRONAGE ULTIMATELY SHAPES CORPORATE STRUCTURES
As mentioned in our previous analysis of risk markets, competition among firms for patronage relationships tends to reveal information to political leaders about a firm's liabilities and assets. Competition to reduce risk potentially

exposes sensitive financial information which may increase the risk of expropriation. By contrast, when protected from political opportunism, firms gain from information disclosures that inspire confidence in the investing public. In India, however, firms rationally create complex and opaque corporate structures to protect their capital. Owners, profits, assets, liabilities, and even sources of capital may be disguised. As a result, stock markets are ineffective because information on profitability as well as assets and liabilities must be hidden. Credit markets cannot be efficient or will not be used because patronage costs increase according to the transparency of a firm's access to capital. This is in sharp contrast to economic models that assume futures markets will extend into the indefinite future. Because potential revenue and sensitive information on competitiveness will not be disclosed, futures markets will be underutilized. Stock markets, credit markets, and futures markets will function perversely, increasing rather than decreasing risk in a patronage-based political system.

Insurance firms similarly produce information transparency and are therefore an informational liability. Owners insure their assets by making them nontransparent or by disguising their value. As a result, Indian firms have strong incentives to lobby against all government regulations to impose corporate openness.

When a firm's contractual structure is shaped by patronage (even in a competitive patronage market), rather than by ideal competitive markets, as anticipated in economic models, firms have incentives to invest in patronage and privilege. Their "market" position is not dependent on their productivity. In Indian firms, the result is that products are uncompetitive in open or international markets. Consequently, firms have incentives to lobby for protectionism and oppose the liberalization of the economy.

As a result of expropriation risks and lack of transparency, India's patronage economy generates demand for corporate relations with *foreign* firms. Scale and scope economies using the Indian corporate structures are difficult to undertake. Affiliation with foreign firms can help overcome these weaknesses because these firms' structures are outside the country; however, patronage-based politics contains an important populist motif that militates against the introduction of foreign interests.

Business organization in any society is highly sensitive to irrationalities in the administration of law and taxation. In India, the need for secrecy is a rational risk-reducing response to regulatory and fiscal uncertainty. However, secrecy results in excessively high levels of firm-specific capital that has a negative effect on productivity.

Property rights are made impenetrable to outside scrutiny to avoid discretionary governmental interventions, thus preventing the development of a liquid market for those rights. Unreliable information concerning the assets and liabilities of individual firms limits the market for claims on their liabilities or assets. By delaying the evolution toward professionally managed, rationally structured administrative hierarchies, secrecy further disrupts efficiency.

When formal alliances between firms are uncertain, intermarriage remains a more effective way to seal business deals than a contract. As a result, India's private sector organizations are dominated by family businesses, and firms remain small despite the availability of technical expertise and skilled labor. The family holding company is the preferred method of concentration, as its opaque accountability is best suited to cope with the risk of government opportunism. The private corporate sector of India is dominated by a relatively small number of large, family-controlled business houses. "The top 37 houses were drawn predominantly from families who belonged to the major traditional trading communities of India" (Kochanek 1987, p. 1281). In the family holding company, the majority of shares are owned by the family; only with great difficulty can shareholders monitor firm performance. The separation of management from ownership, which underlies the international dominance of German, Japanese, and American firms, is not possible where whimsical government intervention makes property rights uncertain.[20]

Capricious interventions by government motivate firms to develop idiosyncratic forms of institutional capital: heavy investment in political corruption compounds uncertainty by intensifying the risk of the repudiation of agreements when government changes hands. Rival political parties may require that deals consummated under a previous government be reexamined. When elections determine the status of property rights, political risk escalates to the level of that under a dictatorship. Contracts, which depend on the previous leader's discretion, can easily be annulled by a successor.

High information costs, asymmetric information, and collusion are part of the strategic calculation of individuals and firms faced with great uncertainty. Economic actors have good reason to fear the violation of economic rights by those exercising political power. To overcome the uncertainty, private firms in India are driven to demand protectionism and monopoly profits.[21] The sources of that uncertainty—weak policy credibility and excessive government discretion—must be removed before entrepreneurial structures can flourish.

Since liberalization, business has benefited from more meaningful consultation. The need to give gifts to bureaucrats when negotiating a deal is less important, especially as businesses become more educated; both sides are more likely to view each other as equal. The trading class is beginning to break the bonds of its family culture. The new high-tech firms are also breaking these patterns as they produce technologies that exist outside traditional government controls. Nevertheless, the past still weighs heavily on the structure and behavior of business interests.

Hidden Patronage Costs to Firms

India's patronage system makes it difficult for government to play the benign role assigned to it by economists using the Arrow-Debreu model as their reference. The expectation that market failure observed in neoclassical economic models—public goods, natural monopolies,[22] and externalities—can be ameliorated by government intervention will not be fulfilled when government officials use their positions for private wealth extraction. Officials in patronage governments do not derive their authority from the provision of public goods, and they cannot be expected to surmount market failure by government action unless that action simultaneously offers private gain. Hence, public goods are often of low quality and are not strategically placed to assist markets. Economies of scale and scope (natural monopolies) are extremely difficult to evaluate in India. As we have shown, information on fixed costs is not transparent, and monopolies may be channels for government patronage. Devisable output per worker (economies of scope) may be stifled because of low investments in human capital, resulting from the low gains from investments in education. In addition, patronage may create "dummy" natural monopolies: large firms with patronage relations to the government may experience less risk, lower variable costs, and lower fixed costs. Monopolies created by government regulation contribute to market failure and may conceal sectors with potentially competition-based natural monopolies. Regarding externalities, Stiglitz writes, "In economies in which [risk] markets are incomplete and information is imperfect, externality-like effects arise and are pervasive" (Stiglitz 1994, p. 62). Hence, externalities should, theoretically, be pervasive in India. The numerous externalities in India can be neither eradicated nor ameliorated through redistribution methods such as redistributive tax schedules (e.g., pollution vouchers). In sum, analyses of distribution cannot be separated from analyses of efficiency when patronage motivates the behavior of politicians and the policies they promote (Stiglitz 1994, p. 45).

WHY FIRMS POSSESS DISINCENTIVES TO SEEK LEGAL ARBITRATION

It is natural to conclude that Indians could seek redress through their legal system. India's court system is notorious, however, for not addressing the needs of business in a timely fashion. Less well documented are the incentives for firms to avoid disclosure of their own assets by bringing a suit in court to prove bureaucratic mismanagement. Disclosure of assets may cause politicians to demand higher bribes from this particular firm in the future, and it may also lead to judicial system rent-seeking. Also, delay characterizes court rulings: the typical court case in India lasts approximately ten years. Delay protects patronage relationships (which are often the source of the grievance) and increases a firm's court costs (capital costs) and opportunity costs. Disclosure of assets, capital costs, and opportunity costs all discourage corporate legal arbitration in India.

The manner in which the state publicly disposes decision-making rights has a direct bearing on the shape and character of society's productive capacity. Governments that conduct public business according to accepted universal criteria can encourage effective organization within the private sector. The emergence of universal standards of bureaucratic honesty and legal entitlement will prompt firms to adopt transparent accounting and disclosure procedures, and ownership structures. Without the institutional preconditions of transparent governance in place, the predictions of models concerning the effective use of the price system and the outcomes of competition do not pertain. When patronage determines the allocation of economic rights by government the price system will not function because only those with connections to the political system can protect their property rights (Root 1994, pp. 3, 10, 46, 233–36, 247–48; 1996, 128–36).

Economic models are based on the assumption that in a market system those who can use a right more effectively will obtain it from those to whom it was originally allocated. The ideal of efficient market allocation assumes that there are no barriers to trade. Thus, efficiency results despite the original distribution.[23] Efficiency-enhancing deals do not occur when property rights depend on political contacts that cannot be freely and openly traded to prospective buyers. When individuals hold economic privileges because of their special relationship with power brokers, these privileges cannot be traded to groups that lack political favor. Hence, the market for property rights is constrained; those with the highest-valued capabilities cannot bid for the rights possessed by politically privileged owners.

When resource allocation is at the disposal of political patrons, the expectation of arbitrary behavior motivates resource holders to restrict information. When beneficiaries of patronage withhold information from others in order to increase payments to themselves, those who hope to make effective policies do not have access to the pertinent information. Poor information makes the patron's role as neutral reformer or supreme arbiter untenable. Poor policies based on poor information are inevitable.

Overcoming the lack of trust is the primary design challenge for the next generation of India's political reformers. Reform must concentrate on the establishment of rules and procedures to ensure accountability to those at the bottom of the hierarchy. It is not enough to lay down bureaucratic regulations; for a liberal market system to flourish, assurances must be in place to guarantee that they will be carried out in the interests of those at the bottom.

Patronage politics engenders an economic system based primarily on distribution, providing limited incentives for production. Decision making is biased toward political over economic goals, generating a weak economy and thereby depriving political sponsors of the resources they need to stay in power. Governments that attempt to stay in power through expanding patronage do so at the expense of ballooning inflation and deficits. Finally, patronage ultimately conflicts with the ability of the bureaucracy to perform its task of creating public goods, which ultimately undermines legitimacy. On both accounts, patronage politics is a formula for continuous political instability and economic uncertainty. Policy prescriptions grounded in Arrow-Debreu models, which assume that both bureaucrats and politicians see their roles as creators of public goods, ignore the consequences of these risks for economic calculations. Assumptions of bureaucratic neutrality, common to economic models, are unrealistic for most developing countries. This chapter has focused on the recent history of India, the world's largest democracy, to illustrate the impact of patronage politics on the economic calculations of firms and individuals. As economic regulation grew during the 1960s and 70s, the economic ideal of shifting risks through competitive markets was eclipsed by the increased allocation of total goods and services via patronage networks.[24]

In the ideal competitive economy the initial distribution of ownership does not matter. However, as India's patronage economy expanded, information asymmetries prevented "the market" from reallocating assets to efficient owners. Thus, the weakness of India's market economy has its origins in the patronage systems that get politicians elected.

Notes

1. "Man has almost constant occasion for the help of his brethren, and it is in vain for him to expect it from their benevolence only. He will be more likely to prevail if he can interest their self-love in his favor, and show them that it is for their own advantage to do for him what he requires of them. . . . He intends only his own gain, and he is in this as in many cases, led by an invisible hand to promote an end which was no part of his intention. Nor is it always the worse for society that it was no part of it. By pursuing his own interest he frequently promotes that of the society more effectually than when he really intends to promote it" (Smith 1961).

2. *Pareto efficient* means no additional person can be made better off without someone else being made worse off.

3. This concept is not meant to describe a particular country's political system at a specific period of time. Rather, it is intended heuristically to illustrate possible interrelationships that might exist among a broad set of variables or categories of political behavior. Patronage can exist alongside rule-bound, merit-oriented competitive systems.

4. This theory defines under which conditions a pure market economy can deliver an efficient equilibrium. A society organized entirely through market mechanisms attains efficient allocation of resources in which the welfare of any economic agent could not be improved without the welfare of another deteriorating.

5. Atomistic competition prevails in which the traders are so numerous that none can exert monopoly power; consequently, they adjust passively their supply and demand according to relative prices, without strategic behavior.

6. The rational expectations literature shows that only one rational path exists to the "steady state." Stiglitz argues that even if there is only one unique path, unless futures markets extend indefinitely far into the future, there is no reason to believe the market economy can rationally choose this path (Stiglitz 1994, p.19). The theory assumes a complete set of contingent markets capable of solving the intertemporal choices of consumers and producers. Consequently, loss associated with uncertainty is removed and the historical path is irrelevant.

7. Assumptions of the second theorem: the second theorem of welfare economics argues that "every Pareto-efficient allocation of resources could be attained through the use of market mechanisms" (Stiglitz 1994, p. 45). In the second welfare theorem any Pareto optimum can be obtained as a market equilibrium. But, one condition is necessary: "the government [must] engage in some initial lump-sum redistributions" (Stiglitz 1994, p. 45; Musgrave et al. 1959). The second fundamental theorem assumes government's capacity to make lump-sum redistributions. According to Stiglitz, "This theorem is widely interpreted as meaning that we can divorce the issue of efficiency from distribution. It is not an argument against markets that the resulting distribution of income is undesirable. If society does not like the distribution of income, the government's distribution branch (to use Musgrave's terminology) just alters the initial endowment of resources, through lump-sum redistributions" (p. 45). In assuming redistribution by the government, the Arrow and Debreu model shows that market mechanisms can attain Pareto efficient allocation of resources.

8. Bueno de Mesquita provides evidence that India did not progress under Congress rule from being an "uneasy amalgamation of interests" to becoming a "politically integrated nation" (Bueno de Mesquita 1978, p. 279). One of the reasons that Congress failed "in its efforts to integrate India's population into a single political framework"was its reliance on locally based patronage networks (p. 287).

9. Although the civil service is grounded in the constitution, accountability is ultimately to the politicians. The prime minister appoints the commissioner without the constraint of congressional hearings, as in the United States.

10. In Rajastan during one year, 40,000 transfer orders were carried out in the education department alone. Fees help explain this merry-go-round. Each transfer cost its bearer Rs 1,000 to 3,000. The post of a superintendent engineer went for Rs 50,000 (de Zwart 1994, p. 81).

11. Police stations are repeatedly auctioned; officers of rank bid for the rights based on corruption prospects. As a result, honest officers have limited hopes of rising to the top.

12. Not all posts are for sale, and not all careers are made through graft. Many situa-

tions exist in which the bidding is based on technical competence, making it possible for highly motivated and competent individuals to rise in the system and serve at the highest levels. They, too, must labor with the overall breakdown of integrity at lower levels of service and perhaps can ultimately be counted on to support reform from inside.

13. Each state has its own administrative cadre that can bid on posts that exist in any region within the state. Some of the states are larger than most countries.

14. In the early 1980s, transfer policies laid down norms calling for postings of three years, but numerous independent studies reveal that this norm is not followed. One study shows that 80 percent of IAS officers held posts for less than two years, and a majority stayed for less than one year; only 20 percent stayed for two or more years (Potter 1986, p. 218).

15. The transferring authority is accountable for transfer decisions only to the immediate officer; no justification for one assignment rather than another need be given to anyone else. Who the transfer officer is depends on the rank of the transferee and on the distance of transfer. Procedures do not exist by which individuals are entitled to be consulted or even to express their preferences. No reasons need be given, and no appeal procedure is available (Wade 1985).

16. Just as the political influence of business in India is exercised in a particular manner, in this arena, too, group representation of interests is not encouraged.

17. (Wade 1985, p. 485.) Canal managers are under pressure to behave virtually antithetically to their ostensible job objectives: instead of reducing water uncertainty, they artificially increase it if they wish to maximize bribe revenue; instead of maintaining the canals in good condition, they leave large stretches of canal unmaintained to save maintenance funds for other uses. Agricultural officers are under pressure if they wish to have congenial postings, to adulterate the special inputs they are given charge of to sell the balance on the black market, and to approve the substandard seeds or fertilizers of private dealers.

18. "By far the most important conflict between patronage politics and development is the control of public services: police and fire services, clean streets, and schools with teachers do not have to be provided. Services that can be turned off selectively are more desirable than services that go to everyone. There would be no obligations on election day if the politicians provided services that everyone received" (Root 1997).

19. This formulation can be found in Marshall: "The more nearly perfect the market is the stronger is the tendency for the same price to be paid for the same thing at the same time in all parts of the market" (1890).

20. See Fukuyama (1995) for a discussion of the common aspects of firm organization among the world's industrial leaders.

21. Industries that rely on imported inputs are likely to behave differently.

22. Natural monopolies may not fall under many standard conceptions of market failure. The literature notes that natural monopolies are nonconvexities in the econ-

omy, caused by prohibitory fixed costs; therefore, government intervention in the market is required (Stiglitz 1994, p. 52).

23. The Coase theorem reveals that only when transaction costs from the subsequent transfer of the right exceed the potential benefits of its exploitation will the original allocation prevent efficient utilization. The transaction costs resulting from patronage politics fall into this category of informational impediments to trade that prevent markets from allocating goods effectively.

24. The relative size of the Indian public/government sector at independence in 1947 dramatically increased from 7.6 to 24.9 percent of gross domestic product, its share in the net domestic product increased from 7.5 to 24.9 percent, and its share in final consumption expenditure increased from 8.2 to 15.6 percent. Its share of gross domestic capital formation, as a proportion of GDP, rose from 10.2 percent in 1950–51 to 24.6 percent in 1990–91. But in gross domestic savings, its share decreased from 17.2 to 4 percent. Jagdish Bhagwati (1995, p. 6) attributes the dramatic decrease in government savings to the unprecedented increase in the 1980s of budgetary expenditure on defense, government wages and salaries, and subsidies.

The 244 economic enterprises of the central government alone, excluding railways and the utilities, employed as many as 2.3 million workers in 1990 (Bhagwati 1995, p. 63). The public sector enterprises in manufacturing, mining, construction, transport and communications, and banking and insurance provided nearly 70 percent of the 26 million jobs in the large-scale "organized" sector in 1989 (Baghwati 1995, p. 64). In the steel industry, all steel production in 1950–51 was centralized in the private sector, but in 1991–92, 85 percent of aggregate steel output came from the public sector. However, despite the growth of the steel industry in the public sector, India still needed to import steel worth over Rs 2,000 crore every year (Prasad 1995, p. 2).

During the 1950–91 period, combined public finances (revenues and expenditures) of the central government, states, and union territories rose 218-fold. Tax revenue as a percentage of GNP rose from 6–7 percent to 17–18 percent, and expenditure as a percentage of gross national product rose from 9.4 percent to 43.7 percent. The state of Indian public finances reached crisis proportions by the end of the 1980s. The public debt-to-GNP ratio increased through the 1980s, jumping drastically toward the end of the decade to nearly 60 percent, a near doubling of the ratio in 1980 (Bhagwati 1995, p. 66).

5. INDUSTRIAL PROSPERITY UNDER POLITICAL INSTABILITY
AN ANALYSIS OF REVOLUTIONARY MEXICO

Stephen Haber and Armando Razo

What is the relationship between political instability and economic growth? The political science and economics literatures largely maintain that instability is harmful to growth. The empirical literature on this topic, however, has a number of limitations. First, it is not clear which way causality runs: Do countries have slow rates of growth because they are politically unstable, or are they politically unstable because they have slow rates of growth? Second, the evidentiary base on which arguments are made about instability and growth is weak. Third, the literature does not present a model (a string of logically consistent, if-then statements) of how, *exactly,* political instability dampens economic growth, which can be operationalized using empirical data.

This chapter reexamines the question of political instability and economic growth using insights from the New Institutional Economics applied to a canonical case: revolutionary Mexico.[1] The extant literature argues that the more unstable a country's political system, the more likely it is that property rights will not be enforced and that regulatory policies will change in an unpredictable manner. This serves to decrease private investment, which, in turn, dampens growth. Revolutionary Mexico is an extreme case of the set of conditions likely to give rise to decreased investment and growth: the political system moved from a prolonged period of stability to a prolonged period of instability, punctuated by one of the great social revolutions of the modern world; regulatory policies changed in ways that should have worked to discourage private investment; and property rights became less certain (assets were subject to expropriation).[2] In short, if the implicit models in the literature are accurate depictions of how real world polities and economies interact, we should expect to find dramatic disinvestment and economic stagnation in Mexico during and after the revolution of 1910.

We focus our analysis on Mexico's manufacturing industry, for both practical and theoretical reasons. First, focusing on manufacturing allows us to demonstrate the causal connections between political instability, changes in the institutions that mediate economic activity, and changes in the structure and performance of the lines of economic activity at which those institutional reforms were aimed. Manufacturing was highly sensitive to domestic political and institutional changes: it relied on high levels of trade protection; changes in labor laws had dramatic effects on its costs of production; and the threat of expropriation could not be easily mitigated by the lobbying of foreign governments. Other lines of economic activity, such as petroleum extraction, mining, and smelting, were capital-intensive, foreign-owned enclaves that had the ability to hire mercenary armies to protect their property rights and to bring to bear diplomatic and economic pressure from foreign governments, thereby mitigating the effects of political instability.[3]

Second, focusing on manufacturing allows us to operationalize implicit economic models in the literature related to investor expectations. One of the central assumptions of the literature is that politically unstable environments work to decrease the expectations of investors about the future profitability of assets, which, in turn, decreases the value of those assets. This mechanism, however, is almost always assumed rather than empirically demonstrated. The fact that quite a few of Mexico's manufacturing firms were publicly traded means that we are able to study investor expectations through the analysis of real (inflation-adjusted) stock prices.[4] Moreover, the manufacturing sector is an ideal focus for this type of analysis because it faced a credible threat of expropriation, but that threat was ultimately not carried out. Other sectors with large numbers of publicly traded, joint stock companies, such as banking, were expropriated quite early in the revolution; consequently, they cannot be studied throughout the period of prolonged instability that characterized Mexican politics until the 1930s.

We develop data sets from published and archival sources at both the firm and industry levels in order to assess the impact of political instability and institutional change on investor expectations, rates of ownership turnover, new investment in plant and equipment, output, industrial structure, labor productivity, and total factor productivity. Our data sets include information from virtually all the extant mechanized manufacturing industries in Mexico during the period under study, including the steel, cement, tobacco products, paper, beer brewing, cotton and wool textile, and soap and glycerin industries. The data sets pertaining to Mexico's largest and most geographically dispersed manufacturing industry, cotton textiles, are unusually detailed and we therefore focus much of our discussion on the econometric analysis of that industry.

We argue that investment and growth during and after the revolution were less affected by political instability than one might predict based on the extant theoretical and empirical literature. Investment was dampened, and growth in output and productivity declined, during the period of greatest political and institutional uncertainty: the years 1914–1917. These years also coincided, however, with the interdiction of factor and product markets because of revolutionary violence and hyperinflation. Once the functioning of the market was restored, investment increased and output and productivity grew (even though the country continued to be politically unstable for another fifteen years), the threat of expropriation loomed over the country's factory owners, and the direction of institutional change, particularly the laws regarding labor relations and the tariff, was indeterminate.

The degree to which the extant literature overstates the political requirements of long-run growth depends on which hypothetical Mexican economy one posits as the appropriate counterfactual. The literature suggests two alternative hypotheses about environments such as existed in revolutionary Mexico. One hypothesis suggests that Mexico's manufacturing sector would not have grown at all (and likely would have shrunk) because of the political instability and institutional uncertainty brought about by the revolution. This hypothesis is easy to reject: new firms entered the market, there was substantial new investment in plant and equipment, and productivity continued growing after the revolution. A second, weaker, hypothesis suggests that the rate of growth of Mexican industry was slowed by the political instability and accompanying institutional uncertainty brought about by the revolution. This hypothesis is more difficult to evaluate because it depends on which hypothetical Mexican economy one believes is the most appropriate counterfactual: the rapidly growing economy from 1890 to 1905 (when a rise in tariffs and the reform of general incorporation laws permitted the creation and rapid expansion of industries), or the Mexican economy from 1905 to 1910 (when the effects of those innovations had already been exhausted and the manufacturing sector was growing at a more modest pace). If one accepts the view that the 1905–1910 economy is the most appropriate counterfactual, the second hypothesis can be dismissed as well. If one insists that the 1890–1905 economy is the appropriate counterfactual, then the results are indeterminate. We suggest, however, that this counterfactual is implausible. The Mexican manufacturing sector scarcely existed in 1890; therefore, the 1890–1905 growth rates were the product of growth from a small base that had already slowed from 1905–1910.

Our analysis suggests two points on which the extant literature overstates the political requirements of long-run growth. First, there is no necessary connection between political instability and the security of property rights: governments may change with amazing rapidity, but property rights are unaffected; or governments may be extremely stable, but property rights may be insecure. Second, entrepreneurs are far less sensitive to institutional change than the extant literature suggests. As long as rights to property in their particular lines of economic activity are not abrogated, they will continue to invest, even if entrepreneurs in other lines of activity are being expropriated.

This chapter is divided into five sections. The first discusses the extant empirical literature on political stability and economic growth. The second section discusses the theory that underlies our analysis. The third section presents a brief history of political and institutional change before, during, and after the

Mexican Revolution of 1910–1919. The fourth section develops econometric evidence to assess the theory presented in the second section. This is accomplished through a detailed analysis of the structure and performance of industry during and after the revolutionary years. The fifth section contains our conclusions.

PRIOR EMPIRICAL STUDIES

The first scholars to address the question of the interaction between revolution and economic growth were historical sociologists and comparative political scientists interested in how revolutions affected the political roles played by various social classes in the transition from agrarian economies to modern industrial ones. This literature indicates that revolutions may have either positive or negative long-term economic consequences (depending on the particular economic and social policies of postrevolutionary governments). In the short run, however, revolutions create dislocations that are largely negative for economic development.[5]

The ability of this literature to pin down the causal connections between revolutions and growth, however, is limited in its analytic orientation, its methods, and the body of evidence it considers. First, the historical-comparative method used in this literature means that it is far better at describing revolutions than explaining their economic impact.[6] Second, the lack of a falsifiable model means that this literature is limited in its ability to make coherent and testable arguments about the relationship between political and economic change. Arguments about the political ascent or descent of particular social classes are often posited (but are not often empirically demonstrated) and then offered as explanations of various long-term economic policy changes. The exact relationship between changes in the balance of class forces within the state, economic policies, and the economic outcomes of those policies, however, is usually left unspecified and untested. Arguments about short-term economic dislocations are similarly convoluted and nonspecific. This precludes propositions whose truth or falsity can be easily deduced. Finally, the economic evidence presented is of an impressionistic nature. The literature rarely, if ever, presents systematically retrieved and analyzed economic data (Dunne 1972; Moore 1966; Skocpol 1979; but for an exception see Paige 1975).

In recent years a second body of literature, often identified with growth theory, has developed; this literature has stressed the negative consequences of political instability for economic growth (Alesina, Özler, Roubini, and Swagel 1996; Barro 1991; Londregan and Poole 1990, 1992). This literature has not yet developed a theoretical model of how growth and political stability interact (in fact, there is no consensus on a theoretical framework to guide empirical work on growth) (Levine and Renelt 1992, p. 943). The implicit model in this literature can, however, be summarized as follows: when political systems are unstable, there is an increased probability that economic policies will change in an indeterminate direction or that entrepreneurs will become subject to expropriation (property rights will become less stable). This discourages long-term investments in physical capital, thereby dampening the rate of economic growth (Alesina, Özler, Roubini, and Swagel 1996).

This body of literature proceeds inductively, employing cross-sectional and pooled regression techniques to identify the statistical relationships between various economic and political features of societies and their economic performance. There are, however, a number of well-known limitations to these kinds of regressions. First, as Alesina and colleagues have pointed out, while many studies have demonstrated a negative correlation between economic growth and political instability, it is not clear which way causality runs (Alesina, Özler, Roubini, and Swagel 1996; Barro 1991). Second, there are econometric considerations that make these estimates dubious. As noted by Londregan and Poole (1992), slow rates of growth may be attributable more to the presence of unconstitutional rulers than to political instability.[7] In addition, Levine and Renelt (1992) have shown that the statistical results of these exercises tend to be highly sensitive to the number of observations, the choice of cases, and the specification of the regressions. Moreover, measurement error remains a key problem because the instruments available to measure political stability or the security of property rights are poorly developed.[8] Finally, there is a more fundamental concern about the stability of the statistical relationship between economic and political variables. Adding a political dimension comes at a cost. Under political stability, the underlying structure of a given specification may break down altogether because even a regression equation that incorporates expectations may not be invariant to time and structural changes. Adding a political instability variable may be inappropriate; the specification may no longer hold precisely because of the existence of instability. This can be a serious problem because in the pooling of countries with different relationships between politics and economics, only a subset of unstable countries within a larger data set may be sufficient to cause a miscalculation in the estimated cross-country equations.[9]

THEORY: POLITICAL STABILITY, INSTITUTIONS, AND ECONOMIC GROWTH

This chapter employs insights from the New Institutional Economics to understand the interaction of political instability and economic growth. The New Institutionalism argues that, all things being equal, societies that create institutions (the laws, rules, and informal agreements within societies that guide economic or other types of social behavior) that clearly specify and enforce property rights, that ease the enforcement of contracts, and that force governments to make credible commitments to limit their ability to manipulate economic rules to their own advantage will achieve faster rates of economic growth than those that do not (Greif 1997; Hurwicz 1993; North 1990, especially ch. 1; North and Weingast 1989). We extend this analysis with definitions of political system and what constitutes a political equilibrium and revolutionary change. We then explore the consequences of political instability for policy making and industrial performance.

Political System

We define a political system as a closed system that includes the stock of formal institutions not only to guide its current functioning as well as its future evolution, but also to provide the governance structure of society.[10] The combination of these internal and external rules makes the political system the primary source of formal, legally sanctioned, regulations and institutional change. One notable feature of a political system is that after it is first put to work, all subsequent institutional changes are endogenous to the system.

The internal rules defining the current functioning and evolution of the political system define the processes through which formal institutional changes take place. These include constitutional amendments, review of proposed policies and laws, and general guidelines as to what constitutes acceptable levels and frequency of institutional change. The existence of these rules does not exclude the possibility that a system may choose to replace itself; rather, the internal rules simply provide means to preserve the continuity of the system when it is socially desirable to do so.

The governance structure of society refers to the set of formal mechanisms that serve to mediate and organize political interests. First, it delineates a division of labor to perform government tasks. Over time, societies have implemented these divisions because of the various practical impediments to having all members of society cast votes on all government decisions. More fundamentally, as social choice theory has shown, there may not exist a social rule that satisfactorily aggregates all individual preferences (Arrow 1951). Second, concomitant to this division of labor, the governance structure provides rules about political organization that determine how people may organize themselves to promote their political interests.

One major purpose of political systems is to decrease uncertainty about two types of political change. The first involves changes in governments.[11] These changes are related to the group of institutions that define the mechanism through which governments are replaced. Institutions that define government selection mechanisms (such as election laws) have an important role in the formation of expectations about who will come to power and what type of institutional changes will be expected. The second type of political change involves fundamental changes in the underlying structure of the political system. These include changes to the internal rules governing the evolution of the political system as well as changes to the more general mechanisms available for political interaction.[12] This second group of institutions (of which constitutions as coordinating devices are a prime example) are useful in shaping the strategies of individual agents or interest groups to promote their political interests in future periods. In particular, they assist individuals in deciding whether or not to promote their political interests within the existing political system.

In sum, the political system serves as a mechanism to mediate conflicting social demands and produces as output specific rules or policies to govern different types of social interactions, including and extending beyond the political arena. In the case of politics, it provides a division of labor between the public and private sector. It also delineates the basic rules of political organization that govern a society. In the case of economics, it provides institutions that guide and restrict economic behavior.

Interaction of Politics and Economics

First, the enactment of regulations and general policies, as output of the political system, affects the scope of action of economic agents. In societies subject to some form of rule of law, the codification of formal rules lies within the political arena that is also responsible for their enforcement and refinement. The political system functions as the institutional umbrella under which economic agents operate.[13] In particular, the political system provides codified rules about property rights, regulation, and other factors that directly affect the functioning of the economic system.

Second, the political and economic systems are linked through their common need for external financing. On the political side, the general costs of government include the costs of enforcing laws, carrying out public projects, compensating government employees, and maintaining the continuity of the political system. On the real economic side are the costs of investment and production, including the costs of acquiring inputs, technology, and internal organization. The basic point to be made is that both types of activities, governmental and economic, are costly and often require external financing beyond the resources of the parties directly involved. Governments have, of course, a choice between (a mix of) taxation or outright confiscation and borrowing. In many cases, however, the tax base is not sufficient to cover all the costs of government. Then, governments will rely, to varying degrees, on the financial system to supplement their receipts. Private economic agents also face a similar constraint. When their personal funds are not sufficient to cover investment and production costs, they will recur to external sources. In short, both the public and private sectors may need to resort to external financing from the available financial institutions.

The nature of the financial system has important implications for the role and actions of the public sector. First, it is useful to recall that the financial system actually stems, or acquires legal relevance, from the political system. This places the government, as the agent of society that manages the political system, in a privileged position and a predicament. As a result, the government can use its authority to engage in opportunistic behavior to satisfy its financial needs. For example, it can force public financial institutions to print more money indiscriminately or provide alternate means to obtain additional credit. Most important, governments can force loans from the private sector. The degree of independence—not just legal but political as well—of the financial system with respect to current governments will prove essential in determining how the financial system responds to government loan demands.[14] The type of government, predatory or not, and its particular objectives may also influence its actions in dealing with external finance sources. In general, the more the government can manipulate the financial system, the fewer the constraints on government behavior. For example, a government strong enough to protect property rights and to enforce institutions is also strong enough to confiscate property and engage in predatory behavior. This internal conflict of governmental activity actually prevails in all interactions between the government and private sector and is referred to as the "sovereign dilemma" (North and Weingast 1989).

Third, economic agents take political factors into account. In general, the efficient functioning of markets hinges on an effective legal system that preserves private property rights. The economic agent's dilemma is one of engaging in productive activities without knowing whether the government will confiscate the benefits. Certainly, agents can be fooled in the short run by new governments. In the long run, however, the issue of credibility in the government's protection of property rights and the provision of an institutional environment that fosters economic growth cannot be disregarded. Economic behavior will then depend not only on economic fundamentals but also on individual perceptions of the government's commitment to enforce those rules and to refrain from predatory practices.

Fourth, economic agents may directly affect political outcomes. The definition of a political system derives from the mediation of various elements of society. These include economic agents who can invest efforts in effecting the policies that regulate them (Becker 1983).

Political Stability and Political Equilibrium

At any point in time, a political system is stable, or self-preserving, if there is common knowledge about the selection mechanism to replace governments and the rules that manage political action, and if the institutional arrangements that specify this political system become self-enforcing. The first condition pertains to people's beliefs and expectations of what constitutes the political system and the dynamics that govern its evolution. It places at the core of our analysis the social relevance of a political system: how people, in the decisions they take, internalize the rules the political system prescribes. Of course, even when people have common knowledge about a system, this does not mean that they will support it.[15] Therefore, an additional requirement is that individual agents must find it in their own interest to sustain a particular political system and not another. In turn, these two conditions imply that there is one and only one political system in place at any given time.[16] Over time, the political system may produce institutional changes that alter its internal functioning. The system may also be subject to external shocks or threats. The self-preservation condition implies that people are agreeing to support the political system in advance of these potential changes or shocks. Thus, the key feature of stability is *continuity,* in the sense that the political system in place can always be anticipated because of common agreement. Because the political system is in some sense the primary and fundamental source of formal institutional changes, this allows agents to adapt to both expected and actual changes.[17]

A political system offers two types of temporal rules for social behavior. First, in delineating the current governance structure of society, it provides a set of effective rules that apply to current situations. Individual agents take these institutions as fixed. At the same time, it serves to approve institutional changes that apply to future periods.

Institutional change under conditions of political stability is necessarily endogenous.[18] A political system reflects, at any given time, a compromise of social demands. Besides the social contract that guarantees the ratification of changes occurring through the political system, there is no additional warranty that any particular agent may be happy with the outcome. Particular demands are by no means resolved, and they may indeed change from time to time for different reasons. What is certain, however, is the mechanism for their present and future resolutions.

The stability of the system derives essentially from, and primarily because of, the common agreement to allow the political system to mediate conflicting goals in current and future periods. It is this common agreement at any point in time that we denote as political equilibrium.[19] Moreover, it is the overlap of intertemporal governance structures, those effective in the present and those occurring in the future, that relates political stability to political equilibrium. A political system is stable when its continuity is perceived as long-lasting. Because it is difficult to foresee the structure of a political system and whether it will actually remain effective, we rely on the identification of a current binding commitment that the political system will be effective, irrespective of structural changes. This is precisely the condition that defines political equilibrium. It follows, then, that if a political system is currently in political equilibrium, it is stable.

Political Instability

A political system becomes unstable when its continuity is no longer sustainable. That is, it may be the case that particular institutional changes, or demands for such changes, cannot be endogenized within the existing system. These unfulfilled demands can trigger new strategies in political organization as people regroup to secure their interests in the future. Depending on the rules governing political organization and particular objectives, people will ascertain the probability of obtaining benefits from participating through the system. To the extent that they do not perceive this route as an effective one, they will instead fight for their interests outside the system. Whether this alternative mechanism will succeed depends as well on the government's own ability to fight the challenge. It may be the case that the government is unable to successfully defeat attempts to change the institutions that govern political action. The result is political instability.

We differentiate between two types of political instability, depending on which of the two defining conditions of political stability break down. The first type, occurring when there is only lack of common knowledge about the political system, is denoted *weak instability*. It corresponds to the case where there are, in effect, multiple alternate political systems competing for the governance of society because different agents perceive different institutional environments. The second type, *strong instability,* occurs when the system loses its self-enforcement quality. This may or may not be accompanied by lack of common knowledge. The basic notion is that some political shocks, which would otherwise be internalized or dissipated, become credible threats to the continuity of the political system, making the social contract no longer binding. The nature of these threats is that they lead to a situation of multiple competing systems where institutional change ceases to be endogenous and is instead subject to the outcome of a systems war, thus creating uncertainty as to which system will ultimately prevail.

Although both cases of instability lead to incomplete information regarding the future governance structure, the second one involves agents who purposefully deviate from the original equilibrium, relying instead on violence and/or diversion of productive resources to influence the determination of the next prevailing political system. We further denote instances of *strong instability* as *ex ante revolutions* because by being potentially capable of removing the current system, they bring about a discontinuity in the evolution of the political system.[20] Stability is restored upon determination of the new political equilibrium, and it may actually return to its original unperturbed state. It is a case of *ex post revolution,* however, when the restored unique system involves substantial institutional changes with respect to the old equilibrium.

Our purpose in emphasizing timing issues is to correct what we view as a fundamental problem of the literature. Scholars focus primarily on the magnitude and direction of change in defining revolutions. The problem is that large swings in the magnitude and direction of institutional change—for example, a massive reduction of private property rights or redistribution of wealth—do not imply by themselves that an ex post revolution has occurred. Even structural changes are not unique to unstable politics: it is perfectly conceivable that drastic institutional transformations can be brought about through evolutionary change within a stable political system. We argue that it is important to focus not solely on the magnitude and the direction, but on the structural dynamics of the political system. What determines an ex post revolution is a particular sequence of events. First, there must be an ex ante revolution that causes a discontinuity in the regular evolution of the political system and creates political instability. Second, the period of instability (in which the institutions governing the economy and polity cannot be known ex ante) must be followed, when stability is restored, by institutional changes that depart from the status quo. Thus, an ex post revolution occurs with the emergence of a structurally different political equilibrium following a period of political instability.

An unstable period is a transition period between two stable political equilibria when the second political equilibrium is not known a priori. From a theoretical point of view, studying the impact of instability on economic performance is different from comparing the economic impact of two different political equilibria—which could be a difficult task but conceptually is simply an exercise in comparative statics. Instability is characterized primarily by the indeterminacy of institutional change, and its exact nature depends on various factors, including timing and duration, the number and types of competing systems, and the information sets of individual agents. By definition, institutional change ceases to be endogenous under conditions of instability. In short, under instability the direction and magnitude of institutional changes becomes indeterminate.

Implications for Policy Making and Economic Performance

Political instability implies both a reduction in the effectiveness of current governance structures as well as an inability to predict the course of future political developments. This is problematic for at least two reasons. First, instability may produce a vacuum in the current exercise of government, depending on the fragility of existing institutions, leaving room for disorderly social conduct and autarky. By changing the reward and punishment system inherent in the previous political structure, instability matters because incentives increase to engage in opportunistic behavior with impunity.

Second, political choices and institutional development with long-term horizons are affected negatively. Individuals and organizations who engage in political projects whose payoffs depend on the continuity of the existing system will probably limit their activities. For instance, a group of people may have found it optimal to invest resources to create and maintain a political party, given their expectations of future political development. To the extent that there is uncertainty about the future, political organization may be hampered because people are reluctant to support political institutions whose future remains extremely uncertain.[21] In addition, in both the short and long run, the lack of effective political institutions affects the enforceability and functionality of the legal system. This, in turn, affects other institutions that are regulated through the legal and political systems. In short, instability can have profound effects on subsequent political and institutional development.

More specifically, political instability affects economic activity by forcing economic agents to adjust their investment rules to incorporate increased uncertainty concerning the return of both productive and financial assets. The problem is more severe than a mere increase in risk, which could in principle be incorporated in investment strategies. The added dimension is that uncertainty effectively taxes property rights: even when the expected value and risk of a project can be calculated, exercising the right to possess the return is subject to the degree of confiscation by future governments. However, uncertainty is driven by political processes, and these are indeterminate during political instability.[22]

We advance the following propositions concerning the impact of political instability on policy making and the protection of property rights.

Proposition 1: Regular processes of institutional change are altered under conditions of political instability.   Political instability may change the nature and timing of institutional changes.[23] In stable systems, all proposals for formal institutional changes have to go through a battery of institutions and decision mechanisms that force compromises and amendments in initial formulations.[24] In most cases, the outcomes of these processes are policy changes that are less drastic than initially proposed. The exact outcome in any society will, of course, depend crucially on the bargaining power of participants in the political arena. In unstable situations, however, new governments are especially positioned to rewrite the constitutional order because the regular constraints available under stable systems are nonexistent or ineffective.

Another important distinction between stable and unstable political systems relates to the timing of institutional changes. As a regularity, policy changes take time to be implemented in politically stable systems. Thus, even if a drastic institutional change is accepted within the realms of a stable political system, the lag from formulation to implementation gives agents time to anticipate and adapt. There may not be a lag under political instability because governments established during or after an unstable period could implement changes overnight without previous announcements to society.

Proposition 2: Under political instability, new governments cannot by themselves make credible commitments to limited government and the protection of property. One crucial area that highlights the inability to make credible commitments is the government's own need for finance. When new governments come to power, especially if they want to take measures to promote growth, they want to send a strong signal to the private sector. One such signal is the honoring of previous government debts, even if the current government has no direct and ideological ties to former governments. Acceptance of these loans, however, places financial strains on current expenditures. When new governments limit the resources that can be spent to fulfill promises they may have made to other constituencies, they are prone to losing popular support. Moreover, if powerful political factions remain, vast resources need to be spent as well on the military defense of their government. Credible commitments to limited government and the protection of property rights are therefore more difficult to make in a restored political equilibrium than if instability had not occurred. Although the exact course of political events may not be known a priori, political factions and individuals (especially creditors) can foresee the challenges that new governments will face. They can anticipate that the new political situation will require new governments to change their objectives and strategies. Therefore, any promise by potential or existing governments made during the course of instability cannot be credible.[25]

Proposition 3: Political instability does not imply a global reduction of property rights. The security of property rights depends on the ability of governments to protect or confiscate them. Weak governments are not strong enough to arbitrate property rights among individuals. Not only are they unable to enforce the protection of property rights, but their weakness may also imply that they are not strong enough to abrogate those rights. The actions of governments are constrained by the political support upon which they rest. No government can be sustained by alienating all sectors of society. In seeking alliances, new governments must make strategic concessions to powerful political groups. As they rely increasingly on these alliances, their scope of action will diminish, along with their desire to confiscate private property—especially that of their supporters. Moreover, according to proposition 2, new governments are inherently weak because their threats cannot be credible.

The general proposition argued in the extant literature—that political instability reduces property rights—therefore does not apply at the global level. For example, it is perfectly conceivable that if economic activity is concentrated in a small elite group (and if this group is able to defend its interests when new governments come to power), aggregate economic activity may remain unchanged. In fact, aggregate activity would plausibly increase if the elite group were able to obtain a more favorable treatment from new governments. Political instability, however, does lead to local reductions in the security of property rights as a consequence of not having a governance structure. Given the heterogeneity of agents, some will be more capable than others of engaging in opportunistic behavior and taking away property belonging to others. In short, the overall impact of instability on economic performance can be either positive or negative, depending on particular arrangements between the public and private sectors.

Proposition 4: Economic agents can mitigate the effects of political instability. Economic agents can respond through three mechanisms to mitigate the negative impact of political instability. First, if instability is long-lived, agents may be able to observe regularities in the unstable environment and adapt accordingly. For example, with time, the complexity and indeterminacy of instability may diminish as competing systems are weeded out of the game and it becomes easier to predict potential winners. This allows agents to anticipate, at least partially, future institutional changes. Second, agents may purposefully invest resources to mitigate the negative impact of instability. For instance, agents may make payments and/or ally themselves with particular factions in return for a promise that property will not be destroyed or confiscated. In particular, political instability entails changes in the access to political and economic power. Those economic agents better positioned to secure their interests within emerging political arrangements can prosper even when a country is politically unstable. The implication of these two mechanisms is that it is unexpected shocks of instability, other things being equal, that have the most negative impact on economic performance because they do not allow agents to prepare. Third, economic activity may continue despite the negative impact of instability because agents may be forced to recoup sunk investments. Thus, instability may have different impacts on different industries because of asset specificity considerations.

In summary, instability can have a short-term negative impact, but its net magnitude may depend on the nature of instability and the response of economic agents. The long-term effects of political instability are harder to identify because they become entangled with institutional changes following restoration of a new political equilibrium. One way to disentangle these effects is through empirical analysis of economic activity in an unstable society.

POLITICS AND INSTITUTIONS BEFORE
AND AFTER THE MEXICAN REVOLUTION

From 1876 to 1911 Mexico witnessed a long period of political stability and economic growth under the dictatorship of General Porfirio Díaz. Díaz confronted a polity that had seen seventy-five presidents in fifty-five years, that had been successfully invaded by the United States and France, and that had fragmented into a number of de facto subnational polities ruled by local political and military bosses. Díaz therefore set out to bring political peace and the centralization of political authority to Mexico through a shrewd combination of rigged elections, strategic concessions to provincial political bosses, the creation of a political machine, and outright repression (Katz 1986; Perry 1978).

Díaz also undertook a wholesale revision of Mexico's economic institutions in order to promote investment in an economy that had scarcely grown since Mexico's independence from Spain in 1821 (Coatsworth 1978; Instituto Nacional de Estadística Geografía e Informática 1994, pp. 401–402; Salvucci 1997). The basis of these reforms was the specification of more clearly defined property rights. In 1883 and 1884, private claims to land titles and subsoil rights were strengthened. The government also renegotiated its external debt in 1888 and virtually eliminated its fiscal deficits from the mid-1890s onward, thereby allowing it to make a credible commitment that it would honor its obligations to its creditors, something Mexican governments had not done in the past (Marichal 1997). A modern commercial code was also introduced that year to correct the contract enforcement problems of the colonial Ordenanzas de Bilbao. In 1889, this commercial code was amplified to allow for the creation of joint stock, limited liability corporations. In 1890, the government rewrote the laws governing intellectual property, creating incentives for developing and investing in new technologies. In 1896, the federal government dispensed with the system of internal tariffs that had long segmented the Mexican market. Other laws encouraged industrial investment (through tax incentives) and regulated the growing banking industry (Beatty 1996; Coatsworth 1978, 1997; Holden 1994; Maurer 1997).

The result of Díaz's institutional reforms was a period of rapid economic growth. Foreign investors poured nearly $2 billion into Mexico during the Porfiriato (the period 1876–1911), investing in railroads, ports, urban tramways, export agriculture and ranching, mining and smelting, and petroleum extraction. This was accompanied by a wave of domestic investment in banking, manufacturing, agriculture, and urban real estate. By the 1890s, Mexico was achieving real rates of growth in gross domestic product of 2.5 percent per year.[26]

The Pax Porfiriana contained the seeds of its own collapse. The laws modernizing the security of property rights produced large-scale commercial agriculture; they also produced an increasingly militant peasantry that clamored for the return of land they considered theirs but had lost because of their lack of titles. The growth of large-scale manufacturing, transport, and mining enterprises produced a working class that began to organize and strike. Even portions of Mexico's elite grew disaffected because their increasing wealth could not be translated into political power in Mexico City.[27]

The commercial and agricultural elite of the northern border states, seeking limited political goals, began the revolution of 1910. What started as a political rebellion, however, soon became a full-blown revolution as the ranchers, plantation owners, and merchants of the north found they could contain neither the peasants and workers whom they had mobilized to defeat Díaz nor the politically ambitious generals who controlled the army.

From 1911 to 1917 Mexico was engulfed in civil war as various factions fought for control of the state. Francisco Madero, the moderate reformer who led the anti-Díaz rebellion, was overthrown and assassinated within fifteen months of taking power. His counterrevolutionary successor, Victoriano Huerta, was defeated on the battlefield by a coalition of reformists and revolutionaries and fled Mexico City in July 1914. The victors then organized the famous convention of Aguascalientes in order to determine the institutional rules of the postrevolutionary state, but they soon fell to fighting among themselves. By the close of 1914 Mexico was embroiled in an even more vicious civil war, as the peasant followers of Emiliano Zapata and the agricultural and mining workers who followed Pancho Villa squared off against a coalition of reformists from the elite classes of Mexico's northern states, represented politically by Venustiano Carranza and led militarily by Alvaro Obregón.

The outcome of the 1914–1917 civil war was a gruesome demonstration of the efficiency with which breech-loading howitzers and machine guns could annihilate peasant armies that relied on traditional tactics and weaponry. The result was a military victory for the northern elite. It was, however, an incomplete victory. While the peasants and workers had been defeated on the battlefield, they had not been politically defeated—and they were still armed. Even after Carranza was installed as president in March 1917, Zapata fought on in the state of Morelos, until he was assassinated in 1919. Villa continued to be militarily and politically active until 1923 when he was assassinated. Carranza, too, was assassinated, after being overthrown by his own generals in 1920. Carranza's successor, Alvaro Obregón, served as president from 1920 to 1924 and was assassinated in 1928 the day after he was elected to a second term as president (Womack 1986). Obregón and his successor, Plutarco Elias Calles (1924–1928), were largely occupied with trying to stabilize the political system: they were forced to put down military insurrections in 1923, 1927, and 1929, to confront the various military strongmen who controlled much of rural Mexico, and to fight a three-year-long civil war with religious elements of the peasantry (1926–1929) over the anticlerical elements of the constitution of 1917 (Meyer 1986). One outcome of this action was a six-year period (1928–1934) in which Calles installed three different puppet presidents, none of whom managed to serve a full term. Another was the creation, in 1929, of the precursor to the contemporary Partido Revolucionario Institucional. It was through the transformation of this personalistic entity, run by Calles, into a corporatist party in the mid-1930s that social and political peace was finally brought to Mexico. That transformation required, however, that the new president (Lazaro Cárdenas) arm the worker and peasant leagues, carry out sweeping agrarian reform, encourage the growth of unions favorable to his government, and deport Calles to Los Angeles.

Political uncertainty was not confined to the federal government. In the provinces, local political and military bosses fought over state governorships, sometimes establishing authoritarian fiefdoms of long duration, sometimes remaining in power for only a few weeks or months. As was the case with the federal executive, the formal selection mechanisms for state executives were often ignored; violence or the threat of violence replaced the ballot (Benjamin and Wasserman 1990; Falcón 1977, 1984; Ojeda 1984, p. 41; Wasserman 1993).

The Mexican Revolution also produced a number of far-reaching institutional reforms, most of which worked against the interests of Mexico's manufacturers. Some of these resulted from the negotiations that produced the constitution of 1917 (a compromise of commercial, peasant, and worker demands). Other reforms came out of decrees by various state governors or the president during the postrevolutionary years.

From the point of view of industrialists looking for clearly defined rules of the game (even if those rules were unfavorable), postrevolutionary Mexico was problematic. First, a number of legal changes directly threatened their interests, particularly changes in property and labor law. Second, the direction of institutional change was indeterminate because the new laws often were not enforced. In fact, Carranza himself made it clear that even though his government was the first to operate under the constitution of 1917 he had no intention of carrying out many of its provisions. His successor, Obregón, did much the same, openly flouting the constitution's rules limiting the president to one term by running for a second term in 1928. Complicating matters further were state governors who sought to curry favor with local constituencies by enacting state-level reforms or by enforcing federal laws in arbitrary ways (Rancaño 1987). On top of it all, the selection mechanism for the government remained arbitrary and subject to mediation with .45 caliber pistols.

One area where institutions changed dramatically was labor law. In 1910 unions were small and persecuted, workers could be fired at will, and the only laws that protected workers, as members of the Mexican government often boasted, were the laws of supply and demand (Anderson 1976, p. 36). Article 123 of the constitution of 1917 brought the eight-hour day and the six-day workweek, gave workers the right to organize and strike, provided for a legal minimum wage, and mandated equal pay for equal work (Bortz 1997). By the end of the Obregón presidency (1924) Mexico's industrial workers had become politically powerful; in fact, Luis Morones, the head of the CROM (the national labor federation), was the minister of industry, commerce, and labor, a position he used to enrich himself by extracting rents from both factory owners and factory workers. State governors, recognizing the importance of their labor constituencies, also became champions of the labor movement.[28] At the national level, the government began mediating industrywide agreements between capital and labor that set standard pay rates by job classification, raised daily wage rates, and laid down detailed work rules (Bortz 1995, 1997).

Paralleling these changes in formal institutions were changes in the informal institutions that governed labor relations in the factories. The breakdown of elite hegemony in Mexico in 1910 meant that workers could openly challenge the authority of factory owners, who could no longer call in the army and the rural police to repress strikes or hang labor leaders. This resulted not only in waves of strikes that lasted from 1911 to the early 1920s, but also in a level of worker militancy that had never before been seen in Mexico (Bortz 1997).

The revolution also brought sweeping reforms in the specification of property rights. Article 27 of the constitution of 1917 reversed Díaz's reforms of the land and subsoil laws. The residual claimant on all property rights became the government. The obvious targets of these reforms were Mexico's agrarian elite and the foreign companies that dominated petroleum and mineral extraction, but their implications were not lost on the country's industrialists, who feared that the government would expropriate their factories as well.

There were good reasons for Mexico's factory owners to fear expropriation. In the countryside, peasants carried out the agrarian reform on their own, invading land, executing landlords, and then later following the legal steps necessary to obtain title. The government also nationalized the parts of the railroad system that remained in private hands (Maurer 1997, p. 240). Mexico's industrialists had also witnessed the de facto nationalization of the banking system from 1915 to 1917, in an effort by the Carranza government to finance the war against Villa and Zapata (Maurer 1997, ch. 6). The government eventually returned the banks to their owners in 1921, but only nine of them were ever able to reopen. These events struck especially close to home for Mexico's industrialists; like the bankers they had supported the Huerta counterrevolution (Rancaño 1987, pp. 195–230). Indeed, the owners of the banks and the owners of the factories were often one and the same group (Maurer 1997, ch. 5; Ojeda 1985, pp. 11–12, 202–219).

The threat of expropriation was driven home to the factory owners in the summer of 1917. In order to combat runaway inflation, the Carranza government completely removed the tariff on common cloth with less than seventy threads per square centimeter and lowered the tariff on fine-weave, printed cloth to only 25 percent of its former value (Rancaño 1987, pp. 209–210). Without protective tariffs, Mexico's textile industry had no hope of competing against foreign manufacturers (Beatty 1996, pp. 64, 74; Graham-Clark 1909, p. 38; on relative costs of production in different countries see Clark 1987, pp. 141–174). The industrialists of Mexico City responded to the lowering of tariffs by declaring a lockout, throwing 4,000 mill hands out of work. Carranza upped the ante, sending a telegram to every state governor and asking for a list of the paralyzed factories. He drafted a law, based on articles 27 and 123 of the constitution, approved swiftly by Congress, allowing the government to seize control of the factories (Rancaño 1987, pp. 213–217). After prolonged negotiations between the government and the industrialists, the seizure of the factories was blocked; the government made it clear that it would not back down on articles 27 and 123 of the constitution, but it did restore the old levels of tariff protection (Primer Congreso Nacional de Industriales 1918, pp. 177, 181; Rancaño 1987, pp. 227–258). The point had been made, however; Mexico's industrialists faced the twin threats of expropriation and downward revisions of the tariff. Moreover, because it was difficult to predict the course of political change in Mexico, these threats could reemerge at any time. At the same time, however, Mexico's industrialists realized that the incumbent government, at least, was willing to partially mitigate the erosion of their property rights by compensating them with private goods (protective tariffs) that lowered the standard of living of the rest of society.

THE STRUCTURE AND PERFORMANCE OF INDUSTRY

What impact did the political instability of the revolution and the decade thereafter, along with the institutional changes that were brought about by the revolution, have on Mexican manufacturing? How well does the actual record of investment, growth, and economic performance correspond to the implications of the model developed in the second section of this chapter?

Surviving the Revolution

We have two reasons for beginning our empirical analysis with the determinants of firm survival. First, we want to avoid a sample selection problem in which our results may indicate that existing firms had good performance despite the revolution when, in fact, they may have survived the revolution simply because they were more efficient than the firms that failed. Second, we want to test the hypothesis that when political conflict involves the use of force, property is destroyed. Indeed, traditional historiography has suggested that the revolution destroyed the physical plant of the Mexican economy. Scholars looking at this period have described it in terms of "a wrecking process," "revolutionary ruin," "lost years for Mexico," or "utter chaos."[29]

Surprisingly, the data we have retrieved on manufacturing indicate that the vast majority of firms survived the revolution. We also find evidence that the rate at which firms failed was not particularly affected by the revolutionary period and that most of those firms that did go out of business were very small enterprises.

In the steel, cement, paper, glass, wool textile, beer, soap and glycerin, tobacco products, and dynamite and explosives industries, monopolies or oligopolies dominated their product lines in the decades prior to and following the revolution (de Allende Costa and Calva 1991, pp. 198–203; Haber 1989, ch. 4). With the exception of one of the three cement firms which dominated the Mexican market (Cementos Cruz Azul) and the single firm which dominated dynamite and explosive production (Compañía Nacional Mexicana de Dinamita y Explosivos), all these firms survived the revolution. Moreover, the two firms that failed were not destroyed by military action. Cementos Cruz Azul was taken over by its creditors and was later merged with another cement manufacturer after the revolution. The Compañía Nacional Mexicana de Dinamita y Explosivos closed its doors because the Carranza government terminated the very lucrative tax concessions under which the firm had operated since 1902. Its physical plant was purchased by the Du Pont de Nemours Company and reopened in the 1920s (Haber 1989, pp. 91–92, 143, 188).

The cotton textile industry, for which we have detailed data on firm sizes and failure rates, allows us to examine the issue of firm survival systematically. The results indicate that most firms survived the fighting intact and those that failed were small enterprises. Prior to the revolution, typically 6 to 8 percent of firms failed in each five-year period. During the period 1910–1915, however, 16.5 percent of firms closed their doors permanently. These were very small firms, collectively accounting for only 7 percent of total industry output. In the period 1915–1920, the percentage of firms that failed fell to 5.7 percent, which was lower than the rate that prevailed before the revolution. These firms accounted for only 2.7 percent of output.[30] As striking as the low rate at which firms failed during the revolution is the fact that these firms were replaced by new entrants of roughly comparable size—a phenomenon we return to shortly.[31]

Are there any systematic patterns to the data on the cotton textile industry that explain which firms survived and which did not? We estimate probit and logit regressions to predict the probability of survival from 1900 to 1910 and from 1910 to 1920 as a function of several firm characteristics. We test for the effects of size (measured by market share), location (by geographic region), age of firm, total factor productivity, and the capital-labor ratio (see Table 5.1).[32] To determine whether these regression results have historical verisimilitude, we analyze the characteristics of those firms that failed during the revolution.

Our probit regression results for the period 1910–1920, reported in Table 5.1, indicate that size was the overwhelming factor in determining firm survival during the revolution. All the other variables either are not statistically significant or have extremely small magnitudes. Our samples are unbalanced (four to five survivors for every firm that exited the market), so we used an alternate logit model to cross-check our probit results.[33] The logit regressions show similar qualitative results: size remains the major determinant of survival during the revolutionary years. Surprisingly, the technical efficiency of firms had no impact on firms' ability to survive the revolution. In both models, the

Table 5.1. *Probit Survival Regressions, 1900–1920 (t-Statistics in Parentheses)*

	1900–1910			1910–1920		
	Spec. 1	Spec. 2	Spec. 3	Spec. 1b	Spec. 2b	Spec. 3b
Intercept	1.023	3.499	1.651	−0.451	−0.640	−0.349
	(3.349)	(2.799)	(1.569)	(−1.108)	(−0.767)	(−0.550)
Size—measured as share of	31.113	31.548	12.185	213.923	168.614	156.368
industry output	(0.719)	(1.155)	(0.371)	(2.890)	(2.117)	(2.046)
Region—dummy for firms in states of DF,	0.082	−0.046	−0.196	0.445	0.704	0.869
MX, Puebla, Veracruz, and Tlaxcala	(0.250)	(−0.083)	(−0.335)	(1.247)	(1.632)	(1.860)
Joint stock—dummy for public, limited	0.402	−0.653	−0.383	0.578	0.749	0.808
liability firms	(1.039)	(−1.138)	(−0.757)	(1.292)	(1.257)	(1.363)
Vintage—dummy for age of firm				−0.543	−0.931	−1.213
				(−1.101)	(−1.595)	(−1.553)

	(1)	(2)	(3)	(4)	(5)	(6)
TFP (production proxied by real value of output)[a]	−0.013 (−1.881)				0.004 (0.958)	
TFP (production proxied by meters of output)[a]			0.000 (0.088)			0.000 (0.496)
Capital-labor ratio[a]		−0.018 (−0.627)	0.002 (0.053)		−0.004 (−0.272)	−0.006 (−0.730)
N	76	125	72	108	90	87
Adjusted R^2	0.14	0.02	0.01	0.29	0.30	0.29

Note: Dependent variable: survival (1 if firm survives entire period; 0 if firm disappears from the industry). TFP = total factor productivity. [a]For the period 1900–1910, TFP and capital-labor ratio data were taken from the 1896 census. For the 1910–1920 observations, TFP and K/L were taken from the 1912 census. In both cases, we assumed that the input mix and productivity of firms remained constant in the short run). Source: See note 31.

contribution of total factor productivity (output per input of capital and labor) and capital intensity (the ratio of workers per machine) is negligible and not statistically significant.

Figure 5.1 graphs the marginal and absolute effects of size on the probability of survival. A striking feature of this graph is that it indicates that once a firm reached a market share of just over 1.5 percent, the probability of survival approached 100 percent.[34] The graph also indicates that the marginal impact of size on survival was most important at the smallest firm sizes.[35]

Our regression results for 1910–1920 are corroborated on examination of the characteristics of textile firms that did not survive the revolutionary years. The median size of firms that went out of business during the revolution corresponded to a market share of only 0.3 percent. In fact, only two firms failed that had market shares greater than 1 percent.

There are several hypotheses that potentially explain why larger firms had a greater probability of surviving the revolution than their smaller competitors. One possible explanation is that very small firms were more likely to go out of business because they were technically inefficient (they were of a size below the minimum efficiency scale). The revolution merely hastened their demise. There are two problems with this interpretation. First, we would expect that firm survival would always be correlated with firm size. We therefore estimated similar regressions for the period 1900–1910. The coefficient on firm

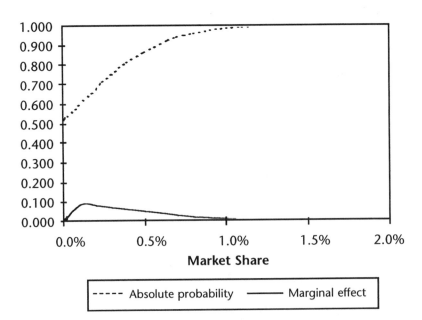

Figure 5.1. Size and probability of survival

size has the right sign and magnitude, but it is not statistically significant (see Table 5.1). Second, one would expect that survivorship would be correlated with technical efficiency. As specifications 2, 3, 2b, and 3b make clear however, differences in total factor productivity are extremely poor predictors of firm survival.

A more likely explanation for the correlation of firm size with firm survival during the revolution is that larger firms had the financial resources to weather the severe economic crisis of 1914–1917. Owners of smaller firms likely had less liquid wealth to buttress their enterprises during hard times (in fact, their more modest wealth explains the small size of their firms). Therefore, they were less likely to be able to purchase stocks of raw materials to sustain business during prolonged periods when inputs were unavailable, less likely to be able to go for long periods when they could not earn revenues from production, and less likely to be able to pay ransoms or forced loans to passing armies. This interpretation is buttressed by the documentary evidence we have from company histories and the correspondence of factory owners with Mexico's Department of Labor, both of which indicate that revolutionary armies rarely destroyed the mills they occupied (Haber 1989, pp. 132–134).

More serious than the threat of occupation by revolutionary armies was the fact that it was difficult to obtain raw materials or move product to market because of the collapse of the national railroad system and the disappearance of a national currency.[36] The implication is that once normalcy returned to the transportation and monetary systems, production regained its prerevolutionary levels. The available evidence supports this view. Data we have retrieved on the steel, cement, beer, and cotton textile industries all display the same basic pattern: there were dramatic declines in production during the violent phase of the revolution, followed by a quick recovery once the fighting stopped (see Tables 5.2 and 5.3). In fact, by the early 1920s production in most industries had regained its prerevolutionary levels.

In summary, we find no quantitative evidence for the destructive power that the traditional historiography has attributed to the Mexican Revolution. Furthermore, our analysis indicates that it was not superior performance that determined survival, but rather small size. Therefore, our results are not biased because of sample selection.

Investor Confidence

It is one thing to determine, ex post, what effects the revolution had on firm survival; it is quite another to determine how factory owners at the time viewed the situation. Did the revolution exert a powerful adverse effect on the confidence of investors, thereby discouraging new investment?

Financial theory states that the price of assets is a reflection of the expectations of investors concerning the future ability of those assets to produce prof-

Table 5.2. Industrial Production in Mexico, 1900–1933

Year	Steel Industry (in thousands of metric tons)		Cement Industry (in thousands of metric tons)		Beer Industry (in thousands of liters)	
	Capacity	Output	Capacity	Output	Cervecería Cuauhtemoc	National Output
1900	—	—	—	—	4,866	—
1901	—	—	—	—	4,685	—
1902	—	—	—	—	5,581	—
1903	110	22	—	—	5,925	—
1904	110	36	—	—	6,865	—
1905	110	4	—	—	8,884	—
1906	110	25	66	20	13,344	—
1907	110	16	66	30	14,005	—
1908	110	17	66	40	11,183	—
1909	110	59	86	50	11,582	—
1910	110	45	151	60	13,275	—
1911	110	71	152	50	14,172	—
1912	110	33	177	40	16,519	—
1913	110	12	177	30	11,732	—
1914	110	0	177	25	3,359[a]	—
1915	110	0	177	10		
1916	110	0	177	20	2,758	—
1917	110	12	177	30	4,640	—
1918	110	21	177	40	4,977	—
1919	110	21	177	40	7,735	—
1920	110	15	222	45	14,929	—
1921	110	42	222	50	16,689	—
1922	110	24	222	70	13,156	—
1923	110	44	222	90	12,335	—
1924	110	19	222	107	11,564	52,003
1925	110	49	222	110	15,736	53,673
1926	110	62	222	151	21,521	67,925
1927	110	41	222	158	23,201	71,613
1928	110	51	246	204	22,229	67,911
1929	110	60	291	158	23,174	71,973
1930	110	58	291	227	21,760	72,065

Note: [a]*Combined value for 1914–1915. Source: Steel industry calculated from Fundidora Monterrey, Informe Annual, 1900–1938. Cement industry figures were obtained from un-published data from the Camara Nacional de Cemento. Beer industry figures were obtained from unpublished data from Cervecería Cuauhtemoc Sales Department and Dirección General de Estadistica,* Anuario Estadístico de la Republica Mexicana, *1942, p. 958.*

Table 5.3. Mexican Cotton Textile Industry, 1900–1930

Year	Estimated Nominal Value Output[a]	Estimated Real Value Output[a]	Estimated Meters of Output[a]	Estimated Spindles	Estimated Worker Equivalents[b]
1900	35,459	35,459	261,397	588,474	27,767
1901	33,877	33,877	262,044	591,506	26,709
1902	28,780	28,780	235,956	595,728	24,964
1903	36,907	36,907	262,170	632,601	26,149
1904	42,511	42,511	280,710	635,940	27,456
1905	51,214	51,214	310,692	678,058	30,162
1906	51,171	51,171	349,712	688,217	31,673
1907	51,686	51,686	428,284	613,548	33,132
1908	54,934	54,934	368,370	732,876	35,816
1909	43,370	43,370	314,228	726,278	32,229
1910	50,651	50,651	315,322	702,874	31,963
1911	51,348	51,348	341,441	725,297	32,147
1912	63,802	72,834	319,668	762,149	32,209
1913	54,002	33,978	298,897	752,804	32,641
1917[c]	25,125	12,266		573,092	22,187
1918	48,567	15,111	180,453	689,173	23,067
1919	80,781	23,333	305,509	735,308	21,877
1920	120,492	27,840	298,829	753,837	24,691
1921	93,342	66,826	338,346	770,945	25,485
1922	85,023	53,040	330,601	803,230	26,451
1923	97,563	44,214	303,090	802,363	26,419
1924	96,435	44,155	285,594	812,165	25,155
1925	102,527	56,839	380,041	840,890	33,262
1926	88,766	60,562	327,487	832,193	27,476
1927	73,179	51,156	308,940	821,211	27,492
1928	89,630	52,529	300,425	823,862	25,348
1929	105,055	67,861	389,147	839,100	27,598
1930	84,876	58,426	305,512	803,873	27,729

Note: [a]Output reported in thousands. [b]Number of workers adjusted for changes in the length of the workday: 12 hours from 1850 to 1913, 10 hours from 1914 to 1917, 8 hours from 1918 to 1933. [c]Spindles and workers data for 1917 was taken from Instituto Nacional de Estadística Geografría e Informática (1994), p. 616. Source: See note 31.

its. Reduced expectations concerning the ability of assets to earn positive returns will therefore result in a decline in the market value of those assets. Therefore, one way to approach the question of investor confidence is to study the
price of common stock in Mexico's publicly traded manufacturing companies.
We have therefore retrieved year-end stock prices from the Mexico City financial press for all the publicly traded manufacturing firms and produced a real
(inflation-adjusted) stock price index.[37] We estimate the index using both real
(inflation-adjusted) pesos and real dollars in order to make certain that our results are not driven by the price index. Our data set includes the four largest
cotton textile producers (CIDOSA, CIVSA, CIASA, and CISAASA, which jointly accounted for roughly one-third of national output), the country's steel monopoly (Fundidora Monterrey), the single largest wool textile manufacturer
(Compañía Industrial de San Ildefonso), two of the country's three most important beer brewers (Cerveceria Moctezuma and the Compañía Cervecera de
Toluca y México), the country's only large-scale producer of soap and glycerin
products (Compañía Industrial Jabonera de la Laguna, which controlled 90
percent of the soap market), one of the two important producers of paper products (Compañía Industrial de San Rafael y Anexas, which monopolized the lucrative newsprint market), and two of the three firms that dominated the production of tobacco products (El Buen Tono and La Cigarrera Mexicana).

Regardless of the price index employed, the data indicate that the revolution made investors extremely uncertain about the future. All twelve firms in
our index saw dramatic declines in their share prices from 1910 to 1918. We
estimate an index (1910 = 100) of the average stock prices. Calculated in real
pesos, the value of share prices fell by 79 percent from 1910 to 1918. Calculated in real dollars, the index fell by 67 percent.

Equally striking, however, are two other features of the stock price data. The
first is that investors were already becoming uncertain well before Díaz was
overthrown. The pattern for all the companies in the sample was a gradual rise
in stock prices until 1906–1907, and then a sharp decline, produced by the
transmission of the U.S. financial panic of 1907 to Mexico. On average, firms
lost 23 percent (measured in real dollars) or 32 percent (measured in real pesos) of their value from 1906 to 1910. The second striking feature is that stock
prices recovered rapidly after the fighting stopped. From 1918 to 1919 the stock
index jumped from 21 to 36 (in real pesos) and from 33 to 39 (in real dollars).
It then continued rising through 1925, when it reached 44 and 50, respectively.
This indicates that if investors were uncertain about the future, their uncertainty was largely confined to the period until 1918—the years when revolutionary violence threatened the physical safety of firms' assets. We also suggest
that the lack of a market response to the failed military rebellion of 1923 (in
which two-thirds of the army sided with the generals against the government)
is equally striking. Investors seemed unconcerned that the government might

topple, even though there was the very real threat of another round of civil war (Meyer 1986, pp. 160–161).

These stock indexes are downward-biased over time. First, the firms in the index were notable for the fact that their board members and founding stockholders tended to be politically well connected. They were therefore able to persuade the government to transfer to their firms valuable rights in the public domain (particularly the water rights necessary to generate hydroelectric power), and they were able to exert influence on tariff policies (Haber 1989, ch. 5; Moreno 1996). Part of their market value prior to 1910 may therefore have been capitalized rents from the political influence of their board members, and the drop in stock prices from 1910 to 1918 may have expressed this decline in political influence. Second, the stock indexes do not capture new, more efficient, privately owned firms that entered some product markets in the 1920s (most notably in beer brewing and tobacco products) and that outcompeted their Porfirian competitors. The result was a dramatic fall in the share prices of three of the twelve firms in our sample, which is independent of the effects of political instability.

Another way to approach the question of the impact of the revolution on investor confidence is to examine the rate at which all firms, including small, privately owned ones, changed ownership. In an environment characterized by uncertainty, we would expect a higher rate of turnover of assets, as entrepreneurs who were uncertain about the future would likely sell their assets to those entrepreneurs who either had better information about political and market developments or were willing to bear greater risk. Presumably, in these cases the sale prices would reflect a discount for increased risk.

Our data set on the cotton textile industry permits us to undertake a partial analysis of this scenario. Unfortunately, we do not have data on the prices at which mills owned by sole proprietors or partnerships changed hands. We do know, however, the size of those mills and when they were sold, which enables us to calculate the rate at which firms changed hands before and after the revolution.[38] During the years 1910–1915, 27 percent of firms changed owners, and during the period 1915–1920, 16 percent of firms changed owners. These rates of ownership turnover were little different from the rates that prevailed before the revolution. Between 1895 and 1900, 29 percent of firms changed hands; between 1900 and 1905, 27 percent; and between 1905 and 1910, 18 percent. The change in the rate of ownership in the decade following the revolution was also not dramatically different from that prevailing before the revolution: 21 percent of firms changed hands between 1920 and 1925, and 20 percent changed hands between 1925 and 1929.

What does appear to have been different, however, was the *size* of firms that changed hands during the revolution. There was little difference in the size of firms that were sold before and after the revolution. There was, however, a sizable decline (on the order of 50 percent) in the average size of firms that were sold during the decade 1910–1920. This result is consistent with the finding that small firms had a lower probability of surviving the revolution intact. One implication of this finding is that the relative price of small firms would fall. We would therefore expect to see a great rate of ownership change among small firms, which is precisely the result we obtain.

New Investment

One implication of our analysis of investor confidence and firm survival is that industry should have continued to grow after the revolution. A logical outcome of recovered investor confidence after 1918 would be new investment in plant and equipment. We have been able to retrieve data on new capacity or investment in the cement, steel, and cotton textile industries. We have also retrieved detailed data on U.S. industrial machinery exports to Mexico, which is an excellent measure of aggregate new investment because virtually all of Mexico's capital goods had to be imported.

Productive capacity in the cement industry continued to expand both during and after the revolution, growing from 66,000 metric tons per year in 1906 to 151,000 in 1910, 177,000 in 1912, 222,000 in 1920, and 246,000 in 1928. This rate of growth in capacity is especially impressive in light of the fact that capacity utilization was almost always less than 60 percent, implying that firms were confident enough about the future to invest well ahead of demand (see Table 5.2).[39] Data on the nation's integrated steel-producing monopolist, Fundidora Monterrey, tell a similar story. During the years of military conflict, Fundidora Monterrey closed its doors and spent no funds on plant and equipment. As soon as normalcy returned to the market, however, the firm invested in a dramatic fashion: the value of its physical plant grew 41 percent from 1919 to 1921, even with capacity utilization at less than 40 percent (see Table 5.2).

One might argue that the recovery of these construction goods industries is not surprising. The physical destruction caused by the revolution might have stimulated demand for exactly these kinds of goods in the postrevolutionary period. It might therefore be the case that these two industries are unrepresentative of the manufacturing sector as a whole, which tended to be more heavily weighted toward consumer goods production.

This interpretation is not sustained, however, by the analysis of data on the country's most important consumer goods industry: cotton textiles. As Table 5.3 indicates, the number of active spindles (the machines that spin carded cotton into yarn) fell by 25 percent from 1913 to 1917.[40] Much of this loss was clearly produced by firms that temporarily closed their doors during the worst phases of the fighting. Indeed, the only way to explain an increase in capacity of 28 percent from 1917 to 1919 is that these firms reopened as soon as the military conflict ended. The recovery from the revolution went well beyond the reopening of old capacity, however. New plant and equipment was being purchased as well. By 1921 the industry was 10 percent larger than it had been in 1910 (and roughly equal to its 1913 level), and in the four years from 1921 to 1925 the industry grew an additional 9 percent, making it 20 percent larger than it had been in 1910. This increase in industry capacity cannot be explained as the result of population growth. The Mexican population was 5 percent smaller in 1921 than it had been in 1910.[41] The growth rate of industry capacity then slowed in the late 1920s as a general decline in the economy's growth rate caused by the collapse of the prices of Mexico's major commodity exports was translated into a decline in the demand for domestically produced textiles.[42]

The patterns displayed by the cotton textile industry are corroborated by data on U.S. exports of industrial machinery to Mexico. In Table 5.4 we present an index of estimates of the real (inflation-adjusted) value of exports of manufacturing, petroleum and mining, and other nonagricultural types of machinery from the United States and United Kingdom to Mexico. During the early years of the revolution (1910–1913), evidence relating to the growth of investment is ambiguous. As a whole, the index of machinery exports fell from 100 to 92 in 1913. However, specific categories such as industrial, textile, and petroleum and mining grew in these early years. Starting in 1914 a similar pattern applies to all series. Machinery exports collapsed dramatically during the years of intense military conflict. By 1918, however, machinery exports to Mexico increased rapidly. In fact, the period 1919–1921 appears to have set records for machinery exports, indicating that Mexican firms were rapidly investing in new plant and equipment. Throughout the rest of the 1920s machinery exports to Mexico were at higher average levels than those which had prevailed during the final years of the Porfiriato.

One might argue that it is not surprising that industrialists reopened their mills after the fighting ended. The capacity that existed prior to the revolution represented sunk costs. As long as industrialists could cover their variable costs, it paid to put capacity back into production. One might also argue that incremental investments by industrialists were not surprising either: if investments in small increases in productive capacity could, at the margin, allow for the efficient use of existing capacity, then it would have been in the interest of industrialists to undertake these investments, even if the general business environment was uncertain.

There are two problems with this argument. First, the data on U.S. exports of industrial machinery to Mexico indicate that firms were doing much more than undertaking incremental increases in productive capacity: the flow of new machinery to Mexico after the revolution exceeded the levels attained before the revolution. Second, this argument cannot account for the fact that new firms entered the market both during the revolution and afterward. In the cotton textile industry, for example, from 1910 to 1915 ten new firms entered

Table 5.4. Total Factor Productivity

	Manufacturing				Other types
Steam Engines, Boilers, and Pipes and Fittings	Industrial Machinery	Textile Machinery	Total Manu- facturing	Petroleum & Mining Total	(not including agricultural) Total
26	40	134	40	6	140
23	33	52	28	6	93
29	21	71	31	7	96
30	56	42	36	10	67
26	59	113	41	14	65
27	94	76	45	23	63
63	120	101	78	37	98
63	150	135	87	160	161
63	145	135	86	115	88
71	94	150	83	96	68
100	100	100	100	100	100
57	156	95	80	103	98
56	108	112	71	88	85
67	212	7	89	95	103
54	44	2	47	86	23
16	17	1	15	25	5
34	63	2	37	38	8
101	129	10	97	73	16
5	218	25	48	499	4
446	409	47	399	612	23
1,146	675	131	954	1,024	421
45	587	40	148	577	454
143	250	318	181	270	291
145	218	170	162	295	69
143	206	181	159	330	66
146	267	262	181	353	—
96	927	318	277	287	—
84	830	305	249	211	—
72	770	321	230	244	—
121	1,189	195	333	239	74
74	1,129	184	287	144	55

Source: *U.S. data were obtained from Department of Commerce,* The Foreign Commerce and Navigation of the United States, 1902–1935. *U. K. data were obtained from* United Kingdom, Annual Statement of the Trade of the United Kingdom with Foreign Countries, *1902–1937. Price deflator is the wholesale price index for all commodities, published in Department of Commerce,* Historical Statistics of the United States: Colonial Times to 1970, *p. 200.*

the industry (eight of these during the turbulent years 1913, 1914, and 1915), adding 4.7 percent to the industry's capacity. From 1915 to 1920, in fact, more firms entered the industry than exited: five firms closed their doors, but fourteen new firms entered (accounting for 4.4 percent of output). From 1920 to 1925 seven new firms entered the industry (accounting for 2.2 percent of output), and from 1925 to 1929 twenty-five new firms entered the industry (accounting for 5 percent of output). In fact, these rates of entry during and after the revolution are indistinguishable from the rates of entry that prevailed during the five years before the revolution (see note 44).

We do not have the kinds of systematic data on entry and exit for other industries that we have for cotton textiles. The partial data we have, however, indicate entry into a number of industries by new, large, capital-intensive firms in the early 1920s. In the tobacco industry, for example, a huge, new, capital-intensive firm (El Aguila, S.A.) entered the market in 1924 and in short order drove its old established Porfirian competitors into bankruptcy. In the dynamite industry, the Du Pont de Nemours company acquired the works of the old Compañía Industrial Nacional Mexicana de Dinamita y Explosivos. In the cement industry, Cementos Monterrey was founded, soon merging with Cementos Hidalgo to form the mammoth Cementos Mexicanos. In the beer industry, the huge Cerveceria Modelo was established in Mexico City, quickly establishing itself as one of the largest brewers in the country. Ford Motor Company entered the market as well, opening an assembly plant in Mexico City in 1925 (Haber 1989, pp. 143–144).

Industry Concentration

Our analysis of firm turnover and new investment might not capture the fact that purchases of new capacity or purchases of competitors' capacity might have taken place among a few large firms. It might have been the case, for example, that the contraction of the banking sector gave rise to privileged access to capital for a small group of entrepreneurs tied to the financial institutions that survived the revolution, thereby allowing them to purchase their competitors' capacity at bargain prices. Perhaps it was the case that some entrepreneurs had political ties to the postrevolutionary governments that allowed them to obtain valuable rights in the public domain (such as the rights to use particular rivers to generate hydraulic or hydroelectric power, or the rights that afforded them discounted freight rates on the government-run railroads), thereby obtaining cost advantages that translated over time into faster growth rates of new investment and increased market shares. Or perhaps it was simply the case that large firms could afford to be less risk-averse than smaller firms, and that they consequently added new capacity at a more rapid rate than their competitors. Any or all of these factors might have produced substantial changes in the competitive structure of industry.

Testing this hypothesis is difficult in most industries because, for technological reasons, they were already highly concentrated prior to the revolution.
The paper, glass, steel, dynamite, and soap industries were monopolies or near-
monopolies, while the beer, cement, and cigarette industries were each dominated by two or three producers (de Allende Costa and Calva 1991, pp. 198–
203; Haber 1989, ch. 4). The cotton textile industry, however, provides an opportunity to assess the independent impact of the revolution on industry structure because there were more than a hundred producers in the industry before
the revolution broke out. In addition, it would not be possible to explain
changes in concentration in this industry as a function of production technology. Textile manufacturing is perhaps the archetypal case of an industry
characterized by constant returns to scale technologies, capital divisibilities,
and the absence of barriers to entry.

As shown in Figure 5.2, we have been able to measure changes in the structure of Mexico's cotton textile industry from 1840 to 1932 by estimating the
two standard measures of industry concentration: the four-firm ratio (CR4) and
the Herfindahl index. Our analysis indicates that the Mexican cotton textile in-

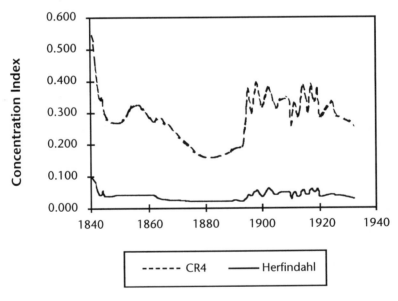

Figure 5.2. Concentration in the cotton textiles industry, 1840–1932
Note: *The 4-firm ratio (CR4) is calculated as the percentage of the market
controlled by the four largest producers. The Herfindahl index is calculated
as the sum of the squares of the market shares of all firms in the industry.
Because it uses data from all firms and because it weights firms by size, the
Herfindahl index is generally regarded as a superior index of concentration.*

dustry was characterized by very high levels of concentration.[43] At the end of the revolution in 1919, Mexico's four largest firms controlled 37.5 percent of the market, which was more than twice the level controlled by Brazil's four largest textile manufacturers and more than five times the level controlled by the four largest textile producers in the United States. Our analysis also indicates, however, that these high levels of concentration predated the revolution by two decades. As one of us (Haber) has examined at length elsewhere, differential access to capital produced by the concentrated nature of Mexico's banking system and financial markets when they began to develop in the 1880s and 1890s gave rise to a rapid increase in concentration (Haber 1991, 1997). To the extent that one can find a trend after 1900, it is in the direction of a modest decline in concentration. The average four-firm ratio was virtually the same during the revolutionary years (1911–1920) as it had been in the decade before the revolution (0.332 versus 0.326). During the decade 1921–1930 concentration was actually lower than it had been before the revolution (0.299).

Productivity

Although there was little destruction of physical capital during the revolution, one might imagine that the dramatic changes in institutions that it brought about had adverse consequences for industrial productivity. The changes in institutions that governed labor markets (the rise of unions, increases in wages, shortening of the workday, increase in worker militancy on the shop floor) all should have worked to raise the unit costs of labor. Similarly, the partial nationalization and disappearance of a major portion of the banking sector, the decline in lending by the surviving banks for productive activities, and the increase in risk premia associated with new investments in the postrevolutionary era should have worked to increase the unit costs of capital. The net result might have been a decline in both labor productivity (output per worker) and total factor productivity (TFP, output per unit of capital and labor).

The detailed data we have retrieved on the cotton textile industry allow us to test this hypothesis directly. We therefore estimate labor productivity and TFP using the following standard methods. We selected two different measures of aggregate industry output: the real (inflation-adjusted) value of production, and the volume of production (measured in meters of cloth). Both proxies of output have different advantages and disadvantages: real output is sensitive to the price index we have developed; the volume of production solves the price index problem, but it understates productivity growth because it cannot capture changes in the quality of cloth over time. We therefore employ both measures in order to provide a cross-check on our results. Following Kane, we employ spindlage as a proxy for capital.[44] Following the work of Atack and Sokoloff on the United States and Bernard and Jones on international productivity comparisons, we employ the number of workers as a proxy for the labor input (Atack 1985; Bernard and Jones 1996; Sokoloff 1984). In order to make appropriate comparisons of pre- and postrevolutionary labor productivity and TFP, we adjust the number of workers to reflect the reduction in daily work hours that occurred as a result of the revolution, from twelve hours per day prior to 1914, to ten from 1914 to 1918, and to eight thereafter.

Estimating labor productivity is relatively straightforward: it is simply the real value of output or the physical volume of output divided by the number of worker equivalents (workers adjusted for differences in the length of the workday before and after the revolution).

Estimating TFP involved several more steps. Ideally, we would have had censuses enumerated at the firm level covering both the pre- and postrevolutionary years, allowing us to employ panel-data techniques to estimate time trends for TFP growth across different subperiods. Unfortunately, after 1913 the censuses no longer enumerate at the firm level. We therefore had to proceed in two stages. First, we used the 1850–1913 firm-level censuses to estimate a Cobb-Douglas production function of the form $Y = A \cdot K^{\gamma} \cdot L^{1-\gamma}$ with constant returns to scale, where K and L represent the capital and labor inputs and A is a function that captures improvements in technology over time. In order to use linear estimation procedures, we took natural logarithms of a normalized production function of the form $y = k^{\alpha}$ where $y = Y/L$ and $k = K/L$ and added explanatory variables to arrive at the following model.

$$Ln\, y = \alpha + \beta_1 \cdot Ln\, k + \beta_2 \cdot Ln\, L + \beta_3 \cdot time\ trend + \delta \cdot \text{dummy} \\ + \gamma \cdot \text{interaction term}$$

We then estimated TFP directly from output and input data for all years for which we have cross-sectional census data using the weights for capital and labor estimated from the 1850–1913 production function. For any given time t, where we had data on output, spindles, and workers, we estimated TFP employing the following formula:

$$TFP_t = \frac{\sum_i Output_{t,i}}{\left(\sum_i Spindles_{t,i}\right)^{\alpha} \cdot \left(\sum_i Workers_{t,i}\right)^{\beta}}$$

where α and β are the (normalized) shares of capital and labor as estimated in the panel regression procedure described above and the subscript i identifies the inputs and output of reporting unit i (Brown 1993; Hall 1995).

Labor productivity was adversely affected by the Mexican Revolution, but the phenomenon of productivity decline appears to have been concentrated in the years of actual violent conflict (see Figure 5.3). When we proxy output by its real value, output per worker in 1918 was roughly one-third of what it had been in 1913. It then climbed rapidly, nearly regaining its 1913 value by

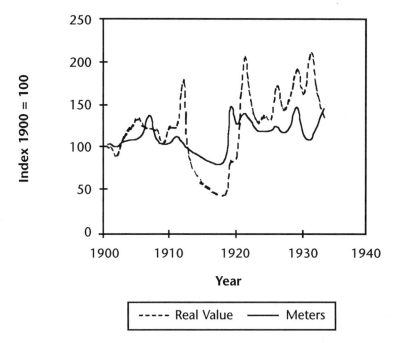

Figure 5.3. Labor productivity

1921, and then continued growing in a somewhat volatile fashion for the rest of the decade. If we proxy output by meters of cloth produced, labor productivity fell far less dramatically during the revolution, the index moving from 111 in 1913 to 83 in 1918. The data also indicate a rapid recovery: by 1919 output per worker was at an all-time high. On average, during the 1920s output per worker was 17 percent higher than it had been during the period 1901–1910.

Our estimates of TFP tell a slightly different story (see Figure 5.4). TFP fell anywhere from 40 to 74 percent (depending on whether we proxy output by physical units or real value, respectively) from 1913 to 1918. Like labor productivity, however, TFP then recovered quickly, regardless of how output is proxied. When measured by its real value, TFP continued growing through the 1920s. When measured in physical units of cloth produced, however, the results indicate little TFP growth in the 1920s.

Although TFP is the one area where we can identify some measurable change caused by the revolution, the mechanism that induced that change was not a drop in new spending on plant and equipment caused by uncertainty among investors about the security of their property rights. Rather, it was the consequence of a change in the formal regulations governing the length of the workday. Manufacturers mitigated the change in working hours somewhat by in-

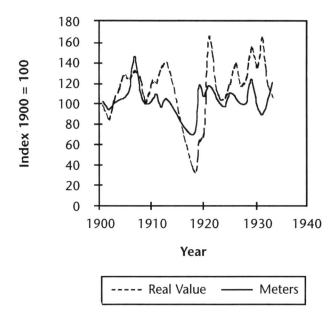

Figure 5.4. Total factor productivity

creasing the capital-labor ratio, which was 38 percent higher in the decade 1920–1929 than in the decade 1901–1910.

Our analysis indicates that in the short run the Mexican Revolution exerted a powerful effect on investor confidence, output, and productivity. It is not possible to separate the effects of the interdiction of factor and product markets caused by military action from the effects produced solely by political instability during the years 1914–1917. Our analysis of the periods of instability before and after 1914–1917 indicates, however, that it was most likely the inability to move goods to market or to obtain spare parts and supplies that dampened economic activity during the violent phase of the revolution. The periods 1910–1913 and 1918–1934 were characterized by political instability, changes in institutions that should have dampened investment and growth, and uncertainty about the future trajectory of political and institutional change. Yet, the evidence we have retrieved indicates that investors were far less sensitive to these factors than the extant theoretical and empirical literature indicates.

The implications of this analysis are three. First, our analysis suggests that the relationship between political stability and economic growth is in need of theoretical refinement. There is no clear one-to-one relationship between political instability and the perception of investors that their property rights are insecure. In fact, one can easily imagine that causality runs the other way: when polities are weak they are less likely to be able to abrogate the property rights of powerful interest groups who may be especially positioned to promote their interests within new political arrangements.

Second, our analysis suggests that the theoretical literature on institutions and growth is in need of refinement as well. There are two alternative hypotheses that the New Institutionalism would suggest about environments such as existed in revolutionary Mexico. One hypothesis suggests that Mexico's manufacturing sector would not have grown at all (and likely would have shrunk) because of the changes brought by the revolution. Based on the data we have been able to analyze here, this hypothesis is easy to reject: new firms entered the market, there was substantial new investment in plant and equipment, and productivity continued growing after the revolution. A second, weaker, hypothesis suggests that the revolution should have *slowed* the rate of growth of Mexican industry. This hypothesis is more difficult to evaluate because it depends on which hypothetical Mexican economy one believes is the most appropriate counterfactual: the rapidly growing economy from 1890 to 1905 (when a rise in tariffs and the reform of general incorporation laws permitted the rapid expansion of new industries), or the Mexican economy from 1905 to 1910 (when the effects of those innovations had already been exhausted and the manufacturing sector was growing at a more modest pace). If one accepts the view that the 1905–1910 economy is the most appropriate counterfactual, the second hypothesis can be dismissed as well. If one insists that the 1890–1905 economy is the appropriate counterfactual, then the results are indeterminate.

Our results are consistent with what we know about the history of Mexico's most important export industry, crude petroleum, in which output climbed every year throughout the revolution (Brown 1993; Hall 1995). They are also consistent with the macroeconomic model estimated by Clark W. Reynolds, which indicates that the revolution's economic costs had been mitigated by the 1940s (Reynolds 1970). In short, pending the outcome of other empirical studies of the type conducted here, we are left to wonder if perhaps the New Institutional Economics has not overstated the institutional requirements of economic growth.

We posit the following hypothesis as an explanation for the persistence of investment and growth in the midst of political instability. Institutional changes can often have multiple, and unforeseen, consequences, as well as interact in ways that cannot be easily anticipated by policy makers. One possibility is that particular institutional reforms may (purposefully or not) lock in future changes onto paths that prevent further reforms. Perversely, these reforms create mechanisms that allow new governments to make credible commitments or, otherwise, restrict their predatory behavior. Indeed, under such circumstances, both economic agents and policy makers realize that the government—indeed, any government—cannot carry further sets of drastic reforms, regardless of its stated goals. Agents therefore perceive that some important subset of their property rights cannot be abrogated, despite the particular identity of the government. They will therefore continue to invest even when the political system is unstable.

We identify such a commitment mechanism in Mexico during the 1920s. Mexican manufacturers were concerned about three particular government actions that could reduce their property rights: reforms to the labor laws that created the eight-hour day and that provided for collective bargaining; reductions in the tariff; and expropriation of their assets. Following the end of the civil war, the government could not have made a credible commitment to restrain itself from engaging in these activities. In fact, this same government had previously engaged in predatory behavior before the enactment of the constitution of 1917. Indeed, the new government pressed forward on the reforms affecting the hours and conditions of work, in large part because organized labor played an important role in the revolution. Industrialists fought this first challenge to their private interests throughout 1918, culminating in the Convention of Industrialists in November of that year. They were, however, defeated by the powerful alliance of labor and government.

Industrialists did not cease investing, however, because the labor reforms led to the emergence of a powerful labor movement which changed the incentives of the new government. Although it was not fully understood in 1918, one of the secondary consequences of the growth of organized labor was the creation of a commitment mechanism that constrained the government from carrying through on other potential reforms, including the confiscation of assets. No postrevolutionary government in Mexico, regardless of its ideology and regardless of its stated goals, could reduce levels of trade protection, because this would have negative effects on the very workers and unions that supported the government. Manufacturers therefore came to perceive—rather quickly—that by ceding ground on the issue of the eight-hour day and collective bargaining, they had forestalled tariff reform. In fact, they came to perceive that they could pass along to consumers any increase in operating costs that came out of the labor reforms. From their perspective, therefore, the reform of labor institutions created a commitment mechanism that prevented the government from carrying out other reforms that would reduce their property rights. They also perceived that the increase in production costs that the reforms entailed would be mitigated by the fact that all manufacturers in any product line would face exactly the same labor costs (because all had to adhere to the eight-hour day and contracts were negotiated on an industrywide basis). These increased costs did not matter so long as tariffs protected them from foreign-produced goods. Finally, because the issue of the tariff was taken off the table, the related issue of the expropriation of assets was also removed from consideration. So long as manufacturers remained committed to keeping the work force in the factories employed, the government had no incentive to expropriate them. In fact, the only factory the government expropriated during the Great Depression (the Cruz Azul cement company) was handled in this way precisely because it had thrown its work force out into the streets. In sum, a commitment mechanism to maintain tariffs and protect private property was created through a set of institutional reforms designed to satisfy the demands of organized labor. It did not matter if the polity was unstable, because new governments could not afford to alienate the labor movement. Manufacturers perceived that regardless of who was in power, their property rights would not be reduced.

Clearly, more work needs to be done on cases of this type in order to further refine the literature on political instability, institutional change, and economic growth. This will require, however, that social scientists engage in the kind of detailed historical analysis that has long been the province of historians, and that historians conduct controlled case studies that are informed by the theoretical and analytic methods of the social sciences.[45]

Notes

Support for this chapter was provided by NSF grant number 34-3163-00-0-79-483, administered through the National Bureau of Economic Research. We thank Moramay López Alonso and Scott Wilson for their invaluable research assistance. We also acknowledge the helpful suggestions of David Abernethy, Terry Anderson, Jeffrey Bortz, Bruce Bueno de Mesquita, Stanley Engerman, Judith Goldstein, Jean-Laurent Rosenthal, Kenneth Sokoloff, and Barry Weingast. The usual caveats apply.

1. Following Alexander George, we employ revolutionary Mexico as a "disciplined-configurative" case study, whose purpose is to evaluate and build general theories. For a discussion of the use of single historical cases in theory building, see Alexander L. George (1979, pp. 43–68).

2. Scholars such as Skocpol (1979, pp. 4–5) have argued that there are fundamental differences between political and social revolutions. Our point of departure is that social revolutions are a subset of a larger class of political conflicts that we usually refer to as "instability." The transformation of institutions in most societies is endogenized within the existing political system, which is to say that conflict is mediated peacefully and without regime change. Some conflicts over institutions cannot be mediated by the existing political system. This may result in an unstable equilibrium: no group can definitively gain the upper hand and either carry through reforms or stop the reform movement. The result may be continual regime change. This is what most scholars appear to have in mind when they refer to political instability. In a subset of these cases, regime change is accompanied by violence, which is what scholars such as Skocpol appear to have in mind when they refer to political revolutions. A subset of these violent regime changes is ac-

companied by the successful reform of institutions, which is what scholars appear to have in mind when they refer to social revolutions.

3. In fact, Mexican crude petroleum output grew more than 40-fold during the revolution. See Instituto Nacional de Estadística Geografía e Informática (1994, p. 559). For the history of foreign petroleum companies in Mexico see Brown (1993) and Hall (1995).

4. This would not be possible in most other lines of economic activity in Mexico: the large mining and petroleum companies were parts of big foreign conglomerates (whose stock prices reflected their worldwide operations); most other domestic sectors, such as agriculture or commerce, were held by private companies.

5. See, for example, Dunne (1972, p. 3); Skocpol (1979, pp. 175–205, 218–229, 265–274); and Moore (1967, pp. 40–110).

6. The fact that these studies tend to select cases on the dependent variable suggests that their ability to explain the causes of revolutions may also be limited. See Geddes (1991, pp. 131–152).

7. Even here, the causality issue is not resolved; it is generally the case that unconstitutional rulers often come to power amid political instability.

8. Barro (1991), for example, employs the number of revolutions and coups per year and the number of political assassinations per million population as measures of instability, and goes on to "interpret [these] variables as adverse influences on property rights" (p. 432). Other investigators have tried to refine these measures. See Alesina, Özler, Roubini, and Swagel (1996).

9. Notably, Alesina et al. (1996) employ a simultaneous equation system to capture the potential feedbacks between economics and politics. Recognizing the inability to properly define instability, they use latent variable methods to model the probabilistic causes of instability. Two questions remain about their analysis, however: first is whether or not the process driving instability and its linkages to economic growth is the correct one; second, even if their specification was the correct one, does our critique that under conditions of instability that relationship may break down still holds.

10. The fact that a system is closed does not imply that the system is immune to external influence. One can incorporate international aspects by including foreign elements in the set of agents operating under a particular system. We can also include other international factors through exogenous shocks, described below under political instability, such as the support of a foreign government to a particular faction fighting for a regime change.

11. Our distinction between a political system and government is similar to the conventional distinction between regimes and governments. However, we prefer the term *political system* because it reflects the ongoing interaction of its elements as opposed to the static definition of *regime* as a form of government.

12. Our framework is not exclusive of rules that regulate a government after its selection, for example, constitutional restraints on the executive branch. We include

these, if they exist, under the second group of rules under which the constituents may agree to be governed by a government if the latter conforms to an agreed-upon set of rules (i.e., a constitutional provision that limits its authority). In other words, the government—if we assume it has its own objectives—can be one of the agents whose actions are being mediated through the political system. In short, the political system provides rules for the interaction (and permissible behavior) of government and society.

13. Informal institutions, such as social norms and customs, although created outside the political system, can sometimes be as important as formal institutions if the formal political system alone does not preclude them.

14. For a more detailed account of this problem, see Weingast (1997b).

15. One may argue that the assumption of common knowledge is a stringent one. This chapter does not intend to resolve the issue of how expectations are formed. In fact, we expect this definition to be refined in that direction. We feel, however, that this characterization is simple enough to illustrate the point that beliefs and expectations matter. Alternatively, instead of common knowledge, we can rephrase the condition as one where all agents arrive at some sort of expectational equilibrium about the nature and evolution of the political system. For a discussion of these issues, see Arthur (1997).

16. Self-enforcement implies only that there are no incentives to deviate, not that everyone is satisfied with the existing political system. For instance, self-enforcement can occur under one of two extreme sets of political conditions: first, all agents, free to make their own decisions, find it advantageous to sustain the system (i.e., cooperation is a Nash equilibrium, or its appropriate refinement, in a game where the different players agree on the system that governs them); or, second, the government, possessing an effective monitoring technology, may impose severe sanctions on players who deviate from the rules (as in a dictatorship) with minimal or null effort. Notice that this would not be a game that defines static rules but rather one where agents agree on *how* to mediate their conflicting interests in the present and future periods. Because this is essentially a repeated game, we also employ the term *stable* in a dynamic sense, meaning that the political system is in a steady state of "cooperation" where small deviations (brought about by internal or external shocks to the system) do not affect its long-run (subgame-perfect) equilibrium. Therefore, we use the terms *stable political system* and *political equilibrium* interchangeably. One potential problem with this game-theoretic characterization, however, is the existence of multiple equilibria in some games, which further warrants discussion of how people support one political system when others are equally valid. Yet another difficulty arises in those cases where there are no equilibria. Efficiency questions aside, all societies operate under an implicit or explicit social contract, as embodied in what we call a political system.

17. This is not to say that endogenous institutional change does not have an effect on the economy. Even if we assume rational expectations, institutional changes—

economic policy, in particular—may have a real effect on the economy if, for example, the government has an informational advantage over private agents or if there are nominal price rigidities. Our statement is simply one of forward-looking agents that are constantly adapting to their perceived institutional environment.

18. This general feature does not change even when we relax our assumptions to allow random shocks to the system. It affects the timing of potential changes but it does not mean that such changes are accepted unconditionally. In fact, because a political system reflects ongoing negotiations of social interests, the necessary ratification of the random changes would effectively endogenize them.

19. This can be expressed in game-theoretic terms as follows. The dynamic evolution of a political system is analogous to a sequence of games. A crucial distinction of ours is that we do not assume these games are repeated; that is, people do not necessarily play the same game over and over. Instead, we see this sequence of strategic interactions as games with potentially different specifications. Because, in fact, institutional changes are continually modifying various elements of previous games, future games can be very different. Thus, members of society are playing a sequence of (structurally) different games. Each of these games is therefore a subgame in that sequence (the whole extensive-form game). That, in turn, requires that each subgame have an equilibrium. It is this subgame-perfect equilibrium, or its refinement depending on the specific model, that corresponds to our notion of political equilibrium, because at that particular point, or period, in time, society is agreeing to abide by the existing rules of the system.

20. Our definitions of revolution focus on procedures, which is consistent with our analysis of institutions as rules that constrain social behavior. Thus, exogenous institutional change is revolutionary only because it is not mediated through the existing system. This is a definition which can be used more systematically than one which focuses on the extent and direction of change, in which there is substantial disagreement about the threshold levels beyond which changes can be classified as revolutionary. Most important, our definition links revolutions and instability in a consistent and systematic way. In contrast, other definitions of revolutions as drastic institutional changes preclude the joint study of stability issues simply because any stable political system is capable in principle of producing such changes. This definition is also a bit different from the one advanced by North (see North 1983, p. 65). There he characterizes revolutionary change as a situation where "the formal rules may change overnight." As such, it is related to uncertainty in a way similar to ours. However, he adds a critical condition: that the underlying informal institutions concurrently remain unchanged. This produces an internal tension in the overall institutional structure that forces subsequent conflict to be finally resolved through a less revolutionary change. This second part relies more heavily on empirical determination of the extent of formal institutional changes.

21. Admittedly, relaxing the constraints of a political system, especially when politi-

cal participation is concentrated, may actually lead to new entrants in the political arena. However, although alternative means of political organization may arise, the question of whether they will be long-lasting remains. In addition, if political organization is costly, the ability of these new political actors to organize themselves will be limited.

22. We follow Frank Knight (1921) in distinguishing between risk, which is a type of uncertainty that can be quantified, and that uncertainty which cannot be quantified. Our use of the term reflects the second type.

23. Uncertainty about future policies is not particularly associated with either political stability or instability. Even under stable political systems, there is uncertainty about future policies because the identity of governments is not known a priori. Elections in the United States are a prime example of this. Preliminary odds and public opinion polls may aid in predicting results, but the uncertainty is not really resolved until the elections are completed. In addition, the direction that institutional change may take is not conditioned by stability or instability. Stable systems do not preclude drastic or detrimental changes.

24. Even in highly centralized political systems—for example, a dictatorship—governments are required to consult with their political supporters about future policy changes.

25. This situation applies even to political factions with established reputations for the protection of property rights. Suppose, for example, that the incumbent government in a stable political system is a protector of property rights and takes actions that promote economic growth. With the onset of a period of political instability, the previously incumbent government is now one of the factions fighting to establish its own political system. Even if it makes a promise to protect property rights once peace is restored, this promise cannot be taken as a credible commitment—for two reasons. First, there is uncertainty as to whether this faction will be able to regain power. Second, even if it does, the constraints that it will face under the restored political equilibrium will be very different from those in which its reputation was established. Once in power, the government may be practically impeded from fulfilling its promises. Furthermore, the ex post perceptions of the new government concerning its ability to sustain power may also have an effect on its behavior. To the extent that the new government perceives its tenure as being limited to a short horizon, incentives may arise for capturing wealth before other governments replace it.

26. For discussions of the Porfirian economic transformation, see Beatty (1996), Bernstein (1964), Cárdenas (1997), Coatsworth (1981), Ficker (1995), Ficker and Riguzzi (1996), Haber (1989, 1992), Maurer (1997), and Reynolds (1970).

27. On the revolution, see Gilly (1994), Hart (1987), Katz (1981), Knight (1987), and Womack (1969, 1986).

28. During a strike in the textile factories in the Distrito Federal in 1917, for example, Governor César López de Lara made it clear to the industrialists that they had a

choice: provide justice for the workers, or spend time in jail. See Rancaño (1987, p. 201).

29. For a summary and critique of this view see Womack (1978).

30. Please see online Table 1 (Exit and Entry) located at: http://www.stanford.edu/~haber/publications/bdmvolume.

31. Data sources on the cotton textile industry are as follows: 1837–1839 and 1841–1842 data were obtained from Secretaría de Hacienda y Crédito Público (hereafter, SHCP), *Documentos para el Estudio de la Industrialización de México, 1837–1845* (Mexico City, 1977, p. 82); data for 1840 were partially retrieved from L. Barjau Martinez et al., "Estadísticas Económicas del Siglo XIX," *Cuadernos de Trabajo del Departamento de Investigaciones Históricas, INAH*, no. 14 (Mexico City, July 1976, table 13), and from SHCP, "Industrialización en México," p. 82; the 1844 census was compiled from L. Barjau Martinez, "Estadísticas Económicas," tables 17–19; data for 1845 were obtained from tables 20–21 of L. Barjau Martinez, "Estadísticas Económicas"; 1850 data were retrieved from Secretaría de Fomento, Colonización e Industria, *Memoria que la Dirección De Colonización e Industria presentó al Ministerio De Relaciones en 17 de Enero de 1852, sobre el estado de estos Ramos en el Año Anterior* (Mexico, 1852); 1854 data were obtained from Gobierno del Estado de México, *Estadística del Departamento de México* (Mexico, 1980); 1857 data were obtained from Secretaría del Estado, *Memoria de la Secretaría del Estado y del Despacho de Fomento, Colonización, Industria y Comercio de la República Mexicana* (Mexico, 1857); 1862 data were obtained from J. M. Pérez Hernandez, *Estadística de la República Mexicana* (Guadalajara, 1862); 1865 data were obtained from Ministerio de Fomento, *Memoria 1865* (Mexico, 1866); 1878 data were taken from Secretaría de Hacienda, *Estadísticas de la República Mexicana* (Mexico City, 1880); 1883 data were taken from A. Garcia Cubas, *Cuadro Geográfico, Estadístico, Descriptivo é Histórico de los Estados Unidos Mexicanos* (Mexico City, 1884–1885); 1888 data were taken from Secretaría de Fomento, *Boletin Semestral de la República Mexicana* (Mexico City, 1890); 1891 data were taken from A. Garcia Cubas, *Mexico: Its Trade, Industries and Resources* (Mexico City, 1893); 1893 data were taken from Dirección General de Estadística, *Anuario Estadístico de la República Mexicana 1893–94* (Mexico, 1894); 1895 data were taken from Secretaría de Hacienda, *Memoria de la Secretaría de Hacienda* (Mexico, 1896); 1896 data were taken from Secretaría de Hacienda, *Estadística de la República Mexicana* (Mexico, 1896); 1898–1913 excise tax data were taken from the Ministry of Finance's periodical reports in the financial weekly *Semana Mercantil*, published in Mexico City; 1912 data were taken from "Extracto de las Manifestaciones presentadas por los fabricantes de hilados y tejidos de algodón para el semestre de enero a junio de 1912," located at the Archivo General de la Nación (hereafter, AGN), Caja 5, Exp. 4 (Mexico, n.d.); 1913 data were also located in the same archives within "Extracto de las Manifestaciones presentadas por los fabricantes de hilados y tejidos de algodón para el semestre de enero a junio de 1913," AGN, Caja 31, Exp. 2 (Mexico, n.d.); 1914 data were taken

from the 4 July 1914 issue of Mexico City's *El Economista Mexicano*; 1915–1932 data were taken from periodical reports of excise tax data found in Secretaría de Hacienda y Crédito Público, *Boletín de la Secretaría de Hacienda y Crédito Público* (Mexico City, 1917–1932); 1924–1933 statewide data were obtained from typewritten reports of the Secretaría de Hacienda y Crédito Público—Departamento de Estadística, "Estadísticas del Ramo de Hilados y Tejidos de Algodón y de Lana," located at the Library of the Banco de México; finally, national data for 1898–1924 were taken from Dirección General de Estadística, *Anuario Estadístico 1923–1924*, Vol. II (Mexico City, 1926).

32. A note on interpreting the regression results is in order. First, to assess the importance of individual explanatory variables in these regressions, we look at their relative magnitudes and statistical significance. Second, the estimate of the intercept provides a benchmark with which to compare the coefficient estimates of the other explanatory variables because it allows us to calculate the probability of the survival of firms which do not have the characteristics of the regressors. Third, as estimated, the model is a probability function for which absolute probabilities can be calculated only if the explanatory variables X are evaluated at particular values of interest.

33. Regression output for the logit equations are shown in online Table 2, located at http://www.stanford.edu/~haber/publications/bdmvolume. We obtain different coefficients in the logit model because we lack the proportionality factor between probit and logit estimates present in more balanced samples. Probit coefficients may be multiplied by a factor of 1.6 to obtain comparable estimates of the logit coefficients when the dependent variable is evenly balanced between 0s and 1s. See Greene (1993, pp. 636–640).

34. The average firm size corresponded to a 0.7 percent market share. The largest firms in the industry had market shares of 5 to 12 percent.

35. We calculated these marginal effects in two steps. First, we used specification 1b in Table 5.1 to calculate a probability equation as a function of size: Prob(survival $= 1 \mid$ size) $= \phi \, (-0.451 + 213.923 \bullet$ size $+ 0.445 + 0.578 - 0.543)$, where ϕ is a normal cumulative distribution function. These are graphed in Figure 5.1 as "absolute probability." Second, we measured changes in probability associated with size increments of 0.01 percent of market share. These changes correspond to the marginal effects of size on the probability of survival. The probability equation corresponds to joint stock firms in the central region. Varying location and firm type (not shown here) produced results almost identical to this equation. To crosscheck our results, we ran separate regressions with an intercept term and size as the only explanatory variables (given that estimates of the other variables in specification 7 were neither robust nor statistically significant). We obtained similar results: marginal size effects were more important for the smallest firms and were exhausted at a size equivalent to 1.5 percent of market share.

36. Mexico's factory owners regularly communicated these problems to the government. See Archivo General de la Nación, Ramo del Departamento de Trabajo: Box

45, file 3, pp. 1–5; Box 52, file 12, pp. 1–3; Box 90, file 17, p. 1; Box 91: file 21, pp. 1–2; Box 96, file 5, pp. 49–53; Box 96, file 9, p. 45; Box 107, file 22, p. 2; Box 107, file 22, p. 2; Box 110, file 28, p. 1; Box 173, file 23, p. 1.

37. Data were gathered from *El Economista Mexicano* and *La Semana Mercantil* from 1896 to 1914. Data from 1914 to 1935 were gathered from the *Boletín Financiero y Minero*. In cases where no shares were traded, the average of the bid and ask prices was taken.

38. See note 39 for reference to tabulated results not shown here.

39. The fact that firms invested ahead of demand is explained by the fact that cement production tends, almost everywhere in the world, to be characterized by local monopolies. The high bulk to price ratio of cement means that it is economical to ship it only over short distances. In order to expand, therefore, firms must erect new production facilities in new areas of the country. Firms also tend to erect more productive capacity than they need in these new markets in order to keep out potential rivals. See Johnson and Parkman (1983).

40. Spindles constitute the most important capital input for the production of cotton textile goods, and thus the literature tends to use spindlage as the measure of capital or capacity. See, for example, Kane (1988).

41. Mexican population data from: Instituto Nacional de Estadística Geografía e Informática, *Estadísticas Históricas de México* (Aguascalientes: Instituto Nacional de Estadística Geografía e Informática, 1994, p. 44). Also, the increase in capacity cannot be explained by wartime production of uniforms and other military demand. With the exception of the federal army, the combatant forces were irregulars. In addition, an interpretation that focuses on war-driven production cannot easily reconcile the sharp decline from 1913 to 1917, the years of most severe combat.

42. For a discussion of the general economic conditions in the late 1920s see Haber (1989, pp. 152–154).

43. See note 33 for reference to tabulated results not shown here.

44. Although some censuses report various measures of capital, the only uniform and consistent definition of capital across censuses was the number of spindles. We know, however, from detailed machinery reports in some of the censuses that spindles constituted the most important capital input for the production of cotton textile goods. This corresponds to the findings of work on the U.S. textile industry, where the literature tends to use spindlage as the measure of capital or capacity as well. See Kane (1988).

45. One reason single case studies do not often contribute to theory development is that historians usually attempt to study all those aspects of the case that they judge interesting or unusual, rather than systematically studying particular issues that are relevant to testing or building social science theories. The result is that social scientists are often forced to conduct their own case studies, but they do so without the detailed knowledge of past societies that is the comparative advantage of historians. See George (1979, pp. 49–51).

6. SOCIO-POLITICAL INSTABILITY AND THE PROBLEM OF DEVELOPMENT

Paul J. Zak

Economic development is fundamentally a process of displacement and change. Traditional agrarian lifestyles in which farmers barter or sell their crops in local markets disappear as the demand for manufactured goods attracts peasants to urban centers. Manufactured goods replace homemade products, and repetitive labor crowds out artisanship even as incomes for laborers rise. Relative income shares of various groups rise and fall as established industries face new competition and the economic and political environments evolve. It is farmers in rural areas and low-skill workers in the countryside and cities who generally see their relative position in the societal income distribution fall with industrialization. This occurs because the urban educated are in the best position to take advantage of the new opportunities that development affords.

As the distribution of income widens during the early stages of development, conflicts over uneven gains from development inevitably arise. Because political structures tend to be immature in developing countries, the inherent displacement which occurs during development seldom has an effective political outlet. Without a political mechanism to mediate disputes, those who find themselves relatively worse off because of development may express their discontent through strikes, riots, and political demonstrations. These factors create *socio-political instability* (SPI). SPI can be considered an institutional failure, because it is prima facie evidence that the methods the government is using to resolve disputes are failing. For the reasons given above, economic development is typically accompanied by SPI. Further, SPI affects, and may undermine, the prospects for successful economic development.

In this chapter I review the sources of SPI and the ways it affects economic decisions that determine the success or failure of development policies. Once the sources of SPI and its effect on development are understood, institutions and policies can be designed that stimulate development without exacerbating SPI. Such institutions and policies are of vital importance in developing countries, because high levels of SPI can doom a country's development prospects. The primary conclusion of this chapter is that development policies cannot be formulated in a vacuum—the social and political environments must be taken into account. Put differently, the potential for SPI constrains the set of development policies that governments can enact. If the social and political effects of policies are ignored, the upheaval that may accompany policy initiatives can undermine a policy's intended purpose, in some cases leading to an economic crisis.

I begin by examining the evidence of SPI's impact on development.

THE CAUSES AND EFFECTS OF SPI

Strong theoretical and empirical evidence shows that SPI hinders development. The seminal modern work in this area was done by Venieris and Gupta (1985, 1986) and Venieris and Stewart (1987), though the notion that social instability affects economic performance can be traced back to Haavelmo (1954) and Adam Smith (1776/1937). Venieris and his coauthors identify the mechanism that produces SPI as the frustrated expectations for income gains that often fail to materialize with development. Although a rising tide lifts all boats, is does not do so at equal rates, so the relative income of some groups will decline even while absolute incomes rise. At the same time, the media in developing countries trumpet the success stories of entrepreneurs who benefit disproportionately from development, which adds fuel to the fire for those whose income gains are meager.

The work of Venieris and his coauthors shows that SPI reduces savings and investment, which has a negative impact on the growth of per capita gross domestic product (GDP). Similar results have been demonstrated by Barro (1991) using various measures of SPI, such as the number of assassinations, coups d'état, and irregular government changes. Extending these results, Alesina, Özler, Roubini, and Swagel (1996) show that not only does SPI affect output, but the level of GDP also affects SPI. In particular, SPI is endemic in poor countries, while rising incomes reduce the incidence of SPI. Zak (1997a) provides the theoretical underpinning for the empirics linking SPI and growth by showing that those with the lowest incomes in a society are the most likely to engage in activities that take physical capital (i.e., plant and equipment) out of production and reduce the amount of output that can be sold. That is, SPI is driven by the trade-offs individuals face between earning income through legitimate work and illegal activities. SPI reduces output for three reasons. First, the disaffected expropriate capital from firms to augment their incomes. Second, capital may be destroyed during strikes and demonstrations, resulting in the loss of productive capacity. Third, the time spent expropriating, demonstrating, and striking removes labor from production, which also reduces output. Thus, Zak (1997a) shows, SPI is driven primarily by violations of property rights—when property that belongs to one individual is stolen or destroyed by another.

Knowing the mechanism through which SPI affects economies permits policies to be designed that decrease the level of SPI, a topic discussed later in this chapter. First, it is worth examining the data to see if the discussion above matches the facts. Another important reason to look at the data before proceeding is to make a determination of the *quantitative impact* of SPI on development. If the effect is small, one can reasonably ignore it. The following section demonstrates that SPI has a quantitatively large impact on development.

The Data

I begin by examining the data on the aforementioned causes of SPI. Zak (1997a) shows that the reward for violating property rights increases in proportion to the difference in the income and wealth of those engaging in expropriative activities relative to those whose property is being stolen. That is, the theory predicts that countries with less equal income distributions will have higher levels of SPI. Using data on income distribution developed by Deininger and Squire (1996) for the World Bank, I use a measure of income inequality called the Gini coefficient to examine the relationship between income distribution and SPI. The Gini coefficient ranges from zero to one, with zero indicating maximal inequality and one indicating perfect equality. Next, a measure of SPI is needed. Here I use the SPI data developed by Venieris and Gupta (1985) that creates an index of SPI using discriminant analysis to weight various constituent factors, including assassinations, irregular government changes, riots, political strikes, and armed attacks.[1] This index is additive, so that a country with an SPI of 0.60, for example, has twice as much instability as a country with an SPI of 0.30. The data set includes sixty-nine countries over a thirty-year time span, 1962 to 1992. Figure 6.1 plots the average Gini coefficient and the average SPI over this period, where the Gini coefficient is multiplied by 100 to aid in the graph's readability. The correlation between these two data series is 0.30. That is, the higher the Gini coefficient on average (more inequality), the higher the SPI.

Figure 6.1 also reveals something else about the relationship between inequality and SPI. There are a number of countries that have virtually *no SPI at all*. Almost all these countries have very low levels of inequality (Gini coefficients are rarely below 0.30 in any country). This naturally leads one to ask about the characteristics of countries that experience no social or political upheavals. The theory in Zak (1997a) indicates that SPI should fall as individuals' incomes rise: If we calculate the correlation between per capita GDP and Gini, we find a correlation coefficient of −0.56. That is, wealthier countries have lower levels of SPI. Income inequality typically increases during the early phases of development and then decreases with continued growth. Rising per capita income can reduce SPI via two channels. First, if growth causes the income distribution to narrow, the relative payoff to expropriation is reduced. Second, as development spreads from educated city dwellers to the less skilled and those living in rural areas, wages of all workers rise, the opportunity cost of engaging in SPI (i.e., taking time off from work) increases, and the incentive

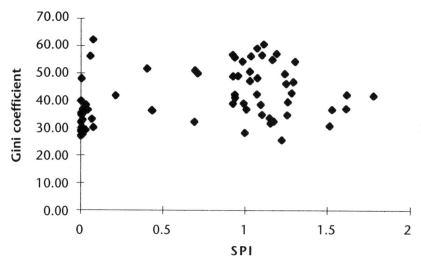

Figure 6.1. Inequality and SPI
Note: *Inequality is measured by the Gini coefficient; SPI is an index of socio-political instability.*

to strike and demonstrate diminishes. Furthermore, economic development typically stimulates political development, so that citizens can express their discontent regarding economic outcomes through political channels instead of by demonstrating or expropriating capital. For all these reasons, SPI typically diminishes with sufficient development and is a significant problem only in less developed nations.

The data plotted in Figure 6.2 show the relationship between GDP per capita and SPI.[2] The figure provides an incomplete picture of the development problem discussed above because it does not relate SPI to the economy's *growth path*. Neoclassical growth theory, as developed by Solow (1956), Cass (1965), and Koopmans (1965), shows that the growth rate of an economy is fastest when the level of per capita GDP is low. Over time, the growth rate decreases monotonically as per capita GDP rises. This is because when there are few factors of production, the increase in aggregate output from each extra productive factor is high. Conversely, for economies that have a large productive base, an additional productive factor has very little effect on aggregate output. A simple example may clarify this concept. Consider a factory with four workers and two machines producing widgets. The addition of one machine will increase output considerably. If the same four-worker firm has one hundred machines and then adds one machine, total output will increase much less than when the factory was smaller. This phenomenon, called *diminishing marginal productivity,* occurs both in factories as well as in entire countries.

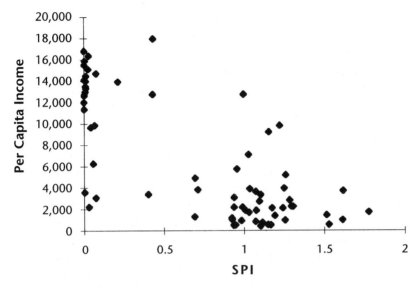

Figure 6.2. Per capita income and SPI

A Model and Statistical Tests

The notion of diminishing marginal productivity is relevant to the analysis of the relationship between SPI and growth because the rate of growth decreases as the level of per capita GDP rises. Therefore, when examining the effect of SPI on the growth, one must statistically control for the level of GDP. In more formal terms, I generalize the growth model of Solow (1956) by including a term which captures the effect of SPI on output.[3]

Table 6.1 presents the results of an ordinary least squares regression of sixty-nine countries over the period 1962–1992 for the growth rate of per capita GDP

Table 6.1. Regression Results Relating SPI and Growth

Independent variables	Coefficient	t-Statistic	Probability
Constant	0.030	5.727	0.000
SPI	−0.012	−2.997	0.004
1962 per capita GDP	−6.92e − 7	−0.856	0.395

Note: *Dependent variable: growth in per capita GDP; observations: 69; R²: 0.143.*

on a constant, 1962 per capita GDP and the mean level of SPI over the sample period. The statistical procedure controls for the effect of the level of GDP on growth so that the analysis across developing and developed countries is comparable. The table shows that SPI has a negative and statistically significant impact on the growth in per capita GDP. The regression analysis indicates that, on average, a doubling of the level of SPI in a particular country will cause per capita income growth to fall by 1.2 percent. This analysis permits us to quantify the impact of SPI on the process of development. It shows that SPI can have an enormous impact on a country's development path over time. For example, a developing country in which per capita GDP is growing at 6 percent per year will double its income in twelve years when there is no SPI. If this country, instead of having no SPI, experiences the average level of SPI, the length of time to double per capita income will rise from twelve to fifteen years. If this country experiences twice the level of average SPI in the sample, it will take twenty years to double income rather than twelve. Three times the average level of SPI increases the time to double per capita income to twenty-six years; four times the average level raises the doubling time to forty-five years.

The projections in this section clearly show the potentially devastating impact of SPI on development. It is essential that any government policy that is designed to stimulate development does not increase SPI at the same time. If such a policy raises SPI sufficiently, the overall effect might be to decrease growth, rather than increase it. Governments therefore face a *policy design* problem. Of the set of policies that raise per capita GDP growth absent SPI, only a subset of these will be effective if policies also increase SPI. Before we can explore the design of such policies, we need to know how SPI affects economic decisions.

THE IMPACT OF SPI ON ECONOMIC DECISIONS

Production

SPI affects the production process in several ways. Although SPI may involve the direct loss of output through expropriation or destruction of capital, output may also fall as a result of labor unrest. Strikes or work slowdowns arise as laborers, frustrated by low wages, government policies, or high taxes express their displeasure by disrupting production. Work stoppages may also occur to protest the political system as a whole. This happened, for example, in South Korea prior to its transition to democracy in 1988. The overall effect of SPI is to shift production inward from the efficient level on the *production possibility frontier* at which firms optimally combine capital and labor to produce a given level of output. Production levels with and without SPI are shown in Figure 6.3. Because SPI is labor-driven, firms will alter the pre-SPI mix of capital and labor used in production to one in which capital is substituted for labor in the pro-

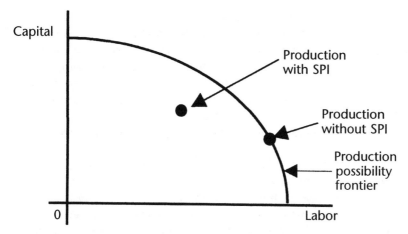

Figure 6.3. Production levels with and without SPI

duction process when SPI flares up. Thus, SPI causes firms to overinvest in mechanized production in response to the lack of a stable labor supply, which may lead to inefficient production methods.

When production is inefficient—that is, when it occurs inside the production possibility frontier—wages and the return to capital fall. Low wages further discourage workers from working, reinforcing the effects of SPI. Without intervention, a cascade of strikes, further wage reductions, and lower levels of output may continue unabated, miring the economy in a low-output long-run equilibrium. SPI also affects profit-maximizing firms' choice of production technologies. In order to reduce the risk of expropriation, firms typically move production toward lower value-added techniques when SPI is high. Lucas (1993) shows that development depends on innovation and a movement toward higher value-added goods production. Thus, SPI stunts long-run development.

Consumption Decisions

If labor income falls as a result of SPI, why do workers engage in strikes and demonstrations? Though psychological reasons for demonstrations certainly exist (see North 1988), the only economic reason to reduce one's current income is because there is an expectation that future income will increase in response to today's protests.[4] Individuals' future incomes may increase because collective bargaining raises wages or, in an effort to reduce SPI and increase production, the government institutes a redistribution of income or services (such as health care or recreational facilities) to workers. Alternatively, the police may be called in to quell labor uprisings. If this action reduces demonstrations and raises output, wages will rise and the incentive to demonstrate will fall. In the extreme, if SPI is sufficiently widespread, the police will be unable to maintain public order and government leaders will be defenestrated. The impact on workers' wages in this case is uncertain. Consumption is roughly proportional to expected lifetime income (this is called the *permanent income hypothesis*), so that factors that raise expected future income will raise present consumption levels. If SPI leads individuals to expect that their future earnings will fall, current consumption levels, and therefore the utility derived from consumption, will fall.

An additional factor affecting consumption decisions is that the market system tends to be underdeveloped in developing countries. Exchange is often fettered by the unenforceability of contracts, monopolies, and high taxes, among other frictions. As a result, there is no guarantee that market transactions will lead to socially optimal outcomes—what Adam Smith called the invisible hand of commerce. Moreover, consumers may seek to circumvent the market system and increase their utility by trying to influence the exchange process. Using one's resources to manipulate the allocation of resources is called *rent seeking*. An example is paying a bribe to a government official in order to effect a transaction. From a societal view, rent seeking is a net loss because these moneys do not add to productive capacity. One reaction to high rates of SPI is to modify the terms of market exchange via rent seeking or to circumvent formal markets by using the black market. All these machinations reduce the gains from free exchange, resulting in socially suboptimal outcomes.

SPI, SAVINGS, INVESTMENT, AND GROWTH

In developing countries, all but the poorest citizens seek to smooth consumption over time by saving, which raises their lifetime utility (see the discussion and evidence in Rebelo 1992). Individuals also save to insure their consumption against losses of income. The primary source of developing country investment capital is domestic saving, and SPI has a deleterious effect on the incentives to both invest and save, which are the basis for growth.

Figure 6.4 demonstrates the reduction in savings and the impact on equilibrium investment resulting from SPI. The capital market is in equilibrium when there is some interest rate, r, such that the supply of funds (savings) balances the demand for funds (investment). In the figure, S denotes the savings schedule without SPI, S' is the savings with SPI, and I is the investment schedule. Savings falls with SPI because (as explained in the previous section) output falls, which depresses wages. The figure shows that the equilibrium level of investment falls with SPI, from I_1 to I_2, putting upward pressure on the equilibrium interest rate.

In addition to reducing available investment funds through its effect on savings and making loans more expensive, SPI has a direct impact on the quan-

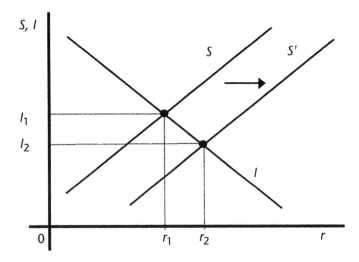

Figure 6.4. The reduction in equilibrium investment resulting from SPI
Note: S *is savings without SPI;* S' *is savings with SPI;* I *is investment;* r *is the equilibrium rate of interest.*

tity and mix of investments. Fixed capital is at greater risk of loss when SPI is high, as expropriation and destruction are more likely. Thus, when SPI is high, investment tends toward the liquid and speculative. Investments in plant and equipment are the foundation of industrialization, but SPI militates against such investments because they tend to be expensive and not easily moved— and therefore carry a larger risk to investors. Countries with high SPI have investments in low-capital, low-productivity industries such as textiles and mining rather than in more capital-intensive industries that allow for sustained productivity gains. Basic industries that are labor-intensive are not amenable to the innovations that lead to higher profits, higher wages, and increases in investment—a human being can weave cotton into cloth on a loom only so fast. Further, countries with high SPI have stock markets that gyrate wildly as speculative funds flow quickly in and out of the country. The low rate of investment in these countries is the primary reason, as shown in the statistical analysis above, that they grow more slowly than do countries with low SPI.

Recall that SPI is caused by the imperfect enforcement of property rights. Investors cannot capture the return from their investment if it is expropriated in uprisings or via government decree, both of which occur in countries with high SPI. As a result, these countries have low investment rates. SPI not only decreases the expected return of investment, it also increases the *risk* of investments. In finance, risk is measured by the variance (or dispersion) of returns. It is easily shown that for two investments with equal expected returns, the one with lower risk will be chosen by risk-adverse investors. Said differently, higher-risk investments will be undertaken only if the expected return from such an investment is sufficiently high to compensate investors for accepting greater risk. When strikes and demonstrations destroy investment in a seemingly random fashion, SPI raises the risk of investment. In a similar fashion, if SPI imperils the political structure, government policies may vacillate wildly, also increasing the risk of investment. Politics sets the "rules of the game" under which investments are made. If low-interest government loans dry up when political priorities change, or if taxes suddenly increase as a result of SPI, the investment risk increases. This can be called the *policy risk* of investment owing to SPI. When risk increases, ceteris paribus, the rate of investment falls. This argument also pertains to foreign direct investment.[5]

In developed countries, the size of financial markets and large number of financial instruments permit investors to insure against many types of risks. A market is called *complete* if it is possible to insure against all contingencies. The low level of financial development in the developing world suggests that capital markets in these countries are incomplete. If a developing country had a complete capital market, SPI would have little impact on investment because investors would be able to insure against it. As this is unlikely, the increased investment risk resulting from SPI cannot be avoided, and its effect on investment may be considerable.[6] To insure against SPI, investors in developing countries commonly move their savings outside their home country. This tactic reduces the funds available for domestic investment, which has a negative impact on a country's growth prospects.

The direct effect of SPI on investment, coupled with its effect on savings, is shown in the depiction of the capital market in Figure 6.5. Investment drops from the no-SPI schedule I to I', the investment schedule with SPI, as the return to, and riskiness of, investments increases. The equilibrium level of investment is now I_3, which is less than I_2, the investment level when SPI affects only savings. The reduction in the demand for investment funds leads to a decrease in the equilibrium rate of interest, which, as shown in the figure, is near that of the no-SPI equilibrium r_1 (though the interest rate can be higher or lower depending on the relative sensitivities of savings and investment to SPI). Most significantly, the effect of SPI on the capital market shows that it unambiguously reduces the equilibrium level of investment.

Growth Dynamics
Financial intermediaries facilitate the flow of funds from savers to investors. Output can be increased only if investment raises productive capacity. It is investment which drives the growth of output. Standard neoclassical models of economic growth do not consider the effects of SPI. Much of the data from developing countries belies the prediction from these standard models. The data

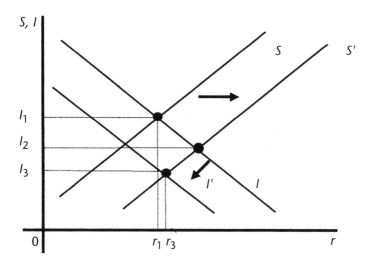

Figure 6.5. The overall effect of SPI on savings and investment
Note: S is savings without SPI; S' is savings with SPI; I is investment without SPI; I' is investment with SPI; r is the equilibrium rate of interest.

show that most poor economies generally grow quite slowly, if at all, while the
standard models predict that poorer countries should grow faster than wealthier
countries. The primary reason for this schism is the typically high levels of SPI in
poor countries. In this section, I discuss how the inclusion of SPI in neoclassical
growth models brings the predictions of these models in line with the data. The
impact of SPI on growth is also shown to depend on the level of SPI; that is, the
growth effects vary depending on whether there is moderate or high SPI.

Figure 6.6 depicts the growth path of two economies as given by a neoclassical growth model. The upper path shows the growth in output in the absence
of SPI, while the lower path depicts the growth path when there is a moderate
amount of SPI. Because the rate of investment falls with output growth as a result of diminishing marginal productivity, the plotted growth rate of per capita
income, y_t, at time t, declines as the economy becomes richer. A *steady state* is
reached when per capita income is constant, $y_t = y_{t+1}$. In the figure, the steady
state is reached when the equilibrium growth path intersects the 45-degree ray
and per capita income ceases to grow. Owing to the lower level of savings and
investment occasioned by SPI, the growth path with SPI is everywhere below
the no-SPI path and, as the figure shows, a developing country with SPI will
have a lower level of steady state per capita income.[7] Said differently, because
of the presence of SPI during the development process, long-run income will
be *permanently lower* even after a country is fully developed. The reason for this
is that resources were taken out of production as this economy developed and,

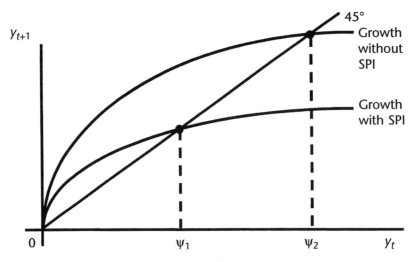

Figure 6.6. Growth with and without SPI
Note: y_t *is per capita income at time* t; $y_t + 1$ *is per capita income at time*
t + 1; ψ_1 *is the long-run level of per capita income when SPI is present;* ψ_2
is the long-run level of income when there is no SPI during development.

even if SPI decreases as this economy grows, it can never recover the lost productive capital resulting from SPI. Thus, such a country's per capita income will
be permanently reduced relative to a country that has undergone less SPI while
developing.

Poverty Traps

The discussion above does not reveal why many developing countries with SPI
not only grow slowly, but often do not grow at all. In the extreme, highly unstable countries sustain *contractions* in per capita income. Zak (1997a) provides
conditions under which SPI causes some countries to contract rather than grow.
Here is the argument: when wages are very low, SPI is typically high; individuals have little to lose by protesting government policies. If average labor income
is low, and the distribution of income is sufficiently unequal, the rate of investment may be insufficient even to sustain the current level of output. The loss of
productive capacity as a result of SPI causes such a country to be caught in a
poverty trap where per capita income declines for extended periods.

Instability begets more instability as ruling coalitions with few resources
cannot implement successful development programs and quickly lose power.
New governments grasp at extreme policies which are rapidly revised to reverse
declining output, adding further to policy risk and discouraging investment.

Unfortunately there are many examples of countries that appear to be stuck

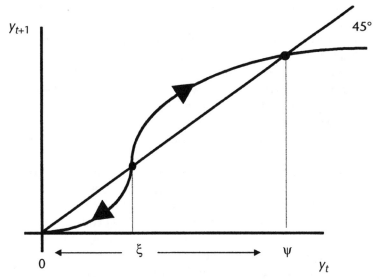

Figure 6.7. An SPI-induced poverty trap
Note: y_t *is per capita income at time* t; y_{t+1} *is per capita income at time* t
+ 1; ξ *is the growth threshold level of per capita income;* ψ *is the long-run value of per capita income.*

in poverty traps, particularly in sub-Saharan Africa. Figure 6.7 depicts the substantial effect of SPI in very poor countries. When the ability to expropriate or destroy capital is efficient and if initial income is less than the threshold value ξ shown in the figure, the economy contracts into a poverty trap at the origin. If the country is not as poor, having an initial income exceeding ξ, then it will grow toward a positive income steady state ψ in the figure, as moderate amounts of SPI do not overwhelm the process of economic growth.[8]

DESIGNING INSTITUTIONS AND POLICIES WHEN SPI IS PRESENT

Olson (1982), North (1988, 1990), and Zak (1997a) make the case that institutions, including those which mediate the conflict of development, have a fundamental impact on economic performance. This is because institutions—both social and political—determine the rules under which transactions are made and thus the types of transactions that are permissible and the return from such exchanges. Given that the distribution of income is generally unequal in developing countries because of unequal development across sectors of the economy, SPI occurs naturally as part of the development process and, as shown above, reduces incomes or may even completely overwhelm the possibility of successful development. As a result, there is a role for government institutions and policies that reduce SPI and stimulate investment. Almost every government policy induces distributive distortions, including taxation, government investment, and monetary policy. These policies may explicitly or inadvertently add to the frustration that causes SPI and can identify the government as the source of inequities and poor economic outcomes. For example, an inflationary monetary policy can wipe out the savings of poor and middle-income groups while it benefits borrowers, often wealthy business owners, by reducing the net of inflation cost of loans. In such a case, "the middle class and poor get poorer and the rich get richer," exacerbating the conditions that cause SPI.

North (1990) argues that well-designed institutions reduce the costs of transactions by defining property rights in an exchange. As Sened (1997) puts it, rules must precede (and define) the market. Government institutions can also mediate disputes between workers and firms in order to reduce SPI and raise output. For governments, the motivating factor in this endeavor is regime perpetuation. Labor unrest and disappointing economic results from government development programs place the ruling coalition in jeopardy of being replaced (Feng and Zak 1999). If this leads to large swings in government policies, uncertainty regarding government policy makes efficient production plans difficult to implement and raises the policy risk of investment. On the other hand, if government institutions lead to stable policies, SPI will generally remain low and economic development will be more rapid. To mitigate the effects of SPI on investment and savings, governments can also provide insurance against strikes and demonstrations when financial markets are underdeveloped. The primary goal of developing country governments is growth—this produces both social stability and political legitimacy (Zak and Feng 1999).

Besides government institutions, politicians can implement specific policies to stimulate growth. Let us call a government action which raises the growth rate of per capita income a *development policy*. The difficult calculus faced by the governments of developing countries is that in the absence of SPI, a development policy may raise per capita incomes, but if such a policy increases SPI, its overall effect may be the opposite. For example, a consumption tax used to fund subsidies for export-oriented industries may stimulate exports, but if such a tax raises SPI and imperils fixed investment in these industries, output may fall after the tax is instituted. The message here is that policy makers cannot ignore the impact that their policies have on SPI if they are seeking to raise the growth rate of output. Thus, governments must navigate a fine line between instituting growth-oriented policies that may raise SPI and instituting policies that directly reduce SPI.

An additional wrinkle appears when designing development policies. Typically, as a country develops, the distribution of income widens, increasing the likelihood of SPI, and, with continued growth, falls (called the Kuznets "inverted U" after Kuznets 1955). Therefore, development policy must be dynamic. Optimally, policies should be adjusted to the evolving economic, political, and social environments in order to maximize their impact on the rate of growth. Irrespective of the mix of development policies instituted, successful development requires that SPI be kept at low levels so that investment is not choked off.

SPI Reduction Policies

Two primary types of policies reduce SPI and lead to better enforcement of property rights: transfers and coercion (Zak 1997a, 1997c). Because low-income individuals make a determination of when to engage in SPI and evaluate the economic environment, policy makers need to keep in mind that these individuals have the smallest opportunity cost of demonstrating. A redistribution of income discourages these people from demonstrating—particularly if the transfer occurs in the workplace. For example, a transfer that is paid for each full day worked discourages workers from taking time off from work to demonstrate. Such a transfer is a signal that "the system works" for the poorest economic agents. The problem with such a program is that the level of transfers needed to reduce demonstrations may be unaffordable in poor countries. In addition, transfers reduce government expenditures on productivity-enhancing programs. Nevertheless, Zak (1997a) shows, transfers raise per capita growth rates in a large cross section of countries.[9]

Coercive policies can also be used to reduce SPI and enforce property rights. Such policies often restrict civil liberties, as is the case, for example, in China and Singapore. A policy that puts more police in the streets does reduce the expropriation risk that fixed investment incurs, but it may also stimulate political demonstrations when civil liberties are compromised (Feng and Zak 1998, 1999). A number of scholars (Feng and Zak 1998, 1999; Haggard and Kaufman 1993; Przeworski and Limongi 1993) have examined the (often temporary) trade-off between democracy and development. These analyses suggest that countries that have successfully industrialized commonly restrict civil liberties at low levels of per capita income in order to maintain public order and then relax restrictions as incomes rise. Zak (1997c) provides evidence that coercive policies generate larger dollar-for-dollar reductions of expropriation than do subsidies. As a result, the trade-off between freedoms and low levels of SPI leans toward the latter for low levels of development and switches to the former as per capita incomes rise.

Optimal Policy Design

Optimal government development policy depends on the policy's impact not only on the economy's growth but also on the incidence of SPI. In this section, I discuss the setting of policy with and without SPI.

Consider a government that seeks to maximize the growth of per capita income by choosing a tax which funds infrastructure investment that raises the productivity of private producers. In this example we will initially assume that there is no SPI. A country will have little or no SPI if there is a broad consensus that funding the policy being implemented is important to the country as a whole and if the income distribution is relatively egalitarian. Suppose the government uses a lump-sum (or head) tax to fund primary and secondary education. Education makes workers more productive, but taxes reduce individuals' incomes from which savings are derived, decreasing available investment funds. Raising taxes shifts the savings schedule in Figure 6.4 from a base level of S' to S, decreasing equilibrium investment. The optimal development policy in this case balances the positive growth effect of an additional dollar spent on education with the negative growth impact of a reduction in investment funds. The optimal policy will be a positive level of funding for education that increases with per capita income (Zak and Feng 1998). Optimal taxes and education levels increase at the same rate as output, continually raising labor productivity and thus output growth. Even though education is important in countries with low levels of per capita income, the taxes used to fund education cannot be too onerous; high taxes adversely affect growth via a reduction in investment as a result of higher SPI.

Zak (1997b) shows that an optimal education policy of the type described above raises the welfare of all individuals in a society (i.e., is Pareto optimal). Furthermore, such a policy will cause the economy to grow steadily without reaching a steady state. That is, education raises per capita income every period as worker productivity increases apace. Education leads to perpetual per capita income growth when there is no SPI, but this result does not necessarily hold in a country with SPI.

Now consider a country with a moderate amount of SPI owing to an unequal distribution of income and an ineffective political structure. If lump-sum taxes are used to fund education as in the example above, the tax paid as a proportion of income is higher for low-income agents than for the wealthy. For example, suppose everyone in the country is taxed $50 per year to fund education. If a household earns $250 per year, the education tax amounts to 20 percent of its income. Alternatively, for a household that earns $50,000 per year, the education tax is only one-tenth of 1 percent of household income. That is, the burden from the tax is oppressive for poor agents and trivial for wealthy agents. If the political structure is unresponsive to the wishes of the poor, they are likely to engage in SPI to express their displeasure with the imposition of such a tax. This displeasure occurs even though such a tax may be in their children's best interest. This is the result of the large-income hit the tax imposes on the poor—given a choice of eating or sending their children to school, the poor will choose to eat and are likely to demonstrate to express their preferences on the issue.[10] If the education tax is imposed without considering its effect on SPI, the loss of output owing to SPI may be larger than the increase in output owing to higher (future) labor productivity. If this occurs, such a development program will not succeed at raising output growth.

There is a different optimal education policy when taxes both raise productivity and increase SPI. Suppose again that education is funded by lump-sum taxes. The optimal education tax balances the growth impetus of education with the economic losses resulting from higher SPI. Such a policy will fund education at a lower rate than it would in the case of no SPI, as taxes cannot be raised as much. The resulting growth rate of output will be lower than in the no-SPI case. Yet this is the *optimal policy when taxes raise SPI,* and such a policy results in higher output growth than would occur without considering SPI when setting taxes. Similar results obtain when other taxes are used, such as income taxes—both proportional and progressive.

The growth effects of education spending when SPI constrains the level of taxation results in a policy that raises output growth, but may not lead to permanently growing per capita income unless SPI falls rapidly with growth. Figure 6.6 illustrates how the growth path of the economy with an education policy lies above the path with SPI and may be above or below the no-SPI path, depending on the relative effects of education in raising output and of taxes increasing SPI, which decreases output. Nevertheless, optimal education taxes taking SPI into account will cause output to grow at its fastest attainable rate (Zak 1997b). In the high SPI case shown in Figure 6.7, there is, unfortunately, no guarantee that a development policy that takes into account SPI provides an escape from a poverty trap (Zak 1997a).

This chapter has shown that SPI arises naturally during the development process as citizens become frustrated with the pace of income gains and/or the distribution of the fruits of development. SPI is exacerbated when citizens do not have adequate political institutions to mediate conflicts over economic and political outcomes. SPI reduces both savings and investment and therefore has a deleterious effect on growth in both the short run and long run. In addition, SPI changes the mix of production inputs, which often leads to the use of inefficient production techniques.

This is where government policy enters the picture. A policy which decreases SPI promotes more rapid growth and political stability as the pressures which incite SPI abate as incomes rise. Such a policy may involve a redistribution of income to reduce inequalities or coercion by the government to limit strikes and demonstrations. Unfortunately, redistribution from the middle- and upper-income groups may stunt growth as the income available for savings and investment falls. Pressures for redistribution toward the poor are greater in democracies because those who earn less than the average income tend to vote for parties which favor redistribution. Such a redistribution policy may threaten long-run income if the negative effect on investment is greater than the increase in investment due to the reduced level of SPI.

Using government coercion to reduce SPI can also be quite costly. Coercion constitutes a pure deadweight loss to society—resources applied to coercion increase neither consumption nor investment—they are simply unproductive. Again, there is a trade-off between using resources for coercion, which reduces SPI and raises investment, and permitting more SPI, which reduces investment but permits greater civil liberties. The determination of the mix between public order and civil liberties depends on a society's preferences and goals. That is, each society must balance the relative value of civil liberties against a desire for faster development.

It is clear from recent history that if the government's role in the economy is too large, then development is stifled. How much involvement, and of what type, is required to engineer successful development? This chapter argues that the primary task of a development policy is to stimulate investment. Because SPI accompanies development, growth slows and long-run income is reduced without policies which prevent SPI. Government development policy, if it is to be effective, must take into account its impact on SPI in order maximize the probability of successful development.

Notes

I thank Bruce Bueno de Mesquita for his comments, which have enhanced this chapter considerably.

1. The statistical technique used by Venieris and Gupta (1985) to create their SPI index optimally weights each separate data series to explain the largest amount of variation across all series.
2. The data set from which the GDP data are taken is the Penn World Tables Mark 5.6, developed by Summers and Heston (1991). These data are corrected for purchasing power in each country so that the numbers are internationally comparable. These data are available from the National Bureau of Economic Research.
3. The formal model is given by $k_{t+1} = s(1 - \pi_t) k_t^\alpha$ where k_t and y_t are per capita capital and output at time t, $s \in (0,1)$ is the constant savings rate. The parameters $\alpha \in (0,1)$ and $\pi \in (0,1)$ denote the productivity of capital and output losses due to SPI, respectively. For simplicity, I assume that capital depreciates fully each period, that population is constant, and that there is no technical progress or learning that takes place in production. The statistical estimation occurs after taking natural logs of the given equation and substituting output for capital using the production function $y_t = k_t^\alpha$. This statistical model is similar to Alesina, Özler, Roubini, and Swagel (1996) and Barro (1991).
4. Feng and Zak (1998, 1999) show that SPI precedes transitions to democracy as in-

dividuals seek to weaken the power of an autocrat. In such cases, current income is traded for an expectation of future increases in civil liberties.

5. The formalization of the discussion in the text is given in this note in the context of foreign direct investment. A risk-adverse investor will invest in country i when the expected return $E(r^i)$ and return variance $VAR(r^i)$ in that country relative to their (nonstochastic) home country return r^{home} satisfy $E(r^i - r^{home}) = 1/(\beta\, E(r^i)) - VAR(r^i)/\beta E(r^i)$, where $\beta \in (0,1)$ is the individual's discount parameter. This equation shows that if SPI raises the variance (or risk) of returns, investment will fall.

6. A discussion of the role of financial development in growth can be found in Greenwood and Jovanovic (1992).

7. I have ignored the effect of technical progress and knowledge spillovers which may cause the economy to grow without reaching a steady state. Models in this class were first developed by Romer (1986) and Lucas (1988). In these types of models, the growth *rate* will be lower with SPI than without.

8. Azariadis (1996) surveys the variety of phenomena that may cause countries to be caught in poverty traps. Political instability is typically high in a poverty trap, including irregular government changes that Londregan and Poole (1990) have dubbed the "coup trap."

9. Alesina and Rodrik (1994) come to a different conclusion regarding the impact of transfers on growth, while Perotti (1996) shows that the data on this issue are inconclusive.

10. Tax-induced SPI can also occur in developed countries. Prime Minister Margaret Thatcher instituted a poll tax in England in 1990 that sparked such vehement demonstrations that it was repealed by her successor, John Major.

7. POLITICAL INSTITUTIONS, ECONOMIC GROWTH, AND DEMOCRATIC EVOLUTION
THE PACIFIC ASIAN SCENARIO

Yi Feng
(with Margaret Huckeba, Son Nguyen T., and Aaron Williams)

The region of Pacific Asia has seen tremendous political and economic change in the past few decades. The area has not only experienced rapid economic growth since the 1960s but also witnessed stunning political development in a number of nations, leading to democracy in such countries as South Korea and Taiwan.[1] By contrast, other East Asian countries, such as China and Singapore, have been frequently referred to as models for generating economic growth under authoritarian rule. These nations seem to offer counterexamples for the argument that democracy provides the best political environment for growth in developing countries.[2] This chapter uses the Pacific Asian case as a template to discuss a political economic theory of growth, and it examines the interaction between growth and politics in this region to evaluate empirical evidence. The general conclusion from this study is that political stability, political consensus, and political as well as economic freedom all promote economic growth, while economic growth has a positive effect on activating party politics conducive to democratization. Political development and economic growth are intertwined. Empirical evidence has shown that the relationship between the two tends to reinforce rather than undermine each other. Considering the current levels of political and economic development among developing countries, the theoretical and empirical results explored in this chapter point to a wide gamut of policy-relevant implications concerning political change and economic prosperity. This chapter attempts to address the nexus between growth and politics in Pacific Asia by examining the uneven growth patterns in the world, exploring theoretical explanations for such patterns, scrutinizing particular cases in Pacific Asia, and extending the study's implications.

GENERAL GROWTH PATTERNS
Uneven economic growth patterns in the world can be easily identified by comparing four groups of countries: Pacific Asia, Latin America, sub-Saharan

Africa, and the G-7 countries. Pacific Asia's developing countries had, on average, a lower level of per capita income than their Latin American counterparts in the early 1960s. Except for Hong Kong, all the Pacific Asian countries lagged behind the Latin American countries in terms of real gross domestic product per capita.[3] What has happened since then is well known. By 1990, Hong Kong, Singapore, Taiwan, and South Korea were ahead of all Latin American countries in national income by a large margin. Malaysia was ahead of all Latin American countries in the comparison group except Mexico and Venezuela. Thailand increased its rate of growth since 1986 and has surpassed Colombia, Jamaica, and Peru in 1990. Figures 7.1 and 7.2 show the relative performance of selected countries in these two regions during the period 1960 through 1990. Pacific Asia's growth path greatly accelerated beginning in 1975. From 1975 to 1990, the average growth rate of real GDP per capita was 5.10 percent for the eight Pacific Asian countries displayed in Figure 7.1, while the eight Latin American countries shown in Figure 7.2 experienced only 0.04 percent growth, and all nineteen Latin American countries (excluding Cuba) underwent −0.03 percent growth during the same period.

Similar statistics were calculated for the ten largest sub-Saharan economies. In 1960, their income per capita was on average much higher than that of East Asia, ranging from 1,120 for Ivory Coast to 2,862 for Mauritius in terms of in-

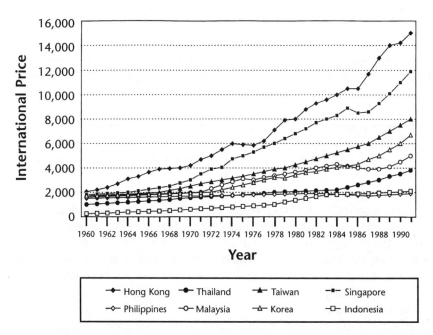

Figure 7.1. Real GDP per capita, 1960–1990: Pacific Asia

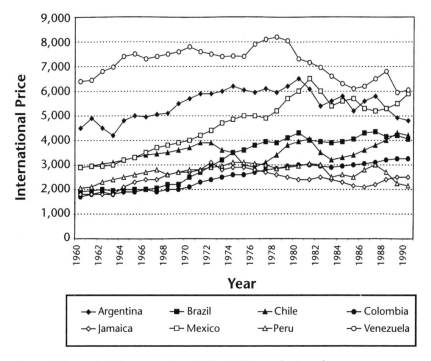

Figure 7.2. Real GDP per capita, 1960–1990: Latin America

ternational prices. Over the years only Mauritius seems to have managed considerable long-run growth, achieving income per capita of approximately 6,000 in 1990. The growth path in the ten African countries listed in Figure 7.3 has not been smooth or stable. Many of the ten sub-Saharan countries experienced negative growth rates in a number of these years, and the income levels in Mozambique and Madagascar were actually lower in 1990 than in 1960. The average growth rate for these ten economies was 0.3 percent over the period 1975 through 1990.

Latin American and sub-Saharan countries share two features in their growth trajectories. First, their growth rates have been low; second, many of these economies have experienced both years of expansion and years of contraction. The former phenomenon implies the existence of some systemic factors that prevent rapid economic growth in these states. The latter feature indicates that the development of some of these countries has been unstable or unsustainable; here, too, some systematic factor or factors must contribute to such uneven growth.

In contrast, a group of nations that has been able to achieve consistent economic growth is the G-7 countries—the highly industrialized nations of

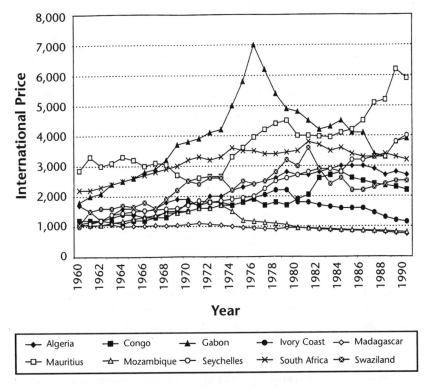

Figure 7.3. Real GDP per capita, 1960–1990: Africa

Canada, France, Germany, Italy, Japan, the United Kingdom, and the United States. Their growth patterns are illustrated in Figure 7.4. These industrialized countries have maintained a continuous growth trend from 1960 through 1990, though their incomes have not grown as fast as the eight Pacific Asian countries. The average growth for the G-7 countries was about half of that of the East Asian countries, at 2.2 percent over the period of 1975 through 1990. Like the Pacific Asian nations, growth in the G-7 is characterized by a pattern of continued transcendence, without the large and abrupt fluctuations typical of the growth trajectories of many African and Latin American countries.

If the growth of an economy is determined entirely by the implications of the convergence hypothesis—that is, the argument that rich countries grow more slowly than poor countries, as a result of diminishing returns—we would find growth patterns different from those indicated in the above figures.[4] Convergence implies that growth in the G-7 countries and the eight Latin American countries will share the same trajectory, and that the eight Pacific Asian countries will experience the same growth patterns as the ten nations of the sub-Saharan group. The absence of or, at best, weak evidence confirming the

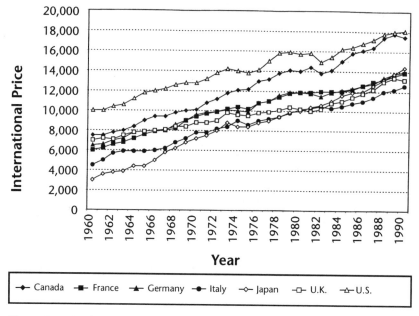

Figure 7.4. Real GDP per capita, 1960–1990: G-7 countries

predictions of the convergence hypothesis drives us to look for other explanations of economic development.

A POLITICAL-ECONOMIC FRAMEWORK OF GROWTH

In addition to economic determinants, political institutions may have pronounced effects on growth.[5] The enigma of erratic and uneven growth introduced in the preceding section is epitomized in one East Asian country. In the 1950s, the Philippines was hailed as an economic miracle and forecast as the most promising in the region for the long run. This optimistic view was attested to by a World Bank report published in November 1957 (cited in World Bank 1993a).

> The Philippines has achieved a rapid rate of economic growth in the postwar period (since 1949). Production has continued to grow at an annual rate of 7 percent, despite the disrupting effects of the HUK movement, which hampered economic activity until 1952. By comparison with most underdeveloped countries, the basic economic position of the Philippines is favorable. It has a generous endowment of arable land, forest resources, minerals and normal potential. Through a comparatively high level of expenditure on education, transport, communications and industrial plant over the past 50 years, the Philippines has achieved a position in the Far

East second only to Japan, both in respect to its level of literacy, and to per capita production capacity. . . . The prospects of the Philippines economy for sustained long-term growth are good. [Apart from] generous endowment of material resources and high level of literacy, other favorable factors are the growth of the labor force, the availability of managerial skills, the high level of savings and investment, rather good prospects for most of the Philippine exports, and considerable possibilities for import substitution.[6]

By comparison, the same report ranked South Korea much lower than the Philippines in terms of its prospects for growth and development: "Korea was another country with poor prospects. In the 1950s, Korea's economy grew by 4 to 5 percent a year, growth largely financed by foreign aid. Domestic savings were barely 3 percent of GNP, and exports were below $30 million a year. Prospects for development were anything but bright" (World Bank 1993a, p. 15).

The Philippines, however, has not lived up to the evaluation and forecast by the experts at the World Bank. The average growth rate of real GDP per capita in the Philippines from 1960 through 1992 was only 1.3 percent, the lowest among the eight East Asian countries. By 1990, the seven other countries had much higher levels of GDP per capita than the Philippines. South Korea, judged to be doomed to lag behind the Philippines, had in 1990 a per capita income level almost four times that of the Philippines. Taiwan, which had about the same level of GDP per capita as the Philippines in 1960, did even better, more than quadrupling the latter (Summers and Heston 1995). What has gone wrong in the Philippines that has forestalled the growth prospects forecast years ago by the economists of the World Bank? A partial answer can be found in the analysis of another World Bank economist. Thirty years after this particular World Bank report was released, Bela Balassa (1991) attributed the poor performance of the Philippine economy to import substitution, protectionism, overevaluation of the currency, excessive debt, and the expansion of the public sector under the Marcos government (Balassa 1991, p. 167).[7]

Something else has eluded the above discussion concerning the roots of the sluggish Philippine economy. An understanding of political institutions in the Philippines provides a key to unraveling the reasons this country, despite all its favorable conditions for development, fell short of the evaluations and expectations of the World Bank. Figure 7.5 shows that the Philippines experienced three periods of negative growth, 1964, 1983–1986, and 1991–1992. The worst period was from 1983 to 1986; the economy shrank more than 10 percent in 1984. This period was one of the most turbulent in the history of the Philippines, beginning with the assassination of the opposition leader Benigno Aquino, and ending with the vindication of the "people power" revolution. The culmination occurred when Benigno Aquino's widow, Corazon, took office, and when the Marcoses went into exile in Hawaii.

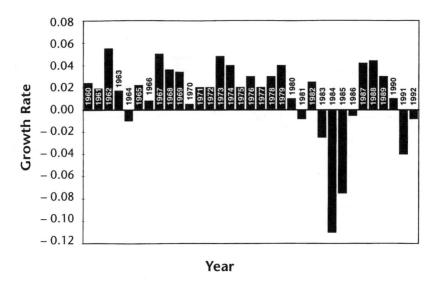

Figure 7.5. Real GDP per capita growth in the Philippines, 1960–1992

Similarly, the two other periods of negative growth coincided with political instability characterized by a transition of domestic power. In 1965, the incumbent president Diosdado Macapagal lost to the Nationalist candidate, Ferdinand Marcos. In 1992, Aquino declined to run for reelection; instead she endorsed the eventual winner, her former defense secretary, Fidel Valdez Ramos. During the Aquino era, though she won a vote of confidence in the legislature in May 1987, military unrest and slow economic growth continued to threaten her government. In December 1989, a military coup d'état erupted against her and was suppressed only with the help of the U.S. Air Force. What emerges from this historical analysis is that economic growth is related to political change. To be sure, the lack of political rights during the period of martial law and the subsequent dictatorship—combined with government corruption, state monopoly, and political polarization and accentuated by the insurgence of groups such as Hukbalahaps and the New People's Army—bode ill for economic development in the Philippines. But the experience of the Philippines also indicates that a country's growth path will also be affected by significant fluctuations of its political order.

Chen and Feng (1996a) and Feng and Chen (1996) discuss three fundamental political conditions that influence economic growth: political instability, political polarization, and government repression. These constitute the basic political environment for economic growth and socioeconomic development. They condition and constrain an individual's economic decision to invest in reproducible capital in the marketplace.[8] Economic growth, a function of accumulation of reproducible capital, increases or decreases as a function of regime instability, political polarization, and government repression. These political factors are the basic political parameters for economic growth and socioeconomic development. The following is an annotation of the mathematical model and its formal propositions in the work of Chen and Feng (1996a).

The characteristics of the political environment are embedded in the investor's reasoning regarding his investment and consumption. When an economic agent makes decisions concerning how much money he should invest and how many goods he should consume, he looks at the current and future political parameters. In particular, he determines how likely the current regime is to be replaced in the future, how polarized the opposing political parties are, and how much political as well as economic freedom is allowed in the society. Both a high likelihood of regime change and a large degree of political polarization lead to uncertainty about the economy, thus reducing the economic agent's incentive to invest.

There is always a probability, no matter how small, that the current regime will be replaced. It is reasonable to assume that the individual investor is uncertain of the policy of any future new government, if installed. Associated with the probability that a new government replaces the current one is the notion that the policies of the future government have not been tested by the marketplace; in other words, the investor is unsure of the implications of these policies. Assuming that the investor is risk averse, he would prefer to wait rather than risking his investment today, particularly if there is a high probability that the current government will be superseded by a new government. In particular, radical political change involving a change in regime adds to the uncertainty of investment decision making, thus reducing capital inflow and economic growth.[9] Feng (1997a) distinguishes between unconstitutional government change, major constitutional government change, and minor constitutional government change, and finds that it is the extraconstitutional change (e.g., a military coup d'état) that has a pronounced negative consequence on economic growth (Feng 1997a).

The effect of regime change on growth is discounted by the investor when political polarization is low, that is, when the difference between the current and future regimes is negligible. *Political polarization* is defined in this chapter as disagreement over public policy between the government and its opponents (Cukierman, Edwards, and Tabellini 1992). It is the incremental change over the social cost imposed by the current government on the society, or the deviation from the level of current government repression by a potential new government. It captures the difference between the new and old regimes in their basic political views of running an economy or organizing a government.[10] If the policies of a future government are predicted to be very different from those of the current government, implying a high level of uncertainty caused by a potentially large policy shift, the investor will typically place a high premium on liquidizing or consuming his assets today rather than committing to long-term investment.

Furthermore, government repression implies that some gains from investment will be expropriated by or lost to the government. Compared to political uncertainty and polarization, the relevance of which lies in the future, government repression is a current choice. Originating in the current government's political and economic orientation, it represents policies that depress private investment (Özler and Rodrik 1992). The government adopts policies from a set of options that range from high to low levels of political, economic, and social freedom; these policies exert an impact on economic agents' investment decisions. Policies that negatively affect investment and growth include infringement on property rights, lack of patent legislation, abuse or misuse of resources to satisfy particular interest groups, and violations of human rights. The government may also make expenditures on public goods such as defense, infrastructure, schools, and a framework for property rights and other institutions necessary for growth. Public goods provided by the government can be regarded as negative social costs; in general, such goods have positive effects on investment. In accordance with the level of government repression, the investor formulates his strategy to maximize his utility by consuming today and investing for tomorrow.

From this admittedly brief analysis, the following theoretical conclusions can be made. First, ceteris paribus, the lower the probability of the survival of the current regime, the lower the growth rate. Second, the more polarized the policy positions between the opposing parties, the lower the growth rate. Third, the more repressive the government, the lower the growth rate.

THEORETICAL IMPLICATIONS AND EMPIRICAL FINDINGS

The framework introduced in the previous section has three sorts of implications for how one should look at the data on growth and what one should expect to find. First, the theoretical discussion introduced in the previous section emphasizes that uncertainty accompanies a substantial change in the government; empirically, we should look at drastic government changes that are likely to produce high levels of uncertainty. Particularly, the focus is on the effect of regime change on growth. Such change typically instills great amounts of uncertainty in the marketplace, compared to routine constitutional government change, which may or may not cause political uncertainty. *Regime change* is defined as a transfer of the national executive from one leader or group to another—a transfer accomplished outside the conventional legal procedures at the time of the event.[11] Second, the previous section suggests that differences in the views of the political groups competing for power reduce economic growth; empirically, we would expect that certain intense political actions (such as political strikes and political assassinations) would decrease economic growth, as they stem from a divergence in political views. Third, the previous section indicates that government repression, political and economic, may have a deleterious effect on growth; empirically, we would expect to find a negative impact on growth of the policies that seriously repress market conditions and activities (Kormendi and Meguire 1985; Özler and Rodrik 1992; Pastor and Hilt 1993).

We examine five variables or indexes as political determinants for economic growth: they are the probability of regime change, political polarization, political freedom, economic freedom, and income inequality. The data on the probability of regime change are from Chen and Feng (1996a) and Feng (1997a), who use the limited dependent variable estimation method to derive a probability of unconstitutional government change based on three broad classes of indicators: economic variables designed to measure the recent economic performance of the government, political variables to account for political events and structure that may lead to regime change, and dummy variables to control for regional differences. The probability of unconstitutional government change measures the latent *tendency* of irregular government change, rather than focusing on the observable evidence of whether the change has occurred. The decision made by the investor is judged to be ex ante; he forms his decisions on the basis of his assessment of the likelihood of political change instead of waiting for the change to happen before he makes a decision.

Political polarization is indexed by revolutions, which are defined as "any illegal or forced change in the government elite, any attempts at such a change, or any successful or unsuccessful armed rebellion whose aim is independence from the central government" (Banks 1979, p. 14). Many political actions can be used to index political polarization: strikes, riots, assassinations, revolutions, and coups d'état. Although the probability of regime change includes the likelihood of a coup d'état, strikes and riots are likely to be underreported because they lack salience. The other problem lies in the paucity of information on the intensity of riots and strikes. Assassinations, which were used by Chen and Feng (1996a) as an index of political polarization, may reflect isolated and individual events that lack broad-based national support. Revolutions typically involve more people than do political assassinations and evince higher political resolve than do political riots and general strikes. This variable is measured by the number of revolutions per year and is expected to have an adverse effect on growth.

Political freedom is measured by the political rights variable in a data set developed by Gastil (1978), who scores nations on a seven-point scale that measures the level of political rights. The countries rated with a score of 1 come closest to political democracy; under Gastil's and Freedom House's (1997) criteria, elections are held freely, fairly, and competitively in these countries, and opposition parties provide a true alternative for voters. None of the seven Pacific Asian countries discussed above has ever received a score of 1.[12] States which receive a score of 2 are regarded as "free," although political violence, discrimination against minorities, military intervention, and political corruption may impair political rights from time to time. Taiwan's clean and fair presidential election of 1996 earned that nation a rating of 2 in the area of political rights for the first time since the Freedom House initiated its world survey in 1973. The Philippines and South Korea are also in this category. Countries that receive a score between 3 and 5 are considered "partly free." In addition to the negative factors that give a nation a score of 2, other forms of political abuse obtain, including civil war, extensive military intervention in politics, the existence of strong royal influence, unfair elections, or one-party dominance. Malaysia and Singapore, for instance, fall in the category of "partly free" countries because of the one-party domination of the United Malays National Organization (UMNO) in the former and the People's Action Party (PAP) in the latter. Countries which receive a score of 6 or 7 are considered "unfree." These countries are likely to be ruled by one-party, military dictatorships, autocrats, or religious groups. Indonesia has been regarded as "unfree" since 1990; their political rights score changed from 5 to 6 in that year, and once again from 6 to 7 in 1993 (Freedom House 1997, pp. 12–13). For the convenience of analysis, the political rights score is normalized in this chapter to a range between 0 and 1, with 1 representing the freest.

For the measure of economic freedom, a composite index developed by Gwartney, Lawson, and Block (1996) is utilized. The index has seventeen components allocated to four major areas: money and inflation; government operations and regulations; takings and discriminatory taxation; and international exchange.[13] Various scholars and experts were surveyed on these components, and different weights were used in summing up the scores of the components. A rating scale of 0 to 10 was used for the index, with 10 representing the highest possible rating and 0 the lowest.[14]

One political control variable to be added is income distribution. Persson and Tabellini (1994) and Alesina and Perotti (1996) found that inequality in income distribution is harmful to economic growth. It has also been found that democracy leads to a reduction in income inequality (Feng 1997c). Therefore, it can be argued that political freedom contributes to economic growth through the channel of income distribution. Also, economic freedom may be conducive to economic growth only when income distribution is controlled for, because skewed income distribution hampers growth even in the presence of economic freedom. This chapter uses the Gini coefficient of income inequality; it ranges between 0 and 1, with 1 representing perfect inequality and 0 perfect equality. The data used here are obtained from the World Bank.

Figure 7.6 presents sample means for several groups of countries: the OECD, the G-7, Latin American countries (exclusive of Cuba), the eight Latin American countries mentioned previously, sub-Saharan countries, the ten African economies discussed above, and seven Pacific Asian countries. The political and economic freedom scores are normalized to take a range between 0 and 1. All variables are examined for the period of 1975 through 1990—with the exception of the probability of unconstitutional government change, the data for which end in 1989. The puzzle on uneven growth patterns raised earlier seems to be solved at least in part by Figure 7.6.

Both the G-7 nations and the Pacific Asian countries have had a very low probability of irregular government change; their respective probabilities are 2 percent and 0.5 percent. Latin American countries have had the highest probability of regime change of all the groups, with a probability of 6.7 percent, fol-

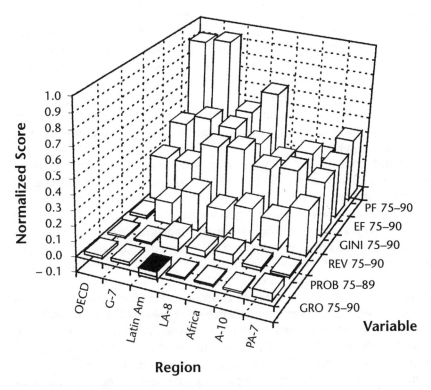

Figure 7.6. Sample means by region
Note: *GRO = growth rate of real GDP per capita; PROB = probability of regime change; REV = revolutions per year; GINI = Gini coefficient; EF = economic freedom; PF = political freedom*

lowed by African countries, with 5.7 percent. Combined with evidence elsewhere, this empirical finding shows a positive association between high growth rates and a low probability of regime change. Investment, which is the engine of growth, requires a stable political regime. The propensity to change within the broad political parameters makes investors cautious about their investment. Furthermore, the high frequency of regime change implies that it is impossible for governments to devise long-term policies, such as research and development, which are needed to guarantee long-run sustainable economic growth.[15]

The G-7 and Pacific Asian countries also enjoy the highest level of economic freedom, with an average score of 5.6 for the former group and 5.7 for the latter. Economic freedom is essential for economic activities. Economic miracles depend on the protection and promotion of economic incentives, at the center of which is the security and free exchange of property rights. Numerous studies have found a positive association between the aggregate rate of economic growth and the degree of economic freedom (Chen and Feng 1996a; Knack and Keefer 1995). Economic freedom reflects the level of government repression in the marketplace. Although Pacific Asian countries do not enjoy the highest level of political freedom, as a region they have the highest level of economic freedom. This type of freedom is linked to such investment risk concerns as government corruption, the quality of the bureaucracy, the repudiation of contracts by governments, the risk of nationalization and expropriation, contract enforceability, and the quality of the communications and transportation system.

Economic freedom that favors only the rich, however, may result in an increase in wealth inequality. Where it efficiently enriches one section of the society while pauperizing others, economic freedom hampers economic growth; it has been found that inequality is systematically associated with low growth rates (Alesina and Perotti 1996; Persson and Tabellini 1994). Therefore, it is likely that the effect of economic freedom on growth is controlled by income distribution. Figure 7.6 shows that both the OECD and Pacific Asian countries have low income inequality, as measured by their Gini coefficients of 0.34 for the former and 0.40 for the latter. In contrast, the average Gini coefficient is 0.50 for the eight Latin American countries and 0.45 for the ten sub-Saharan countries. The relatively even distribution of wealth is conducive to growth, especially when combined with economic freedom, which enhances the prospects of wealth acquisition for all or most segments of society.

One factor that particularly helps promote growth in Pacific Asia is the strategy to reduce political instability and polarization through "shared growth." Governments in these countries secure social support for their policies by advocating growth that benefits every segment of society (Campos and Root 1996). Through such a strategy, the interests of various social groups coalesce.

The governments also adopt tactics to collect, formulate, and share information through various channels in order to develop a national consensus on development. For example, the Malaysian Business Council in Malaysia, the Economic Trend Review in South Korea, the state-sponsored industrial associations in Taiwan, and the National Wages Council in Singapore all have facilitated a broad-based consensus for growth among the government, business interests, and labor, thus minimizing friction and polarization between these groups (Root 1996). The key to the East Asian miracle lies in institutional stability, policy consensus, and economic liberalization.

Two variables, however, differentiate Pacific Asian countries from the G-7 countries. First, the incidence of revolutions is much higher in the former than in the latter group; second, political freedom is much lower in the former than in the latter. However, a closer examination shows that the relatively high frequency of revolutions in the Pacific Rim Asian countries is caused by domestic revolutionary movements in only one country. In the Philippines during the 1970s, two separate forces, the Communist New People's Army and the Moro National Liberation Front, waged guerrilla war on the government. This resulted in the declaration of martial law, the dissolution of the Congress, the arrests of opposition leaders, and the imposition of strict censorship. Scholars have recorded at least one revolution in the Philippines each year from 1975 through 1990, with the exception of 1980. Therefore, statistically, the relatively high average frequency of revolutions in Pacific Asia is due to the Philippines, which recorded twenty-four revolutions during this period. By comparison, Thailand had five revolutions, Korea had four, Indonesia had three, while Singapore and Taiwan had none.[16] Without the Philippines, the average number of revolutions per year in the region drops to 0.135, down from 0.33 when the Philippines is included in the data. In contrast, the average incidence of revolutions is 0.098 for the G-7 countries, 0.262 for sub-Saharan countries, and 0.297 for Latin American countries. It does not seem accidental that the two Pacific Asian nations with the highest economic performance, Singapore and Taiwan, had no occurrences of revolution.[17]

The other political variable that separates the Pacific Asian countries from the OECD countries is the degree of political rights. It should be understood that even though the average level of political freedom in Pacific Asia is not as high as that in OECD countries, or even that in Latin American countries, it is not extremely low either. The average level of political freedom during 1975 through 1990 is 0.454 for Pacific Asia, compared to 0.215 for sub-Saharan Africa, 0.50 for Latin America, and 0.946 for OECD countries. The role of democracy in economic growth should be understood in a broad and complex context. As Feng (1997c) argues, democracy affects economic growth primarily through the indirect channels of reducing irregular government change, promoting private investment, improving human capital formation, alleviating income inequality, and safeguarding economic freedom (Feng 1997c). For countries where the accumulation of physical and human capital is slow, or the probability of a military coup d'état is high, or income distribution is marked with considerable inequality, or economic freedom is lacking, democracy will be most likely to promote economic growth by relaxing these political and economic constraints.[18] But for a country with brimming economic freedom (such as Singapore), an infinitesimal chance for irregular government change (such as Taiwan), abundant savings and investment (such as Malaysia), and vastly improved human resources (such as South Korea), the role that can be played by democracy in promoting growth is limited. However, this does not mean that democracy or political freedom will not exert an effective influence on growth in a country with these favorable attributes. Political freedom will still have a positive impact on growth in such a country, but the marginal gain from having additional political freedom is likely to be limited or diminishing, considering the high levels of positive growth factors already in existence.

The above discussion indicates that regime stability, political polarization, and freedom all contribute to economic growth. These factors have also been evident in other countries. In Colombia, for instance, a political deal was made at the end of the 1950s to determine the president. The individual chosen would hold the office for an eighteen-year period, assuring the country a high level of political stability. Given this scenario, the degree of policy polarization may not be a crucial factor for economic growth for the near future when a person is identified to be the "long-run" president. In Venezuela, the main political parties tend to agree, before any election, to implement the same kind of economic programs, thus producing a high degree of policy consensus. In this case, political uncertainty related to the election outcome is insignificant for economic growth because any party that gains office will adopt the same economic policy (Karl 1991, p. 36).

It is important to note that any single policy variable in the preceding section yields only a partial equilibrium result. None of the three variables (uncertainty, polarization, and repression), by itself, is a *sufficient* condition for economic development. Therefore, an undemocratic country may still enjoy rapid economic growth if the country is politically stable and economically efficient (e.g., Taiwan in the 1970s and the 1980s). On the other hand, a democracy may experience an economic slowdown if it is beset by political instability or polarization (e.g., postcommunist Russia and Poland). Furthermore, regime instability and political polarization may offset each other. When contending parties share very similar political and economic views, government change is likely to have little effect on capital accumulation and growth, even though the probability of a government transfer may be high. For example, coups d'état took place in Thailand in the 1970s and in South Korea in the

1980s; in both cases, economic policies remained consistent between the overthrown government and the new government, causing little disruption in their economies. Similarly, a wide difference between opposing parties may not matter to an individual economic agent if he thinks that the current government is very stable and the probability of its being replaced is close to nil (for instance, Colombia and Malaysia).[19]

HISTORICAL EXPERIENCE: SINGAPORE AND THAILAND

This section is a historical examination of Singapore and Thailand. The former nation exemplifies the fulfillment of the basic conditions for sustained growth, while the latter presents a case of economic growth under a seemingly unstable political system. The comparison and contrast between the two countries is based on the theoretical framework set forth in the second section of this chapter, and the empirical evidence of the third section. The following discusses political stability, policy polarization, and economic freedom in the context of the two nations, respectively.

Singapore

Singapore is an island of approximately 235 square miles, with a population of 2.6 million people. It is one of the smallest states in Southeast Asia and has virtually no natural resources except for its people and its geographically strategic location. Nevertheless, it is a country that has enjoyed remarkable economic growth during the past two decades; it is now one of the most industrialized countries in the region. Judging from purchasing power parities, real per capita income in Singapore increased from $1,777 in 1963 to $7,623 in 1988, putting the country ahead of Spain and New Zealand (Balassa 1991, pp. 2, 83). Such progress is possible due to the country's high political stability, low policy polarization, and the government's commitment to economic freedom.

Singapore has a parliamentary system dominated by a single political organization, the People's Action Party (PAP). Legislative authority resides in an eighty-three-member unicameral Parliament, whose members serve a five-year term by popular election. The leader of the Parliament's majority party or coalition assumes the country's executive leadership as prime minister. The president, chosen by direct election, serves as head of state; the office is more ceremonial than substantial.

Singapore was a British colony from 1819 until World War II, when Japanese forces occupied Singapore from February 1942 to August 1945. In 1946, Singapore became a Crown Colony separate from the Federation of Malaysia. During this period, a strong anticolonial movement created a power struggle marked by several years of violence before the PAP finally came to power.

In 1959, the first government of the State of Singapore was formed, with Lee

Kuan Yew as prime minister and leader of the People's Action Party. Political tension still existed at this time, especially because of Singapore's merger with Malaysia, which made Singapore a constituent state of Malaysia. This uneasy political relationship ended in August 1965 when Singapore became an independent nation. Since then, the political scene in Singapore has been characterized by the dominance of the PAP. No opposition party in Singapore has provided a viable alternative platform for voters. Despite the attempts by several political organizations to vie for parliamentary seats, the PAP has dominated every election since 1959.

The record of the PAP's complete electoral victories was broken in the Anson constituency by-election on October 31, 1981, when a Sri Lanka–born lawyer was elected secretary general of the Workers' Party. This party became the first opposition party to gain a seat in the Parliament in thirteen years. However, this still left seventy-four out of seventy-five parliamentary seats in the hands of the PAP (Gayle 1986, p. 102). In response to pressure from minority parties, in the summer of 1983 the PAP decided to reserve up to three of the seventy-nine parliamentary seats for members of Parliament of other parties, if the opposition parties were not able to win at least three seats from their own constituencies (Gayle 1986, p. 103).[20]

For years, the PAP did not have to worry about such pressures. From 1968 to 1980, the ruling party won every seat in the course of four national parliamentary elections and numerous by-elections. The loss of seats in the 1981 and 1984 elections to the opposition parties was accompanied by moderate erosion in the PAP's share of the popular vote. Their share dropped from 78 percent in 1980 to 65 percent in 1984 and 63.1 percent in 1988, and dipped below 60 percent in 1991. Most observers, including some in the PAP, saw the 1984 election as a political watershed (Tai 1989, p. 197). Despite these minor setbacks, the PAP remains synonymous with political stability in Singapore. To be sure, the party has succeeded through some repression of domestic opposition. But other factors that help to explain the PAP's long tenure are rapid economic growth, improved social welfare, the effective incorporation of potential opposition groups into the ruling party, and the cultivation of a supportive national ideology (Goldstein 1993).

In 1990 Lee Kuan Yew yielded the office of prime minister to Goh Chok Tong, who has proven to be a capable and experienced national leader; his openness and accessibility have given him broad grass-roots support.[21] Goh's victory in the 1997 election has further consolidated his leadership of Singapore into the twenty-first century. In early 1996, Goh admitted that the PAP would have to be satisfied with about 60 percent of the popular vote in the upcoming national election (Mauzy 1996). On January 2, 1997, however, the PAP won 65 percent of the national vote and eighty-one of eighty-three seats in the Parliament, compared to winning seventy-seven of eighty-one seats in the

1991 election. This is a clear indication that Goh Chok Tong has succeeded in strengthening his position in the PAP and in slowing the party's decline in Singapore's politics.

Polarization seems inevitable in Singapore, with its ethnic, cultural, and linguistic diversity. The small state is inhabited by people of Chinese, Malaysian, Indian, Eurasian, European, Iraqi, and Jewish origins; the Chinese, at 77 percent, are the largest ethnic group in the population. In addition, each group tends to live within its own borders, emphasizing their unique identities. Furthermore, ethnic patterns spill into religious affiliations. More than 70 percent of all Chinese profess some attachment to Confucianism, Buddhism, or Taoism. Meanwhile, almost all Malays and many Indians adhere to Islam. Most political and economic elites are at least nominally Christian, though only about 25 percent of the total population claims such a religious affiliation (Gayle 1986, p. 101).

Politically, however, polarization between ethnic or religious groups seems to be insignificant. The government is wary of any policy that divides its people along ethnic or religious lines. Despite the fact that the population of Singapore is largely Chinese, the government chose English as the official national language to unify the various racial, religious, and political sectors. Goh Chok Tong has made it clear that even though China will emerge as a superpower in the next twenty years and Chinese will become an important international language, the Singapore government will guard against an evolution into the Chinese sphere of influence. Singapore has been very careful in dealing with racial and religious issues that could polarize the country.[22]

In accordance with the PAP's effort to avoid racially divisive policies, it has made use of the state apparatus to unify the nation. One of the central goals of the party has been to reduce political polarization and encourage the population to accept its development strategy of combining Singapore's human resources with the investment plans of transnational corporations. Its solution has been to create a party-state apparatus that combines ideological domination, demobilization, and repression to achieve pervasive technocratic control of all sectors of society. As a result, the cadre system within the PAP has been tightened, and a wide range of programs that extend government influence through community centers has emerged (Buchanan 1972, p. 280). The introduction of compulsory expression of loyalty to the state, the initiation of compulsory national service, rigid limitations on employees' bargaining power, and the abolition of trial by jury were among the measures taken by the PAP in the latter half of the 1960s. The effect of such steps has been a significant decrease in the expression of virtually any form of effective political opposition, leading to the extremely high level of social and political conformity in Singapore.

Despite the lack of political openness in Singapore, the country enjoys a very high level of economic freedom.[23] According to the recent ranking compiled by Gwartney, Lawson, and Block (1996), Singapore had the third highest level of economic freedom in the years 1990 to 1993, below Hong Kong and New Zealand but ahead of the United States, Switzerland, the United Kingdom, Canada, Australia, and Japan (Gwartney, Lawson, and Block 1996, p. xx). Singapore has a predominantly market economy based on international trade and finance. Because of a pro-market policy and an absence of political uncertainty, the country has an excellent investment climate and business environment. The fact that the same political party has been in power since 1959 has enabled the government to establish a long-term policy stressing growth-oriented market mechanisms.

Singapore's economic policy has adopted the fundamentals of the capitalist system, encouraging foreign investment and free competition, and protecting property rights with a view to optimizing economic results. The government's firm commitment to rapid economic growth takes the form of generating investment from the private and public sectors along with investment from foreign and local sources. One such source comes from savings. Gross domestic capital formation has been 45.1 percent of the GDP: 39.4 percent from gross national savings and 5.7 percent from net capital inflow (Lim 1988, p. 231).

High economic freedom in Singapore is also reflected by the degree of Singapore's integration in international business. Singapore has developed into a global city through its sea and air links, as well as its telecommunications, trade, and financial connections with the rest of the world. The Singapore economy is highly open to foreign direct investment, labor, and technology. Its heavy reliance on foreign direct investment has led to extensive foreign participation in manufacturing, export, marketing, and technology transfer (Lim 1988, p. 275). Foreign-owned firms account for 55.5 percent of gross output, 41.6 percent of employment, and 66.5 percent of exports.

Thailand

By comparison, Thailand presents a deviant version of the three basic conditions for economic growth. Despite apparently high political instability in Thailand, its per capita income increased more than threefold between 1963 and 1988. Although lower than the Pacific Asian nations where coups have been rare (e.g., Singapore and Taiwan), the growth rate of the Thai economy exceeded that of many other lower-middle-income countries by a large margin (Balassa 1991, pp. 2, 188–189).

The case of Thailand has two unique features. First, Thai military coups d'état do not cause much political uncertainty in the Thai economy, compared to Latin American countries where coups cause fundamental change in political order. Second, the prevalence of the monarchy in the Thai tradition and culture has reduced political instability caused by government change. As a result, a coup d'état does not have the same consequence in Thailand as in nations of other cultures where a permanently unifying political figure does not exist.[24] Thailand has been able to manage economic growth until the recent financial crisis.

In contrast to Singapore's two governments since its inception,[25] from 1932 to 1997, Thailand has had twenty-four governments, often emerging in the wake of major political crises. During this period, the country experienced ten coups and sixteen failed coup attempts (Morell and Samudavanija 1981; Schlossstein 1991). Since 1975, the average tenure of a Thai government has been about twenty-four months; the shortest, under Suchinda, lasted only two months, and the longest survived one hundred months, under Prem. Despite this apparent political uncertainty, the political system in Thailand is basically secure. "Shifts in Thai political power that have resulted in wholesale changes in government tend to reflect differences among the ruling elite rather than any underlying systemic weakness or instability" (Schlossstein 1991, p. 171).

The task of analyzing each of these coups would be cumbersome. An examination of one extreme case should help convey a sense of how the cycle of coups and counter-coups defines Thai politics.[26] In November 1971, Prime Minister Thanom Kittikachorn, the supreme commander of the Thai armed forces, grew concerned about the unruly nature of the parliament. Thanom's dissatisfaction led him to launch a coup. He dissolved the parliament, reshuffled the cabinet, and promised a new constitution within three years (Schlossstein 1991, p. 172).

By October 1973, the absence of a working constitution led a coalition of students and intellectuals to publicly criticize the Thanom dictatorship for its reluctance to produce a new constitution. In demonstrations against the military, thirteen protesters were arrested for causing unrest, denied bail, and accused of being Communists. The government's actions aroused nearly half a million Thai citizens to protest the military regime. The movement prompted the release of the thirteen students and a promise that a new constitution would be written. However, the government's gesture failed to assuage the protesters' concerns. After the protesters refused all the compromises the government offered, the army moved in to quell the unrest. The clash between the army and the protesters resulted in the deaths of over one hundred protesters. The clash further fueled the unrest in Bangkok, which ultimately accelerated to a level that forced Thanom to resign his government and military position and to flee the country in exile. King Bhumibol filled the power vacuum in the following days with the appointment of Sanya Dhammasakdi, who promptly declared a policy of greater political openness.

This example of political change is by any standard an extreme case in Thailand, as coups in this country customarily involve a reshuffling of military leaders. Ordinarily, the coups are outcomes of a power struggle among the Thai military elite of a similar ideological perspective; they amount to nothing more than a battle for the leadership of the country rather than a fundamental change in the course of the nation. Coups seldom elicit significant attention from the Thai citizenry. The frequent leadership turnover through extralegal means has not threatened the legitimacy of the Thai government because the coups "rarely have obstructed government processes or undermined the principal underpinnings of the state: nation, king, and religion" (Neher 1992, p. 650).

Although the example above does not illustrate a typical coup in Thailand, which is usually a bloodless affair, it is a useful illustration of the king's role in Thai politics. King Bhumibol has been the reigning monarch since 1946. The king's official political power is limited; his influence is, however, beyond measure. "The overwhelming sense in Thailand today is that regardless of the form of government, as long as the substance of the monarchy prevails, the people will be happy" (Schlossstein 1991, p. 142). He has provided a unifying center in Thailand, which prevents military coups from having any devastating consequences on life in the country. "When the King intervenes in the political process to restore equilibrium, he serves as a focal point for restraining excesses. He legitimizes the political leadership of the elite so long as they exercise power within tolerable though vaguely defined limits, and he is also considered the system's last resort, accessible by individual petitioner and public opinion alike" (Schlossstein 1991, p. 177).

In general, it can be argued that the characterization of Thai politics as a vicious cycle of coups is an inaccurate description, because the Thai citizenry has reached a level of sophistication that will not tolerate abusive hegemony by the military. Furthermore, despite the military's 1991 attempt to assert itself, it is widely believed that the military has begun to accept a limited role in Thai politics. Finally, the monarchy is a stabilizing and unifying element that prevents apparent instability from having fundamental effects on the politics and economy of Thailand.

Polarization in Thailand has been exceptionally weak. A couple of broad explanations include the dominance of Buddhism and the ethnic homogeneity of the Thai population. Buddhism, the professed religion of approximately ninety-five percent of the population, exerts a significant influence on Thai behavior because it emphasizes the avoidance of personal conflict, thus promoting compromise and cooperation (Schlossstein 1991, p. 189). The religion also minimizes polarization because its adherents are not strongly committed to social issues. Ideology has never played an important role in Thai partisan politics. As aptly put by a Thai political scientist, "Thai politics revolve around personalities, not ideology" (Fletcher and Gearing 1996, p. 22). Finally, the prevalence of Buddhism in Thailand has diminished the possibility of social divisions along religious lines. Ethnic homogeneity has also contributed to the low level of polarization in Thailand. Eighty-five percent of Thailand's population is Thai, and 12 of the remaining 15 percent is Chinese. The prevalence of the Thai population and the lack of conflict between them and the Chinese has provided a social foundation to alleviate ethnic conflict in Thailand.

Gwartney, Lawson, Block (1996) rank the level of economic freedom in Thailand the fifteenth highest worldwide—higher than that of Costa Rica, Denmark, Taiwan, and France (Gwartney, Lawson, and Block 1996, p. xx). A recent indicator of corruption, however, ranks Thailand's level of economic corruption the third highest among the Asian countries examined in this chapter, following the Philippines and Indonesia (Milken Institute 1998). "Thailand's economic development policy hinges on the transition from, and substantial rejection of, a highly interventionist postwar orientation" (Muscat 1994, p. 58). Thailand's economic policies from 1945 to the early 1950s were marked by a high degree of government intervention. Although the United States and the World Bank were heavily involved in formulating the economic policy of the Thai government, the government failed to delineate a coherent policy until the late 1950s, when Thailand made a commitment to laissez-faire capitalism (Muscat 1994, p. 47).

Under the incoherent policy of the late 1940s, the number of government-owned enterprises expanded to nearly 150 (Muscat 1994, p. 57). This expansion can be used as an indicator of the government's willingness to intervene in the private sector. The Thai government adopted a strong interventionist stance in the early postwar period, but by the mid-1950s, the shift away from a capitalist structure had come to a halt. The policy swing toward capitalism was primarily the result of three factors. First, the state's acquisition of private enterprises was not analogous to the socialist movements in European countries. Second, the high failure rate of public ventures demonstrated the inadequacy of heavy government involvement in the private sector. Third, and most important, owing to the political and military elites' lack of knowledge of financial and economic complexities, a small number of professionals were given the opportunity to promote a coherent economic policy that embraced capitalist principles (Muscat 1994, p. 65).

By 1958, this group of technocrats, led by Dr. Puey Ungphakorn, had gained control of economic policy. The technocrats were committed to the concept of a market economy free from government intervention except in cases of stability maintenance and provision of public goods. The technocrats greatly expanded their control of economic policy when the government of Sarit Thanarat turned to them for assistance. The role of the technocrats in the policy process was solidified by their continued dominance under Sarit's heir Thanom Kittikachorn, who ruled until 1973.

The concept of privatization of state enterprises has enjoyed special attention since the early 1980s. In 1958, seventy-four state enterprises existed in Thailand. By 1993, the number was reduced to sixty-eight, seventeen of which operated as infrastructure enterprises. From 1978 to 1989, the output of the Thai public enterprises constituted about 6 percent of GDP, though the percentage edged up to 8.75 for the period 1990 through 1994.[27] In recent years, the agricultural sector output of the Thai public enterprises, one major part of the Thai pubic sector that competes with the private sector, has been shrinking in its share of the total pubic sector output: from 15 percent in 1990 to 11 percent estimated for 1998.[28]

A critical moment in the Thai economy occurred in July 1997 when the *baht* was devalued under the speculation pressure. The shock later spread to other Pacific Asian countries, causing damage to their equity markets and economies. The variation in resilience of these economies may serve as another testimonial to the political economic framework discussed previously.

On the surface, the causes of Asian devaluation were multiple. These countries obtained short-term loans at relatively low interest rates from commercial banks in the United States and other countries. The loans were then reinvested in real estate and equity markets in and outside these countries. However, these loans performed poorly. At the same time, the current accounts of these countries deteriorated, decreasing foreign reserves. All these factors increase the perception of currency devaluation, which drives investors to hedge against the loss of assets by selling domestic currencies—all of which leads to actual currency devaluation. International speculation has also been blamed for the financial crises in these countries. However, speculators are only messengers who reveal institutional problems inherent in these economies.

The markets in such countries as Indonesia and Thailand lack clearly defined rules that maximize the rate of return on capital. As a result, the assessment of investment risk is far from sufficient, and the control of the risk is not a serious option. Cronyism and corruption are practiced at the cost of policy transparency. Furthermore, the basis for the relationship between government and business does not guarantee credible commitments for the state and public officials to honor basic citizen rights, including those "fostering democracy, a stable constitutional order, and economic growth" (see Chapter 3 of this volume). The countries that have been hit hard and will recover slowly are those where political rights tend to be few or the winning coalition is small. A system with a small winning coalition protects leaders from being deposed following poor economic performance or, in other words, does not provide incentives for leaders to make transparent and credible commitments to rules that maximize economic growth. Figure 7.7 indicates South Korea and the Philippines, two democracies, sustained relatively little damage, while Indonesia, an autocracy, incurred loss in the financial crisis.

Figure 7.8 shows the political parameters for economic growth in individ-

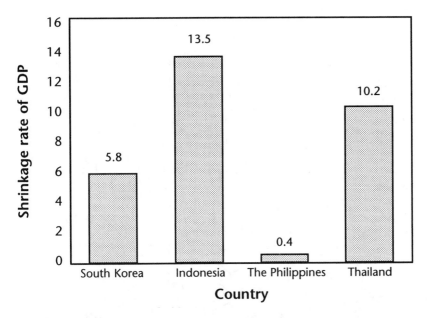

Figure 7.7. Projected GDP growth rates for Pacific Asian countries (Source: Data from Donald Straszheim, "The Realities of Global Competition," paper presented at the annual meeting of International Studies Association, West, in Claremont, October 9–10, 1998.)

ual Pacific Asian countries. Of the seven countries, Singapore, Taiwan, and Korea seem to be poised for continued growth. Even though South Korea was hit hard in the financial crisis because of its deteriorating current accounts and poor performance on short-term loans, its political fundamentals will help its recovery and long-run growth. Its projected growth rate for 1999 is 0.2 percent, up from the projected 6 percent downward growth in 1998. Taiwan and Singapore have not been as adversely affected as other Pacific Asian countries. The economy of Singapore will continue to benefit from its high economic freedom, second in the region only to Hong Kong in the survey by Gwartney and colleagues (1996). Taiwan will maintain its growth momentum if political stability and economic freedom can be assured. One other factor that will definitely help sustained growth in these countries is their relatively low income inequality.

On the downside, Thailand, Malaysia, and Indonesia are confronted with an array of negative factors. These countries need to develop transparent rules and regulations redefining business practice, as well as the relationship between government and the business community. They also all need to decrease political instability. In addition, Malaysia and Indonesia will fare better if they

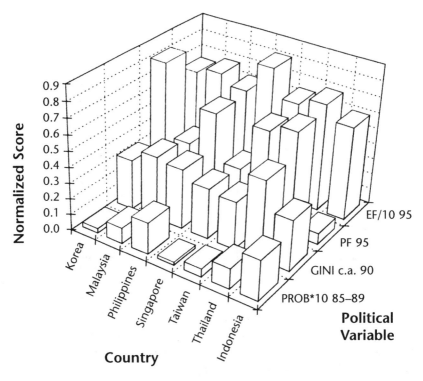

Figure 7.8. Political environment for growth in Pacific Asia
Note: *PROB = probability of regime change; GINI = Gini coefficient; PF = political freedom; EF = economic freedom.*

increase political rights or the "winning coalition" in order to make the government more sensitive and responsive to economic performance. The Philippines, after decades of political violence and polarization, has finally become a full democracy. Despite lingering elements of political instability, the country has largely survived the financial crises, owing to its improved economic structure underlined by improvement in political stability and political freedom, as well as reduction in government intervention in the economy.

All these nations provide examples of the importance and relevance of political institutions to economic development. Statistical data and historical evidence indicate that political stability, policy consensus, and economic freedom have contributed to economic growth in these and other Pacific Asian developing countries. The fact that political freedom is lacking in some of these countries should not be interpreted as a cause for their favorable economic performance; rather, it should be treated in a counterfactual manner. Given a higher level of political freedom, these countries could grow even more rapidly, as has been found in other countries where democracy and political freedom contribute to economic growth by reducing the likelihood of military coups d'état, promoting private investment, improving human capital formation, and enhancing property rights (Feng 1997c).

Although the effect of democracy on growth is not immediate and direct, growth holds a fundamental key to the initiation of democratization and establishment of democracy. Recent research has confirmed the notion that economic growth and development lead to democracy in developing countries (Diamond 1997; Feng 1997a; Feng and Hsiang 1997). The following section theorizes on the relationship between development and democracy, and provides some preliminary empirical evidence on such a relationship in Pacific Asia.

DEVELOPMENT AND DEMOCRACY

The democratization process is a function of the cost of implementing democracy and the accumulation of reproducible capital by agents.[29] The likelihood of democracy in any autocratic country increases as the cost of democracy decreases and as reproducible capital increases. Political learning takes place continuously through comparison, interaction, and induction; in this process, people modify their political beliefs and tactics, thus reducing the costs of overthrowing the dictatorship. As reproducible capital accumulates, potentials for social well-being increase. A higher living standard leads to greater accumulation of usable knowledge in production, which gives rise to a still higher living standard. In this interaction between reproducible capital and the standard of living, people also foster a desire to change the political system such that the political infrastructure will accord with economic success.

In order to slow the democratization process, an autocratic government may adopt a strategy to increase the cost of democracy through greater repression, such as arrests and executions, or to delay the accumulation of reproducible capital by devastating the country's economy. By doing so, however, the government increases political instability, which may result in its own downfall. This assertion has been empirically supported: Londregan and Poole (1990) find that low growth leads to an increase in the likelihood of a coup d'état, and Feng (1997a) finds that lack of democracy raises the probability of a coup d'état (Feng 1997a; Londregan and Poole 1990). Therefore, authoritarian governments are in continuous danger of being overthrown by other potential dictators or being replaced by a democratic government.

The first step toward democratization is the weakening of the dominant party. The work of a number of scholars suggests that the increase in wealth, education, and urbanization associated with development causes the economic agent to lose his societal affiliation with authoritarian rule when making political and economic decisions. Calvert (1994) indicates that the social order of a cooperative equilibrium fails when the underlying conditions induce the agent to act in accordance with his self-interest. Denzau and North (1994) term this loss of identification with mainstream politics the loss of a "shared mental model" which occurs when wealth increases. North (1988) names this process the "loss of the social contract," and Trebilock (1995) argues that democracy is a "psychological imperative" for self-recognition that follows economic growth within the middle class. Finally, the domestic theory of international politics by Bueno de Mesquita and Siverson (1997) implies that political regimes are endogenous to their institutional constraints imposed by economic conditions (Bueno de Mesquita, Morrow, Siverson, and Smith 1999; Bueno de Mesquita and Siverson 1997; Calvert 1994; Denzau and North 1994; North 1988; Trebilock 1995). This information indicates that economic development has the potential to cause political change. The economic rise of the middle class cannot be truly complete without its concomitant political rise (see Chen and Feng 1996b, 1999; Feng and Zak 1999).

According to Zak (1996), systematic poverty creates a large number of frustrated social members who expropriate capital through political action such as revolution. Expropriation is considered a very attractive option by actors when the opportunity cost of expropriation—that is, the loss of wages earned in the production sector—is low. The decision to expropriate is often the result of political turbulence; it can also be the source of regime change. In either case, the society will experience a reduction in growth.[30] While irregular government change decreases growth, the reduction in growth accelerates political upheaval. Instead of the coup traps identified by Londregan and Poole (1990), twin traps make more sense: a coup trap and a poverty trap, which reinforce each other (Chen and Feng 1996b). Economic development increases the chances of peaceful evolution toward democracy; it encourages substantial government change within the framework of the constitution or through peaceful revision of the constitution in accordance with new social and political demands.[31] Development decreases the likelihood of irregular government change, thereby removing this detriment to democracy (Feng 1997a).

The major argument here is that economic growth is likely to lead to a peaceful evolution from procedural to substantive democracy—not revolutions that completely change the political system. This implies that democratic transitions may take place as the result of a political evolution nurtured by economic development. A lack of economic development, in contrast, will weaken the social and economic foundations for compromise and cooperation among various interest groups, making the coordination problem mentioned by Weingast (1997) even more difficult to resolve.

Political development in South Korea seems to attest to the nexus between economic development and political openness. Concomitant with economic success in South Korea has been an ever increasing demand for political freedom. Following a series of massive demonstrations in 1987, President Chun promised democratic reforms, including a direct presidential election. A new constitution was approved by referendum in 1987 and took effect in February 1988, replacing the constitution that had been in place since 1980. Executive power is now vested in a president who is directly elected to a single five-year term. The president, whose powers are limited by the 1987 constitution, may not dissolve the legislature or suspend basic legal rights. The president appoints a cabinet, which is led by the prime minister. Legislative power is vested in the unicameral National Assembly.

The presidential election, held on December 16, was won by the candidate of Chun's party, Roh Tae Woo. In the elections held in April, opposition parties captured a majority of the National Assembly. Even before Roh Tae Woo assumed the presidency, he unleashed a landmark eight-point declaration on June 29, 1987, amid antigovernment demonstrations. The eight points are: assuring the peaceful transfer of power and allowing a direct popular election through constitutional revision; revising the presidential election laws and guaranteeing fair election management; releasing and pardoning political prisoners and restoring their civil rights; upholding human dignity and guaranteeing people's basic civil rights; guaranteeing freedom of the press; guaranteeing self-government and autonomy in all aspects of social life; guaranteeing sound political activities of the parties and cultivating the practice of dialogue and compromise; and eradicating crimes threatening the safety and security of the citizens and correcting social corruption and irregularities (Yang 1994, p. 473). Since then, party politics have shown vitality, and political competition for national office has become open. In 1992, Roh stepped down as the leader of the Democratic Liberal Party amid allegations that his party had bought votes in the March election. In the national election of December 1992, South Korea elected its first civilian president, Kim Young Sam, a former dissident who had joined forces with the DLP in 1990.

In the 1992 election, the DLP won 49 percent of the seats in the parliament. The new governing party was the result of a merger of three political parties: the Democratic Justice Party, the Reunification Party, and the New Democratic Republican Party. Kim Young Sam is the first president in over three decades who has not served in or been connected to the military. Unlike Roh, Kim's victory was welcomed by the South Koreans, although some harbored uneasy feelings concerning his collaboration with Roh in creating the DLP. Since he has assumed office, Kim has effected many political changes consistent with a major government transfer. For instance, he has sought to rid the government and financial institutions of corruption, culminating in the arrest, indictment, trial, and conviction of two former presidents, Chun and Roh. Under his administration, another landmark democratization effort has materialized: for the first time in thirty-four years, South Korean citizens have been given an opportunity to choose governors, mayors, and heads of towns, counties, and wards. The 1995 local elections were a harbinger of major regular government change. All but two of the twenty-five wardships in Seoul, for instance, were captured by opposition candidates. The mayorship of Seoul, the most contested seat in the elections, was won by Cho Soon, an opposition candidate. Furthermore, all the opposition candidates had been fielded by the DLP, which, as the second largest party in Korea, holds 97 of the 299 seats (32.4 percent) in the National Assembly (Koh 1996).

Figure 7.9 presents the trend of real GDP per capita, the relative size of the largest party in the South Korean parliament, and party fractionalization. The relative size of the largest party is the number of seats held by the largest party relative to the number of all seats in the parliament. Party fractionalization is operationalized through a range between zero and one, with one representing the highest degree of fractionalization, which is the antithesis of one-party dominance.[32] The figure shows an increasing trend toward real GDP per capita, an ascending pattern for party fractionalization, and a decreasing tendency toward dominance by the largest party. The parallel between economic development and political development in South Korea carries with it an optimistic message: a democratic transition can happen peacefully and naturally as the result of economic development.

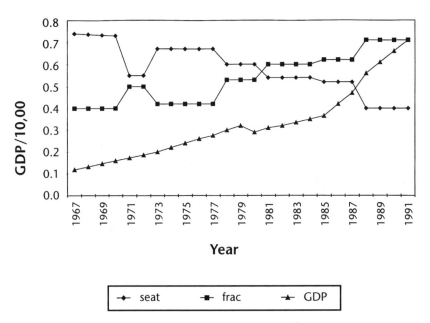

Figure 7.9. Development, major party dominance, and party fractionalization in South Korea

Taiwan is another classic example of a positive relationship between economic and political development. As the country's economy has developed, the political predominance of the Nationalist Party (KMT) has been greatly weakened. In September 1986, Taiwan's opposition groups, also known as *dangwai* (outside the "ruling" party), founded the first opposition party, the Democratic Progressive Party (DPP). Seven years later, in August 1993, the opposition within the Nationalist Party seceded to form the New Party. The Nationalist Party, the DPP, and the New Party are the three major political parties competing for political office in Taiwan today. Compared to the political monopoly of the Nationalist Party under Chiang Kai-shek, his successor and son, Chiang Ching-kuo, adopted a moderate policy toward political openness. When Chaing Ching-kuo died on January 13, 1988, Taiwan was ready for multiparty political competition. Since then, "the emerging political system is both open and inclusionary. The electoral process is open to political parties of every ideological stripe, including communists. . . . Party competition has become institutionalized; the status of the opposition is now formally accepted by the incumbent state elite and protected by statute. Legal requirements for the registration of a new political party are minimal. [T]he opposition parties have been able to develop a grassroots presence and establish links with secondary groups. Most citizens and civil groups no longer worry that ties to an opposition party might make them targets of political intimidation by state agencies" (Chu 1996, pp. 72–73).

The positive relationship between economic development and partisan politics in Taiwan is illustrated in Table 7.1. The opposition parties in Taiwan—the DPP, in particular—have an advantage in local elections, compared to general elections,[33] and in legislative elections, compared to presidential elections. The latter are influenced by international events, as these elections touch upon the sensitive issue of the independence of Taiwan.[34] Nonetheless, the trends in economic development and party partisanship in Taiwan are consistent with the idea that economic prosperity leads to the rise of multiparty politics. The elections selected for the data set displayed in Table 7.1 are those of a more or less general dimension, excluding local elections and presidential elections, for the reasons listed above. The indicators for economic development are GDP per capita and the consumption of electricity. Clearly, the gap between the Nationalist Party and the DPP has narrowed significantly since 1986, when opposition parties were first allowed to exist legally; during this period, one should note, the economy has continued to grow.

Taiwan's economic development has enriched a large proportion of society which, because of the island's demographic makeup, has grown into the political base of the largest opposition party in Taiwan. The DPP represents many natives of Taiwan (the *benshen ren*), whose political and economic interests are distinct from those who came to Taiwan as political refugees in 1949 and later

*Table 7.1. Percentage of Popular Votes of DPP and KMT and Trends
of Economic Development in Taiwan*

Year	Election Events	DPP	KMT	GDP per capita	Power
1986	Legislature and National Assembly	24.60	66.70	32.97	34.927
1989	County and legislature	29.70	59.70	63.79	47.029
1991	National Assembly	23.94	71.17	81.11	51.841
1992	Legislature	31.86	60.50	89.82	55.717
1993	County magistrate	41.30	47.47	104.70	58.041
1994	Gubernatorial	38.72	56.22	108.52	61.156
1995	Legislature	33.17	46.06	115.97	65.214

Note: *The unit for GNP per capita is hundreds of U.S. dollars; the unit for power consumption is 1,000,000,000 kWh.* Source: *Data on elections are from Tse-Kang Leng,* The Taiwan-China Connection: Democracy and Development across the Taiwan Straits *(Boulder, CO: Westview Press, 1996), p. 28; data on GNP per capita and energy consumption are from the Department of Budgets, Accounting and Statistics, Taiwan Provincial Government, Republic of China,* Statistical Yearbook of Taiwan Province, *No. 55 (1996). The values of the economic data take one-year lags from the election events.*

(the *waishen ren*). The former group constitutes a much larger proportion of the population (about 86 percent);[35] therefore it provides a potentially much larger base of political support.[36] Owing to a combination of their social and economic status—which includes their historical background in commercial endeavors, which continued and flourished even under Japanese occupation; their abundant labor source, resulting from their large families; their possession of land; and their business networks—the *benshen ren* have had an advantage over the *waishen ren* in private business activities. In contrast, the *waishen ren* have had an advantage in government, public enterprises, and education because of their positions in, or relationships with, the government and bureaucracies, as well as their training and education.[37]

Over the years, the *benshen ren's* education has improved, particularly at the secondary level. The commercial endowments of the natives of Taiwan, combined with the outcomes of educational improvement and economic development, have strengthened their demands for political representation. The economic rise of the *benshen ren,* which is supported by the finding that controlling for education, the income of the *waishen ren* is only slightly higher than that of the *benshen ren* (Lin and Lin 1993), has been coupled with an increasingly strong demand for the elevation of their political status. The DPP has been working hard to appeal to their interests at the expense of the Nationalist Party. Though the ruling party has not changed in Taiwan since the headquarters of the Nationalist Party moved to the island after they were ousted from power in a civil war on the Chinese mainland, substantive change in governance has occurred in Taiwan. In terms of the percentage of population under jurisdiction, the DPP is the de facto ruling party. With the landslide victory in the magisterial election in Taoyuan County on March 15, 1997, the DPP governed 51.16 percent of the total population on Taiwan.[38]

Singapore, at first sight, seems to offer a counterexample. Despite the rapid growth of the Singapore economy, the PAP remains solidly in power. "In a pseudodemocracy—such as Mexico under decades of rule by the Partido Revolucionario Institucional (PRI) or Singapore under the People's Action Party (PAP)—the ruling party hegemonically controls the levels of power (electoral administration, the registration of parties, the police and justice system, the mass media, not to mention credit, contracts, and jobs) so that opposition parties have no chance of winning power at the national level" (Diamond 1997, p. 4). The changing number of parliamentary seats occupied by the PAP seems to provide evidence to support this argument. From 1968 to 1981, the ruling party has won every seat in four national parliamentary elections; since 1981, the PAP has won over 95 percent of all parliamentary seats. Judging solely by the number of seats in the Singapore parliament, the negative relationship between the level of economic development and the domination of the ruling party does not seem to have any policy-relevant substantive importance to the Singapore experience—though statistically, it may still be significant.

The dynamic change in the strength of the ruling party in the case of Singapore should be measured not in terms of the number of seats lost to the opposition parties, but in terms of the PAP's share of the popular vote. More sensitive to public opinion on political parties, the share of the popular vote is a truer barometer of the popular strength of the PAP than is the number of seats, which is constrained by electoral regulations. The share of the popular vote received by the PAP dropped from 78 percent in 1980 to 65 percent in 1984, 63.1 percent in 1988, and below 60 percent in 1991.[39] Real GDP per capita in Singapore at international prices for those same four years was 7,053, 8,891, 10,316, and 12,224, respectively. While its GDP per capita rose by 73 percent in the dozen years from 1980 to 1991, the PAP's share of the popular vote fell 23 percent. Thus, the Singapore experience is consistent with the notion that development and democracy are compatible.

The argument that economic development prolongs a dictatorship in the long run is not consistent with the data. Though economic growth may be conducive to the maintenance of legitimacy of authoritarian rule in the short run, growth leads to social and economic development that gives rise to new needs and demands by groups that deviate from the ruling authoritarian party. As Alagappa argues, "effective economic performance may strengthen authoritarian rule in the short term, but in the long run it creates tension between the government and the new groups (the middle and working classes and the evolving civil society) unleashed by such development. The new groups, particularly the working class, demand their political incorporation and at a minimum the accommodation of their interests. Since these run counter to the interests of the power holders, challenges lead to the contestation of authoritarian rule" (1995, p. 62).

The findings presented in this chapter lead us to believe that the relationship between political development and economic development in developing countries, as well as the remaining communist countries, such as China, Cuba, North Korea, and Vietnam, tends to evolve incrementally. Political democratization in these countries is likely to be subtle rather than sensational, involving quiet moves rather than quantum leaps. Economic reform creates a political dilemma for authoritarian regimes. When economic reform fails or is absent in an authoritarian government, it is discredited for its inability to improve national welfare and loses its legitimacy. The success of reform, however, nurtures the expansion of political demands leading to democratization. "If we review democracy in developmental terms as emerging in fragments or parts by no fixed timetable or sequence, then the presence of one fragment of democracy can provide space, experience, initiative, or inspiration for the emergence of others. From this perspective, every increment of democratic progress is significant and should be encouraged" (Diamond 1997, p. 4).

Such incremental political development has already taken place in South Korea and Taiwan, and it is now taking place in China, Vietnam, and everywhere else where economic development is gaining momentum. Economic development and political development can be characterized by a positive process of mutual reinforcement. Sustained political development is and must be bolstered by sustained economic development, and vice versa.

Notes

This work is supported by an Edward Teller National Fellowship from the Hoover Institution on War, Revolution, and Peace, Stanford University, 1996–1997. An earlier version of this chapter was presented at the U.S. and World Affairs Seminar, Hoover Institution. The author thanks Bruce Bueno de Mesquita, Baizhu Chen, Larry Diamond, James D. Morrow, Steven Solnick, and Masaru Kohno for insightful comments and helpful conversations. Contributions from Son Nguyen T., Aaron Williams, and Margaret Huckeba to discussions on Singapore and Thailand are gratefully acknowledged. Michael J. Toner has provided editorial assistance, and Ekniti Nitithanprapas has helped obtain data from Thailand. The usual caveats apply.

1. Singapore became the first East Asian developing country to be classified as a developed country by the World Bank, as of January 1996, and Taiwan was classified as a free country for the first time by the Freedom House survey, following its first direct presidential election in April 1996.

2. Three schools of thought can be found in the study of democracy and growth. The "conflict school" argues that democracy hinders economic growth, particularly in less developed countries (e.g., Gerschenkron 1962; Huntington 1987; Johnson 1964; Moore 1966). In contrast, the "compatibility" school of thought implies that democracy enhances economic growth and that democratic government in the Third World is best suited to foster sustained and equitable economic development (e.g., Friedman 1961; Hayek 1944; Lipset 1959; Mises 1981; Riker and Weimer 1993; Smith 1937). Finally, the "skeptical" perspective holds that there is no systematic relationship between democracy and economic development (e.g., McKinlay and Cohan 1975; Pye 1966). For details, see Sirowy and Inkeles (1990).

3. The data used in this comparison are from Summers and Heston (1995).

4. The main reason for this phenomenon in neoclassical growth models is diminishing returns to reproducible capital. Poor countries tend to have low ratios of capital to labor and consequently have high marginal products of capital; therefore, they tend to grow at relatively high rates. See Barro (1991).

5. Many economic variables have been considered as determinants of economic growth, such as investment, human capital, international trade, and inflation. In Levine and Renelt's (1992) systematic study of a wide range of economic factors that may account for long-run aggregate economic growth, trade and investment have been identified as major inputs for growth, though the effect of trade on growth weakens when controlled by investment. They also find that the initial level of development has a negative effect on growth, conditional upon the level of human capital, which has invariably been found to exert a positive impact on growth, though this effect does not hold for the period 1974 to 1989. Barro (1991, 1997) has found that among a multitude of variables, the initial level of GDP, the initial level of human capital, the fertility rate, government consumption, an index of the rule of law, and trade have some effect on growth.

6. Quoted in World Bank (1993a). This section uses the GDP data constructed by Summers and Heston, which may differ somewhat from the World Bank data.

7. Balassa also notes that after the declaration of martial law, in addition to the state-owned Development Bank of the Philippines, the Philippines National Bank, and the Land Bank of the Philippines, the state took ownership of Philippines Airlines; some multinational corporations sold their interests to the state-owned Philippines National Oil Company; and the military took over several privately owned steel mills to create the National Steel Corporation.

8. The theory of reproducible capital focuses on the fact that the way an individual allocates his time over various activities in the current period affects his productivity in future periods (Lucas 1988; Romer 1986).

9. Even when the policy remains the same, investment is still negatively affected by the changing ability of government to carry out the policy. See Feng and Chen (1997).

10. Roemer (1995) uses a deductive model to show that potential government change in a democratic political system creates uncertainty because of the difference in policies between political parties. The difference in policies between opposition parties in an unconstitutional government change should be even greater, thereby creating a higher level of uncertainty. See Roemer (1995).

11. For other similar definitions, see Easton (1965, p. 177) and Sanders (1981, p. 68).

12. Because of Hong Kong's colonial status, Gastil and the Freedom House have not conducted a survey on Hong Kong's political rights or civil liberties.

13. These categories do not directly represent economic freedom as defined by Gwartney, Lawson, and Block (1996). Rather, they are the inferences of economic freedom characterized by the protection of property rights and the freedom of exchange of private goods.

14. Three kinds of weighting systems were presented by Gwartney, Lawson, and Block (1996). The equal impact system involved using a weight which is the inverse of its standard deviation; less weight is given to a component when it has a great deal of variability among experts. This method results in each component exerting an equal impact on the index. The weights were also adjusted for differences in the variation in the component ratings across countries. An alternative weighting system is based on the estimates experts provide on the importance of each component; this survey data is then used as a basis for attaching weights. In accordance with the third system, area specialists are asked to rate countries, and then a regression is run using the economic data. If the predicted value for the subjective rating is correct, then the parameter estimates are used as component weights. The second indicator is used in this chapter, as recommended by Gwartney, Lawson, and Block, on the grounds that it reflects the collectively weighted assessment of various experts.

15. Regime change is treated as an independent variable here. The negative effect of regime change on growth still holds in a model that treats regime change and growth as endogenous to each other. See Feng (1997a).

16. The following list contains the years in which revolutions occurred in particular countries. Indonesia: 1979 and 1990; Korea: 1977 and 1979; Malaysia: 1977; The Philippines: 1975 through 1979, and 1981 through 1990; Thailand: 1976, 1977, 1981, 1984, and 1985. Please note that multiple revolutions occurred in some years. The source of these data is Banks (1996).

17. It can also be argued that economic growth is the reason that no revolution has occurred in these countries and elsewhere. Between revolutions and the likeli-

hood of regime change, it seems that the latter has a more adverse effect on growth. Also see note 18.

18. Feng (1995, 1997b) has found that democracy promotes growth in Latin America and sub-Saharan Africa, where the structures conducive to growth leave a lot of room for improvement with respect to greater political freedom.

19. Case's (1995) study of Malaysia provides an example of a stable government in an environment of ethnic and religious polarization.

20. In the 1997 election, for instance, the opposition parties won two out of eighty-three seats. As a result, a nonconstituency seat was offered to the Workers' Party, which was the biggest loser in the election.

21. *Guojirebao,* January 4, 1997, p. A2.

22. *Guojirebao,* January 4, 1997, p. A5.

23. Some scholars oppose the idea of describing the Singapore state as repressive. They tend to see Singapore as a hegemonic state that promotes "social reform, social organization, and social control, to actually achieve at the same time political legitimation and political domination" (Bello and Rosenfeld 1990, p. 317). "The nexus between a good government and citizenry is familial" (Gayle 1986, p. 109).

24. For instance, coups d'état in Latin American countries have had much more pronounced impacts on their economies than have coups in Thailand.

25. However, it is assumed that the change from Prime Minister Lee Kuan Yew to Prime Minister Goh Chok Tong does not constitute a fundamental change in the government.

26. Chai-Anan Samudavanija (1982) illustrates the process of the succession in what he called the "vicious cycle of coups" that has characterized Thai politics. The cycle comprises six recurring phases: a military coup, followed by the promulgation of a new or resurrected constitution, a period of politicking and elections, a "honeymoon" period of cooperation and all sorts of new legislation, bitter arguing and stagnation among the governmental elite, leading, finally, to another military coup to restore order and stability.

27. International Monetary Fund, *Government Financial Statistics,* 1995.

28. Comptroller's Office, Government of Thailand, *The Income Summary of the Thai Public Enterprises,* 1997.

29. The cost of democracy is defined as the cost of overthrowing the current authoritarian regime or the cost of installing democracy. See Chen and Feng (1999).

30. Expropriation reduces the output in two ways. Time spent expropriating is time not spent in production, and expropriation results in part of the capital stock being removed from production. See Zak (1996, 1997a).

31. After years of economic reforms as priority and a shift away from politics as command, China has recently deleted the antirevolutionary clauses from its constitution and replaced them with national security stipulations. Though this change is more symbolic than substantial, it reflects a move away from ideological purism.

32. Party fractionalization is measured by the following formula: $1 - \sum_{i=1}^{m} (t_i)^2$ where t_i is the proportion of members associated with the ith party in the legislature. Therefore, given a fixed number of members of parliament, the more parties represented in that body, the larger the index becomes; hence, the more fractional the parliament is likely to become. Data on party fractionalization and the relative size of the largest party are from Banks (1996); the party fractionalization index is based on the formula by Rae (1968). The GDP data are from Summers and Heston (1995).

33. In the Taipei mayoral election of 1994, the DPP candidate won 43.68 percent of the popular vote, compared to 25.90 percent by the KMT candidate. In the Taoyuan County magisterial election, the DPP candidate won 54.51 percent of the popular vote, while the KMT candidate won 36.39 percent, and the New Party candidate won 7.66 percent.

34. In the first direct presidential election in Taiwan in April 1997, KMT candidate Lee Teng-hui secured 54.0 percent of the popular vote, compared to 21.1 percent for the DDP, 14.9 percent for the New Party, and 9.9 percent for the independents. The outcome of this election was to some extent influenced by the military exercise of the Communist Chinese, which culminated when three missiles landed near the island as a "warning against the independence of Taiwan." Although mainland China claimed that the military exercise deterred voters from choosing the independent-minded DDP, many people believed that the exercise backfired against China by strengthening Lee's popularity.

35. Of the total population on Taiwan, *minnan* has a share of 75 percent, *kejia* 10 percent, and *waishen* (those who did not originate in Taiwan) 14 percent. See Lin and Lin (1993, p. 104).

36. It has been found that less than 5 percent of nonnative voters voted for the DPP, and that very few natives voted for the Nationalist Party. See Wu (1993, p. 42).

37. Between 1949 and 1950, the number of people of different origins immigrating to Taiwan was between 1.5 and 2 million, adding to the approximately 6 million people who were already living there. See Chang (1993, p. 248).

38. Although the DPP incumbents hold only seven of twenty-one county magisterial or city mayoral offices in Taiwan, the districts they rule are populous, such as the city of Taipei and Taoyuan County.

39. In the 1997 election, the PAP popular vote share bounced back to 65 percent.

8. DEMOCRACY AND THE RULE OF LAW

Robert Barro

In the long run, the difference between prosperity and poverty depends on how fast an economy grows. Much of the recent empirical research on the determinants of growth has concentrated on the role of government policy in fostering this long-term growth. Although the government's influence includes the fiscal and monetary instruments that have been the main focus of macroeconomists, an even more important dimension of policy concerns the character of a nation's political, legal, and economic institutions. Differences in institutions across countries have proved empirically to be among the most important determinants of differences in rates of economic growth and investment. Consequently, basic reforms that improve the quality of institutions provide one of the best routes for transforming a country in the long run from poverty to prosperity.

The question of which aspects of institutions matter for long-run economic performance has proved to be more controversial than the proposition that institutions are important overall. One strand of the recent research has focused on democracy—specifically, on the strength of electoral rights and civil liberties. The second strand has emphasized property rights and legal structures that promote the rule of law. Some scholars, such as Milton Friedman in *Capitalism and Freedom* (1962), argue that these two aspects of liberal institutions are mutually reinforcing and that both are conducive to economic performance. Recent empirical research supports the idea that property rights and the rule of law are key determinants of economic growth and investment but delivers mixed results with respect to the contributions from democracy. Before we turn to this empirical evidence, it is worthwhile to assess the situation theoretically.

ECONOMIC EFFECTS OF PROPERTY RIGHTS AND THE LEGAL SYSTEM

The economic effects of secure property rights and a well-functioning legal system are reasonably straightforward. Because people are, to a considerable degree, self-interested, they tend to undertake hard work and investments only if they have a reasonable probability of enjoying the fruits of their efforts. Thus, when property rights are insecure—for example, because of high crime rates or high rates of taxation or high chances of government expropriation—people tend to work and invest little. The concept of high taxation can be extended from income taxes or other formal levies to include onerous government regulations and licensing requirements, as well as bribes required by corrupt officials.

Vigorous business activity also depends to a considerable extent on a legal system that allows for contracts to be clearly specified and enforced. This contracting potential influences relations of businesses with suppliers, creditors, workers, and customers. For example, if the legal system does not enforce the repayment of loans, then loans will be scarce, and many productive investments will therefore not occur. (The private sector can respond, to some extent, to the public vacuum by creating its own methods of enforcement, such as that provided by the Mafia.)

One way that businesses can react to poorly defined property rights is to reduce their levels of operation. However, another possibility—especially in response to high rates of taxation and oppressive regulations—is to move from the formal part of the economy to the informal or black-market sector. This informality may be better for the economy than a cessation of operations, but it does entail costs. Informal operation tends to be less efficient because businesses must expend resources to conceal their activities. In addition, black-market participants typically lose access to useful government services, such as contract enforcement. Another effect is that the government fails to raise much in taxes on black-market activities, and the amounts collected from legal enterprises must rise to pay for a given level of public expenditures. (For a discussion of these issues, see Loayza 1996.)

The stress on property rights and the legal system does not imply that more government activity is necessarily good or bad for economic performance. Some actions—such as maintenance of internal and external security and enforcement of contracts—entail more government spending and tend to enhance economic activity. Others—such as burdensome regulations and nonproductive expenditures that require high tax rates—hinder the economy.

ECONOMIC EFFECTS OF DEMOCRACY

What effects on the economy would we anticipate from an expansion of democracy, for example, in the form of an increase in electoral rights? One effect, characteristic of systems of one-person/one-vote majority voting, involves the pressure to enact redistributions of income from rich to poor. These redistributions may involve land reforms and various social-welfare programs. Although the direct effects on income distribution may be desirable (because they are equalizing), these programs tend to compromise property rights and reduce the incentives of people to work and invest. One kind of disincentive involves the transfers given to poor people. Because the amount received typically falls as the person earns more income, the recipient is motivated to remain on welfare or otherwise disengage from productive activity. The other adverse effect involves the income taxes or other levies that are needed to pay for the transfers. An increase in these taxes encourages the nonpoor to work and invest less.

One offsetting effect is that an evening of income distribution may reduce the tendency for social unrest. Specifically, transfers to the poor may reduce incentives to engage in criminal activity, including riots and revolutions. Because social unrest reduces everyone's incentives to work and invest, some amount of publicly organized income redistribution would contribute to overall economic activity. However, even a dictator would be willing to engage in transfers if the decrease in social unrest was worth the cost of the transfers. Thus, the key point is that democracy will tend to generate "excessive" transfers purely from the standpoint of maximizing the economy's total output.

Although democracy has its down side, one cannot conclude that autocracy provides ideal economic incentives. One problem with dictators is that they have the power and, hence, the inclination to steal the nation's wealth. More specifically, an autocrat may find it difficult to convince people that their property will not be confiscated once investments have been made. This convincing can sometimes be accomplished through reputation—that is, on the basis of a history of good behavior—and sometimes by relaxing the hold on power. In this respect, an expansion of democracy—viewed as a mechanism for checking the power of the central authority—may enhance property rights and, thereby, encourage economic activity. From this perspective, democracy encompasses not only electoral rights but also civil liberties that allow for freedom of expression, assembly, and so on.

Theoretical reasoning suggests that enhanced property rights and the rule of law will encourage economic activity. The overall effects of expanded democracy, particularly in the sense of voting rights, are ambiguous. To sort out these relationships, we now turn to empirical evidence. The first areas to consider are the measurement of democracy, the rule of law, and related concepts.

MEASURING DEMOCRACY

A number of researchers have provided quantitative measures of democracy, and Alex Inkeles (1991) finds in an overview study a "high degree of agreement produced by the classification of nations as democratic or not, even when democracy is measured in somewhat different ways by different analysts" (p. x). One of the most useful measures—because it is available for almost all countries annually on a consistent basis since 1972—is the one provided by Raymond Gastil (1982–1983 and other years) and his followers at Freedom House. This source provides separate indexes for electoral rights and civil liberties.

The Freedom House concept of electoral rights uses the following basic definition: "Political rights are rights to participate meaningfully in the political process. In a democracy this means the right of all adults to vote and compete for public office, and for elected representatives to have a decisive vote on public policies" (Gastil, 1986–1987 edition, p. 7). In addition to the basic definition, the classification scheme rates countries (somewhat impressionistically) as less democratic when minority parties have little influence on policy.

Freedom House applies the concept of electoral rights on a subjective basis to classify countries annually into seven categories, where group 1 is the highest level of rights and group 7 is the lowest. This classification was made by Gastil and his associates and followers based on an array of published and unpublished information about each country. The original ranking from 1 to 7 was converted here to a scale from 0 to 1, where 0 corresponds to the fewest rights (Freedom House's rank 7) and 1 to the most rights (Freedom House's rank 1). The scale from 0 to 1 corresponds to a classification made by Kenneth Bollen (1990) for 1960 and 1965. The Bollen index differs mainly in that its concept of democracy goes beyond electoral rights.

To fix ideas on the meaning of the 0-to-1 subjective scale, note first that the United States and most other OECD countries in recent years received the value 1.0, which classifies them as full representative democracies. Dictatorships that received the value 0.0 in 1995 included Indonesia, Iraq, Syria, Zaire, and several other countries in Africa. Places rated in 1995 at 0.5—halfway between dictatorship and democracy—included Colombia, Dominican Republic, Ghana, Guatemala, Malaysia, Mexico, Nicaragua, Paraguay, Senegal, and Sri Lanka.

The solid line in Figure 8.1 shows the time path of the unweighted average of the electoral-rights index for the years 1960, 1965, and 1972–1995. The number of countries covered rises from 99 in 1960 to 109 in 1965 and 138 from 1972 to 1995.[1] The figure shows that the mean of the index peaked at 0.66 at the start, 1960, fell to a low point of 0.44 in 1975, and rose subsequently to 0.59 in 1995. Thus, there has been noticeable democratization since the mid-1970s, but 1960's level has not been regained. (This comparison may, however, not be accurate because the data for 1960 are not precisely comparable to those used since 1972.)

The figure also demonstrates that the main reason for the decline in the world average of electoral rights after 1960 is the experience in sub-Saharan Africa. The dotted line shows that the average of the index in sub-Saharan Africa peaked at 0.58 in 1960 (twenty-six countries), then (for forty-three countries) fell to low points of 0.19 in 1977 and 0.18 in 1989 before rising to 0.40 in 1995. This pattern emerges because many of the African countries began with ostensibly democratic institutions when they became independent in the early 1960s, but most evolved into one-party dictatorships by the early 1970s.

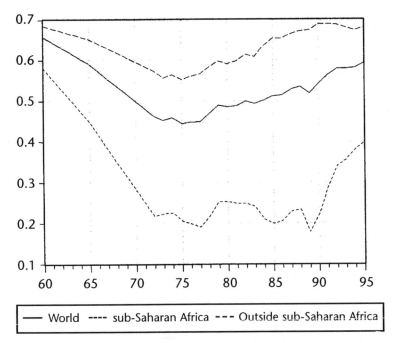

Figure 8.1. Electoral rights, 1960, 1965, 1972–1995

The democratization in Africa since 1989 has been substantial, and some of this development has likely reflected pressures from international aid givers, including international agencies and the United States. Whether this level of democratization will be sustained—unlike in the 1960s—is not yet known.

For countries outside sub-Saharan Africa, the dashed line in the figure shows that the average of the electoral-rights index fell from 0.68 in 1960 (seventy-three countries) to 0.55 in 1975 (ninety-five countries). The index then rose by 1995 to 0.68. Thus, outside sub-Saharan Africa, the democratization since the mid-1970s has been sufficient to reattain the value for 1960.

The Freedom House index of civil liberties is constructed in a similar way. The definition here is "civil liberties are rights to free expression, to organize or demonstrate, as well as rights to a degree of autonomy such as is provided by freedom of religion, education, travel, and other personal rights" (Gastil 1986–1987 edition, p. 7). In practice, the indicator for civil liberties is highly correlated with that for electoral rights. Figure 8.2 shows this correlation in terms of the unweighted averages of the two indexes for 138 countries from 1972 to 1995.

For practical purposes, it makes little difference in the subsequent analysis— for example, in looking at the relation between democracy and economic

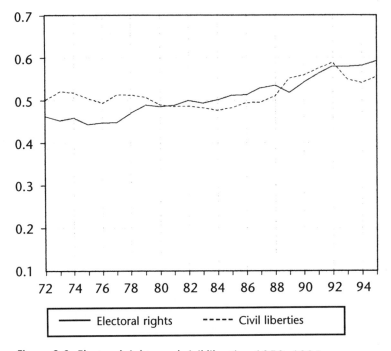

Figure 8.2. Electoral rights and civil liberties, 1972–1995

growth—whether one uses the index for electoral rights or the index for civil liberties. The remainder of this study focuses on the index of electoral rights and sometimes refers to this indicator as simply a measure of democracy.

MEASUREMENT OF THE RULE OF LAW

Many analysts believe that maintenance of property rights and the rule of law are central for investment and other aspects of economic activity. The empirical challenge has been to measure these concepts in a reliable way across countries and over time. Probably the best indicators available come from international consulting firms that advise clients on the attractiveness of countries as places for investment. These investors are concerned about institutional matters such as the prevalence of law and order, the capacity of the legal system to enforce contracts, the efficiency of the bureaucracy, the likelihood of government expropriation, and the extent of official corruption. These kinds of factors have been assessed by a number of consulting companies, including Political Risk Services in its publication *International Country Risk Guide.*[2] This source is especially useful because it covers over 100 countries since the early 1980s. Although the data are subjective, they have the virtue of being prepared contemporaneously by local experts. Moreover, the willingness of customers to pay substantial fees for this information is perhaps some testament to their validity.

Among the various indicators available, the index for overall maintenance of the rule of law (also referred to as "law and order tradition") turns out to have the most explanatory power for investment and economic growth. This index was initially measured by Political Risk Services in seven categories on a scale of 0 to 6, with 6 the most favorable. To make the index comparable with the ones discussed earlier for electoral rights and civil liberties, the rule-of-law variable was converted to a scale of 0 to 1, with 0 indicating the poorest maintenance of the rule of law and 1 the best. To understand the scale, note that the United States and most of the OECD countries (not including Mexico and Turkey) have had values of 1.0 for the rule-of-law index in recent years. However, Belgium, France, Greece, Portugal, and Spain were downgraded from 1.0 in 1996 to 0.83 in 1997. Also rated at 1.0 in 1997 were Hungary, Kuwait, Malta, Morocco, and Singapore. (Hong Kong was downgraded upon its return to China from 1.0 in 1996 to 0.83 in 1997.) No country had a rating of 0.0 for the rule of law in 1997, but countries rated at 0.0 in some earlier years included Ethiopia, Guyana, Haiti, Sri Lanka, Yugoslavia, and Zaire. Countries rated at 0.5 in 1997 included Algeria, Brazil, Mexico, Peru, Uruguay, South Africa, several other countries in sub-Saharan Africa, and much of Central America.

The solid line in Figure 8.3 shows how the unweighted average of the rule-of-law indicator evolved from 1982 to 1997. (The number of countries covered was 88 in 1982–83, 100 in 1984, and 114 since 1985.) The average began at 0.50 in 1982 and showed little change from there to 1991. Then the average rose to 0.71 in 1996 and 0.70 in 1997. Hence, the 1990s have been a period in which the world average of maintenance of the rule of law has expanded.

Figure 8.3 also shows the behavior of two other series constructed by Political Risk Services, one for political corruption and the other for the efficiency of the bureaucracy. For these series, 0 indicates the most corruption and the least efficiency, whereas 1 indicates the least corruption and the greatest efficiency. As the figure shows, these two indicators are closely correlated with the rule-of-law indicator in terms of variations over time and across countries. However, when the rule-of-law measure is held constant, the indicators for corruption and bureaucratic efficiency do not contribute significantly to an explanation of economic growth and investment.

These findings may reflect the two-sided nature of political corruption and bureaucratic efficiency. In some circumstances, corruption may be preferable to honest enforcement of bad rules. For example, outcomes may be worse if a regulation that prohibits some useful economic activity is thoroughly enforced rather than circumvented through bribes. However, the economy is hampered when few legitimate activities can be undertaken without bribes. Thus, the overall impact of increased levels of corruption is ambiguous. Similarly, en-

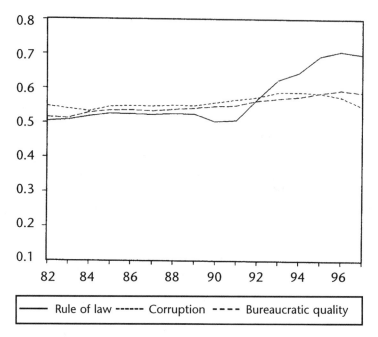

Figure 8.3. Indicators of political institutions, 1982–1997

hanced bureaucratic efficiency has obvious advantages. However, if bureaucrats are carrying out activities from which they ought to be absent, then the economy may suffer from more bureaucratic efficiency. Moreover, there may be a tendency for the bureaucracy to grow larger when it is more efficient. Therefore, the predicted net effect of bureaucratic efficiency is also uncertain.

As an overall tendency, countries that are strong in terms of rule of law (and also in terms of low corruption and high bureaucratic efficiency) tend also to be strong in terms of the democracy indicators, electoral rights and civil liberties. However, the correlation between any of the property-rights/legal-structure indicators, such as the rule-of-law index, and any of the democracy indicators, such as the electoral-rights index, is much weaker than that within either of the two categories. In particular, in many cases the rule-of-law index is high while the electoral-rights index is low, and vice versa. These cross-country differences between rule of law and electoral rights make it possible to distinguish empirically the effects of these institutional characteristics on economic growth and other variables.

Table 8.1 shows countries with large gaps (magnitudes of at least 0.5) between the rule-of-law and electoral-rights indexes. Cases in which the rule of law was high in relation to electoral rights included Chile, Hong Kong, Hungary, Poland, Singapore, and Taiwan in 1982 or 1985 and China, Hong Kong,

Table 8.1. Countries with Large Gaps between Rule-of-Law and Electoral-Rights Indexes

Country	Rule-of-Law Index	Electoral-Rights Index
I. High Rule of Law Relative to Electoral Rights in 1982		
Burkina Faso	0.50	0.00
Chile	0.83	0.17
Ethiopia	0.50	0.00
Guinea	0.50	0.00
Hong Kong	1.00	0.50
Hungary[a]	0.83	0.33
Myanmar (Burma)	0.50	0.00
Niger	0.67	0.00
Poland[a]	0.67	0.17
Singapore	1.00	0.50
Somalia	0.50	0.00
Taiwan	1.00	0.33
II. High Rule of Law Relative to Electoral Rights in 1995		
Bahrain	0.83	0.17
Cameroon	0.50	0.00
China	0.83	0.00
Egypt	0.67	0.17
Gambia	0.83	0.00
Hong Kong	1.00	0.50
Indonesia	0.67	0.00
Iran	0.83	0.17
Kenya	0.67	0.00
Kuwait	0.83	0.33
Morocco	1.00	0.33
Myanmar (Burma)	0.83	0.00
Nigeria	0.50	0.00
Oman	0.83	0.17
Saudi Arabia	1.00	0.00

(continued)

Table 8.1. (*Continued*)

Country	Rule-of-Law Index	Electoral-Rights Index
II. High Rule of Law Relative to Electoral Rights in 1995		
Singapore	1.00	0.33
Syria	0.67	0.00
Tunisia	0.67	0.17
United Arab Emirates	0.67	0.17
Yugoslavia	0.67	0.17
III. Low Rule of Law Relative to Electoral Rights in 1982		
Bolivia	0.17	0.83
Colombia	0.33	0.83
Cyprus*a*	0.33	1.00
Dominican Republic	0.50	1.00
Greece	0.50	1.00
Honduras	0.17	0.83
Israel	0.17	0.83
Jamaica	0.17	0.83
Malta*a*	0.33	0.83
Nigeria	0.17	0.83
Peru	0.33	0.83
Sri Lanka	0.33	0.83
Trinidad and Tobago	0.17	0.83
Venezuela	0.50	1.00
Zimbabwe	0.17	0.67
IV. Low Rule of Law Relative to Electoral Rights in 1995		
Guinea-Bissau	0.17	0.67

Note: *The table shows observations for which the magnitude of the gap between the rule-of-law and electoral-rights indexes was at least 0.5.* *aData are unavailable for 1982 and are shown for 1985.*

Indonesia, Iran, Saudi Arabia, Singapore, and Syria in 1995. These countries maintained high levels of law and order but had relatively little democracy. In the typical case (with Hong Kong as an exception as a British colony), the country was run by a dictator who nevertheless promoted property rights and a reliable legal system. Prototypes of this kind of dictator are Pinochet in Chile, Lee in Singapore, and the Shah in Iran.

Countries in the reverse situation—in which electoral rights were high in relation to the rule of law—included Bolivia, Colombia, Cyprus, Dominican Republic, Greece, Honduras, Israel, Jamaica, Peru, Sri Lanka, Trinidad, and Venezuela in 1982 or 1985. In contrast, in 1995 only Burkina Faso was in this situation. (Countries with gaps of 0.33 in 1995 included Bolivia, Brazil, Costa Rica, Jamaica, Panama, South Africa, Trinidad, and Uruguay.) Countries in this group maintained a high degree of democracy but were relatively weak in terms of property rights and legal protections. Interestingly, the substantial rise in the world average of the rule-of-law index in the 1990s (see Figure 8.3) has sharply curtailed the number of countries that have large positive gaps between electoral rights and the rule of law.

EFFECTS OF THE RULE OF LAW AND ELECTORAL RIGHTS ON ECONOMIC GROWTH

Barro (1997) describes an empirical framework for assessing the effects of various factors on the rate of growth of real per capita gross domestic product (GDP). The growth rate is determined from an equation of the form

Growth rate $= F(y, y^*)$

The variable y represents the starting position of the economy, including the initial level of per capita GDP and the amounts of human capital in the forms of education and health. The variable y^* represents the long-run position toward which the economy is heading. This position depends on government policies and other factors. For example, improved maintenance of property rights raises y^*. For given y^*, the growth rate falls with y because of diminishing returns to the accumulation of physical and human capital. This force tends to generate a convergence pattern, whereby poor countries catch up to rich ones. For given y, the growth rate rises with y^*. Therefore, improved policies—such as better maintenance of property rights—increase the growth rate.

The sample consists of roughly 100 countries observed over three decades—the 1960s, 1970s, and 1980s. This sample includes countries at vastly different levels of economic development, and countries are excluded only because of missing data.

For the rule-of-law index, the empirical relation with the rate of economic growth is shown in Figure 8.4.[3] This type of diagram is constructed so that the effect of the variable of interest—here, the rule-of-law index—is measured after holding constant the influences of an array of other explanatory factors, including the initial level of real per capita GDP, initial amounts of schooling and health, and other variables. The important result shown in the figure is that a higher level of the rule-of-law index generates a higher rate of economic growth. This result is significant in a statistical sense.

The estimated effect of improved rule of law on growth is quantitatively large. Specifically, a rise by one category (among the seven used) in the Political Risk Services index is estimated to raise the growth rate on impact by 0.5 percent per year.[4] A change from the worst rule of law (0.0) to the best (1.0) would contribute an enormous 3.0 percent per year to the growth rate. Of course, this kind of growth dividend from legal reform could arise only for countries, such as Haiti and Zaire, that began as institutional disasters and transformed virtually overnight into institutional marvels. For countries that already have reasonably well-functioning legal systems, such as the United States and most other OECD countries in the 1990s, the potential for this kind of growth enhancement through institutional improvement does not exist.

If we graphed the ratio of investment to GDP versus the rule-of-law index, then we would obtain a relation similar to that shown in Figure 8.4. That is, one route by which stronger rule of law promotes growth is by encouraging investment. However, a positive effect of the rule-of-law index on economic

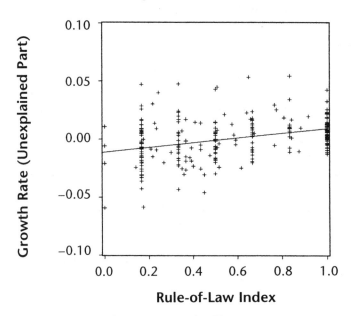

Figure 8.4. Growth rate versus rule of law

growth still appears even when the ratio of investment to GDP is held constant. This effect likely involves improved productivity of resources and the encouragement of investments that are not measured by the standard national-accounts variable.

Figure 8.5 shows the relation between the growth rate and the extent of democracy, as measured by the electoral-rights index.[5] The overall relation between economic growth and democracy is weak. In particular, there are examples of dictatorships (values of electoral rights near 0) with high and low rates of growth and similarly for democracies (values of democracy near 1). However, there is a suggestion of a nonlinear relation—an inverted U-shape—in which growth rises initially with democracy, reaches a peak at a value for the electoral-rights index of around 0.5, and then declines subsequently with further rises in democracy. This relationship, shown by the curve in the figure, is statistically significant. Moreover, the same kind of nonlinear relation emerges if we replace the growth rate on the vertical axis by the ratio of investment to GDP. That is, democracy also has a nonlinear (inverted U) effect on a country's propensity to invest.

One way to interpret the results is that in dictatorships, an increase in electoral rights tends to increase growth and investment because the benefit from the limitations on governmental power is the pivotal factor. But in countries that have already established a moderate degree of democracy, a further increase in electoral rights impairs growth and investment; in these cases, the pivotal factor is the intensified concern with social programs and income redistribution.

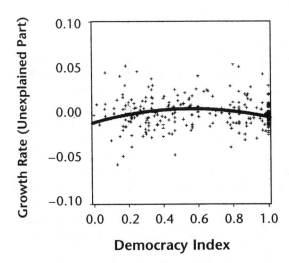

Figure 8.5. Growth rate versus democracy

Specifically, the results suggest that growth would be somewhat reduced by further democratization beyond the levels attained in 1995 in countries such as Malaysia and Mexico (which had index values of 0.5 in 1995). Moreover, by 1995 political liberalization was probably beyond the point of growth maximization in places such as Chile, South Korea, and Taiwan. According to the electoral-rights index, these countries went from levels of 0.17, 0.33, and 0.33, respectively, in the early 1980s to 0.83, 0.83, and 0.67, respectively, in 1995. These results do not point to the conclusion that dictatorship is desirable from the standpoint of economic performance. Some autocrats—such as Pinochet in Chile, Fujimori in Peru, the Shah in Iran, and Lee and several others in East Asia—have produced good growth outcomes. Many more autocrats, however,—including Marcos in the Philippines, Mao in China, Mobutu and numerous other despots in Africa, and many others in South America and eastern Europe—have delivered poor growth outcomes.

History suggests that dictators are of two types: one type focuses on theft; the other emphasizes economic development (and relies to a considerable degree on free markets and property rights to accomplish this objective). More fundamentally, however, a dictator's quest for individual wealth does not imply an indifference to the size of the national pie that can be taxed. Hence, a dictator's self-interest may be consistent with a desire for national economic development—at least, if this development does not threaten the leader's hold on power. The statement that autocrats are of two types is, then, an admission that the theory of dictatorial behavior has not been worked out very well. Possibly the unpredictability of a dictator's behavior is fundamental—in this case, the choice of an autocratic political structure can be viewed as a risky investment at the national level. From this perspective, autocracy will always be an unreliable way to generate economic growth, even when a nation is willing to accept dictatorship on other grounds.

The findings do not support the idea that democracy is necessary for growth—or even that democracy beyond an intermediate range is likely to raise the rate of economic growth. It may be an unpleasant conclusion, but the data suggest that once an intermediate level of democratization has been attained, a further expansion of democracy comes at the expense of economic performance.

DETERMINANTS OF DEMOCRACY AND THE RULE OF LAW

The analysis thus far has dealt with the impact of alternative institutional arrangements—specifically, more or less democracy and the rule of law—on the economy. But nothing has yet been said about how the different institutional arrangements come about and, particularly, how these arrangements are influenced by the state of the economy.

A common view since the research of Seymour Martin Lipset (1959) is that prosperity, measured in various ways, stimulates democracy. This idea is often called the Lipset hypothesis, although Lipset appropriately credits the basic notion to Aristotle: "From Aristotle down to the present, men have argued that only in a wealthy society in which relatively few citizens lived in real poverty could a situation exist in which the mass of the population could intelligently participate in politics and could develop the self-restraint necessary to avoid succumbing to the appeals of irresponsible demagogues" (1995, p. 75). (For a statement of Aristotle's views, see Aristotle 1932, book VI.) The fair thing seems to be to refer to this idea as the Aristotle-Lipset hypothesis.

Theories of the effect of economic conditions on the extent of democracy or property rights are not well developed. Lipset (1959, pp. 83–84) emphasized increased education and an enlarged middle class as key elements, and he also stressed Tocqueville's (1835) idea that private organizations and institutions are important as checks on centralized government power. In some models, an autocrat will voluntarily relinquish authority—for example, by establishing a constitution, allowing power to a legislative body, expanding voting rights, and extending civil liberties—in order to deter revolutions and to encourage the private sector to invest (and, thereby, to expand the pie that the government can tax).

Despite the lack of strong theoretical underpinnings, the cross-country data confirm that the Aristotle-Lipset hypothesis is a strong empirical regularity. In particular, increases in various measures of the standard of living forecast a gradual rise in democracy. In contrast, democracies that arise without prior economic development—sometimes because they are imposed by former colonial powers or by international agencies—tend not to last. Given the strength of this empirical regularity, one would think that clear-cut theoretical analyses ought also to be attainable. (This seems to be a case in which the analysis works better in practice than in theory.)

Table 8.2 summarizes empirical findings on the determinants of democracy, as measured by the electoral-rights index. The system attempts to explain the level of this index for each of the roughly 100 countries at six points in time—1972, 1975, 1980, 1985, 1990, and 1995. The first part of the table uses a basic system that includes as explanatory variables an array of economic and social factors. The nine variables included are described in the table. The results in the right-hand column show the effect of each explanatory variable on the electoral-rights index when all the other explanatory variables are held constant.

From the standpoint of the Aristotle-Lipset hypothesis, the key findings from the basic system are the positive and statistically significant effects on electoral rights from real per capita GDP and primary schooling. These results strongly confirm the idea that a higher standard of living goes along with higher levels of democracy. Moreover, the effects are predictive, in the sense

Table 8.2. Effects of Explanatory Variables on Electoral-Rights Index

Explanatory Variable	Estimated Effect and Statistical Significance
I. Basic System (all variables considered together)	
Five- and ten-year lags of electoral-rights index	Positive and significant (full effect is less than one-to-one)
Real per capita GDP	Positive and significant
Years of primary schooling	Positive and significant
Gap between male and female primary schooling	Negative and significant
Urbanization rate	Negative and marginally significant
Country size (population)	Insignificant
Heavy reliance on oil production	Negative and significant
II. Additional Variables (added one at a time to basic system)	
Years of secondary and higher schooling	Insignificant
Greater income inequality	Negative and marginally significant
Rule-of-law index	Insignificant
Colonial history (distinguished by identity of former ruler among Britain, France, Spain, Portugal, and others)	Prior colony and identity of former ruler are all insignificant
Religious affiliation (broken down into nine groupings)	Muslim, nonreligion, and other religion are significantly negative relative to Catholic (the most prominent category); Protestant, Hindu, Buddhist, miscellaneous eastern religions, and Jewish are insignificant relative to Catholic

that for a given current value of the electoral-rights index, higher values of per capita GDP and primary schooling predict that future values of the electoral-rights index will be greater.

The result shown for reliance on oil production is also consistent with the Aristotle-Lipset framework. The negative effect here means that GDP based primarily on natural resources—in this case, oil—does not provide the same pressure for democratization as that derived from the accumulation of physical and human capital.

Another variable with considerable explanatory power for democracy is the gap in years of education at the primary level between males and females. The negative effect here means that if the education system treats males and females more equally, then it is more likely that electoral rights will be greater (which includes, in part, the extension of the voting franchise to women). The causation here is, however, not clear-cut, because an expansion of electoral rights also makes it more likely that the school system will treat males and females more equally.

Although the simple relation (when per capita GDP, education, and the other explanatory variables are *not* held constant) between electoral rights and urbanization is positive, the effect shown for urbanization in Table 8.2 is negative. (Urbanization has a strong positive correlation with per capita GDP and schooling, but these variables are held constant for the findings presented in the table.) This result may indicate that it is easier to maintain dictatorial powers when the populace is concentrated in cities. However, as a demonstration of the weakness of the underlying theory, some political scientists have argued in reverse, that the urban population is harder to suppress because of its better access to communications and transport.

Country size, measured by population, is not systematically related to democracy. On a theoretical level, the expected relation could go either way, depending on how the technology of suppression relates to the overall scale of operations, that is, to the size of the country.

Finally, the basic system shown in Table 8.2 includes five- and ten-year lags of the electoral-rights index—these effects are positive (and highly significant), indicating substantial inertia in changing democratic institutions in response to changes in the economic and social variables included in the system. In practice, changes in democracy (as measured, and also in reality) are often discrete, with either no change or a substantial shift occurring in a particular year. If, for example, per capita GDP or education rises, then an increase in democracy becomes more likely, and the probability of this increase occurring becomes greater as time passes. Quantitatively, the results imply that (on average) about 25 percent of the full adjustment of democracy to a change in an explanatory variable occurs over five years, and nearly 70 percent occurs over twenty years. Thus, after twenty or more years, the level of democracy is nearly fully determined by the economic and social variables—the kinds of influences stressed by Aristotle and Lipset—and very little by the country's longer-term history of democracy.

Table 8.2 also shows some variables that were added, one at a time, to the basic system. One result is that years of educational attainment at the secondary and higher levels has no predictive power for the electoral-rights index. Hence, it appears to be early education that interacts with a country's propensity for democracy.

The table shows that greater income inequality, measured in some alternative ways, is negatively related to democracy—this finding was also predicted by Aristotle and Lipset. (The data on inequality are compiled by Deininger and Squire 1996.) The main difficulty here is that the limited availability and poor quality of the data on income distribution cause the sample size to contract substantially when an income-distribution variable is included in the system. It seems likely that, with more and better data, the negative impact of income inequality on democracy would show up more clearly in a statistical sense.

One important idea stressed by Milton Friedman and others is that political and economic freedoms are reinforcing. Our interpretation of this idea is that greater rule of law should predict more democracy, and, similarly, greater democracy should predict more rule of law. With respect to the former channel, the results shown in Table 8.2 fail to confirm any reliable effect of the rule-of-law index on the electoral-rights index. That is, given the current state of democracy and the values for the economic and social variables, stronger enforcement of the rule of law does not predict increases in the extent of democracy.

Colonial heritage is a key predictor of democracy if countries have inherited a tradition of valuing electoral rights from their previous rulers. For example, Lipset has argued that British rule over the early American colonies provided a crucial experience in paving the way for democracy in the United States. It is true that former colonies are less likely than noncolonies to become democratic—the average of the electoral-rights index from 1975 to 1995 was 0.69 for 32 noncolonies and 0.46 for 106 former colonies. Moreover, within colonies, electoral rights were higher on average from 1975 to 1995 among former possessions of Britain and Spain than among those of France, Portugal, and other countries (in the present sample, Australia, Belgium, the Netherlands, New Zealand, and the United States).

However, the empirical results summarized in Table 8.2 fail to find these kinds of linkages. Given a country's economic and social conditions—as reflected in the explanatory variables shown in the table—differences in colonial history have no predictive value regarding democracy. Hence, if colonial status matters for democracy, then this influence must operate indirectly by influencing the pace of economic development. This indirect channel is worth exploring but has not yet been documented.

Religious affiliation has also been stressed by some political theorists, such as Samuel Huntington (1991), as an important determinant of democracy. This connection was assessed in Table 8.2 by using data on professed religious affiliation among nine major groups: Catholic (including eastern orthodox), Protestant (including Anglican and some other Christian denominations),

Hindu (including Jains and Sikhs), Buddhist, miscellaneous eastern religions (Chinese folk religions, Shinto, Confucianism, and new religionists), Jewish, no professed religion (including atheists), Islamic and other religions (such as Parsis, Bahais, Spiritists, tribal religions, and indigenous Third World Christians). These data are from Barrett (1982).

The simple relation between religion and democracy is strong—if one classifies countries in accordance with their largest religious affiliation, then the averages for democracy from 1975 to 1995 were 0.9 for Jewish countries (one country), 0.8 for Protestant (twenty-four), 0.7 for Hindu (five), 0.6 for Catholic (forty-nine) and Buddhist (four), 0.5 for miscellaneous eastern religions (three), 0.3 for other religions (seventeen) and Muslim (thirty-two), and 0.1 for nonreligion (one country, China). However, the estimated effect of religion on democracy becomes much weaker when a country's economic and social variables are held fixed, as in Table 8.2. In this context, the significant results are—using Catholic affiliation as a benchmark—negative effects from Muslim, nonreligion, and other religions. The Muslim effect may reflect the strong connection between church and state in Muslim countries. The nonreligion effect becomes less clear-cut when China is eliminated from the sample.

Table 8.3 shows the results from the application of the same kind of analysis to the determination of the rule-of-law index. Because the data on the rule of law begin only in the early 1980s, this system seeks to explain the rule-of-law index at only three points in time—1985, 1990, and 1995. Many of the results are similar to those shown for the electoral-rights index in Table 8.2. In particular, the Aristotle-Lipset hypothesis works also for the rule of law, in terms of the significantly positive effects shown for per capita GDP and years of primary schooling. Also similar are the negative effect of urbanization, insignificant effect of country size, and insignificant effect of average years of schooling at the secondary and higher levels. Greater income inequality, again, has a negative impact, and this effect is statistically more reliable for the rule of law than for democracy. Also as in Table 8.2, the positive effect from the lagged value of the rule-of-law index indicates the gradual adjustment of this institutional feature to changes in the economic and social variables.

Some differences from the results for democracy are that the gap between male and female primary schooling, the oil variable, and the array of religious affiliations have no influence on the rule-of-law index. Also, colonial heritage is much more important for the rule of law than for democracy. Even with the economic and social variables held constant, former colonies have significantly lower values in the rule-of-law index than do noncolonies. Within the colonies, the ordering of the size of the negative effect goes from former possessions of Portugal to those of the group of other countries, to those of Spain, to those of France, and to those of Britain. Hence, colonial powers seem to be-

Table 8.3. Effects of Explanatory Variables on Rule-of-Law Index

Explanatory Variable	Estimated Effect and Statistical Significance
I. Basic System (all variables considered together)	
Five-year lag of rule-of-law index	Positive and significant (less than one)
Real per capita GDP	Positive and significant
Years of primary schooling	Positive and significant
Gap between male and female primary schooling	Insignificant
Urbanization rate	Negative and marginally significant
Country size (population)	Insignificant
Heavy reliance on oil production	Insignificant
II. Additional Variables (added one at a time to basic system)	
Years of secondary and higher schooling	Insignificant
Greater income inequality	Negative and significant
Electoral-rights index	Insignificant
Colonial history (distinguished by identity of former ruler among Britain, France, Spain, Portugal, and others)	Prior colony is significantly negative; among rulers, some indication that this effect is most negative for Portugal, then other countries, then Spain, then France, then Britain
Religious affiliation (broken down into nine groupings)	All insignificant

queath propensities for the rule of law more than they bequeath propensities for democracy. Probably Britain and France were best at making these bequests because they had better-established legal systems than did Spain, Portugal, and some of the other colonial rulers.

Finally, Table 8.3 indicates that the electoral-rights index has no predictive content for the rule-of-law index. This result parallels the finding from Table

8.2 that the rule-of-law index does not predict the electoral-rights index. Putting the two results together, we conclude that—given economic and social conditions—the evolution of electoral rights and the rule of law are largely independent.[6] That is why we found numerous instances of substantial gaps between the two indexes in Table 8.1.

The electoral-rights and rule-of-law indexes do, however, exhibit a significant positive correlation overall across countries and over time. We can explain this relation by noting that movements in the economic and social variables—for example, increases in per capita GDP and years of primary schooling—tend to shift the two institutional measures in the same direction. Specifically, economic development tends to raise the levels of both indexes. Moreover, an independent improvement in the rule of law tends to stimulate economic growth, thereby setting in motion the kinds of increases in economic variables that lead to expansions of electoral rights (as well as to further strengthening of the rule of law). Thus, the findings document this indirect channel whereby an expansion of the rule of law leads to an increase in the level of democracy. The reverse channel is weaker because an expansion of democracy does not necessarily lead to a higher rate of economic growth.

Perhaps the findings about democracy and the rule of law can best be summarized by relating them to U.S. foreign policy toward developing countries. The U.S. focus for many years has been toward promoting democracy—notably, free elections with multiple parties—at all times and places. For example, when Haiti was run by a military dictator, the United States intervened to restore the previously elected president, despite his doubtful credentials. When President Fujimori of Peru disbanded the legislature and assumed dictatorial powers—ostensibly temporarily, to counter a terrorist threat and to enact drastic economic and political reforms—the United States complained bitterly. When President Mobutu of Zaire was finally toppled by a revolution—after more than thirty years of mismanagement and corruption—the United States called immediately for the new leader, Kabila, to organize free elections. Moreover, the United States continually attacked China for its lack of democracy, although it had made major strides in enhancing the rule of law, whereas Russia was applauded for its free elections despite its difficulties in maintaining law and order.

The current U.S. secretary of state, Madeleine Albright, was asked recently whether it was sometimes necessary to sacrifice democracy in the short run in order to promote economic growth. She replied to the effect that there is no such trade-off because democracy is a prerequisite for economic growth. This response sounds pleasant but is simply false. The idea that democracy is necessary for growth is just as false as the proposition that dictatorship is essential for poor countries to escape poverty. The more nearly correct statement is that, on average, the extent of democracy has only a weak relation with subsequent economic performance.

When President Fujimori initiated his self-coup in 1992, the then U.S. secretary of state, James Baker, said "You cannot destroy democracy in order to save it." This proposition turned out to be false for Peru. Fujimori's curtailment of democracy led, in fact, to important economic and legal reforms, to success against a severe terrorist threat, and in a few years to a restoration of democracy. Apparently it is sometimes possible for dictators to accomplish things, including sustainable democracy, although the serious challenge is to predict accurately the behavior of autocrats.

The fact is that democracy is a tricky matter. It is desirable for its own sake, and it tends to arise more often and to a greater extent when countries become richer. History indicates that poor countries have difficulty sustaining democracy—when a democracy arises without prior economic development, it tends not to last. Even if a poor country could beat the odds and sustain democratic institutions, there is no reason to believe that this accomplishment would help much in the quest to escape poverty. The movement from dictatorship to a moderate degree of democracy seems to contribute slightly to economic performance, but this positive effect does not continue once a moderate degree of democracy has been attained. In this sense, a full representative democracy is something of a luxury good—it costs something, but rich countries can well afford it.

For a country that starts with weak institutions—low levels of democracy and rule of law—an increase in democracy is less important than an expansion of the rule of law as a stimulus for economic growth and investment. In addition, democracy does not seem to have a strong role in fostering the rule of law. Thus, one cannot argue that democracy is critical for growth because democracy is a prerequisite for the rule of law.

The problem with the United States recommending democracy in a country such as Zaire (now the Republic of Congo) is not that democracy harms economic performance but, rather, that it has little impact. If a poor country has a limited amount of resources to accomplish institutional reforms, then they are much better spent in attempting to implement the rule of law—or, more generally, property rights and free markets. These institutional features are the ones that matter most for economic growth, and these features are not the same thing as democracy. Moreover, in the long run, the rule of law tends to generate sustainable democracy by first promoting economic development. Thus, even if democracy is the principal objective in the long run, the best way to accomplish it may be to encourage the rule of law in the short run. Perhaps the advice the United States dispenses to poor countries should focus more on the rule of law, property rights, and free markets, and less on the romance of democracy.

Notes

1. The Freedom House data cover more than 138 countries, but some countries were omitted here because of the lack of other historical data, especially on national accounts. The majority of countries omitted are from the formerly centrally planned group (aside from China, Hungary, Poland, and Yugoslavia, which are included in the sample).

2. These data were introduced to economists by Knack and Keefer (1995). Two other consulting services that construct these types of data are BERI (Business Environmental Risk Intelligence) and Business International (now a part of the Economist Intelligence Unit).

3. The values shown for the rule-of-law index apply to each country in the early 1980s. Hence, this variable takes on only one of seven possible values, corresponding to the seven categories used by Political Risk Services.

4. In the framework used, this growth-rate effect persists for a long time. However, the magnitude of the effect diminishes slowly as the economy develops, and the influence in the very long run is on the level of economic activity, not its rate of growth.

5. The values shown for the electoral-rights index refer to averages over several years. Therefore, these values are not confined to the seven possible values that correspond to the categories used by Freedom House.

6. Examination of the residual errors in the equations for the electoral-rights and rule-of-law indexes shows that the contemporaneous correlation of these errors is positive but small.

9. *IMPROVING THE EFFECTIVENESS OF DONOR-ASSISTED DEVELOPMENT*

Bruce Bueno de Mesquita and Hilton L. Root

Variations in economic performance among nations can no longer be attributed to ignorance about what makes an economy grow. The economic means to eradicate poverty enjoy wide agreement among specialists in economic reform. A broad consensus exists on the importance of dedicating resources to the improvement of public sector management, reforming the civil service, strengthening accounting and auditing practices, supporting the decentralization of public services, and establishing an appropriate legal and judicial infrastructure. Productive economies generally enjoy low inflation, low and predictable taxation, private ownership of the means of production, and decentralized decisions concerning the allocation of resources. Governments with transparent laws faithfully enforced and with leaders who are held accountable for their performance in office typically produce economic growth. If this is true, why is it necessary to convince, cajole, and coerce governments into adopting proper policies? The problem is, as noted in all the chapters in this book, that many political systems fail to provide the incentives to produce competitive economies.

The economic policy consensus embodied in international donor assistance presumes large winning coalitions that must be responsive to the interests of a broad base of the population. In democratic OECD nations, government creates a macroeconomic environment that fosters a competitive, merit-based economy. Economic advisors from these countries generally assume that getting the macroeconomic structure right will similarly create a competitive, merit-based economy. These advisors are often disappointed by outcomes because they fail to take into account that in much of the world, a level economic playing field is anathema to the political motives of leaders. The interests of leaders lie in protecting and promoting politically based rather than merit-based allocation systems, despite the lip service paid to the policies encouraged by foreign advisors. Because that leadership must institute the necessary changes to create the level playing field, we can be confident that the standard argument derives from a mistaken premise. Backward thinking, stupidity, and greed are appealing explanations for the economic failures of the world, but they almost certainly are inadequate explanations. In much of the world, fixing the macroeconomic environment alone would result in the ouster of the incumbent political leadership. Leaders, then, sensibly are slow in implementing economic liberalization because they are afraid of creating alternative economic interests that they do not control.

Greed is an inadequate explanation of corrupt practice because greed cannot be fulfilled without first gaining and holding on to political power. Therefore, all leaders must first be motivated to hold office and, then, may secondarily be motivated by greed. Their pursuit of greed, however, is contingent on whether pursuing their venal interests harms or hinders their prospects of remaining in office. Stupidity cannot be an adequate explanation of poor policies because we must then reconcile the apparent contradiction that these allegedly stupid leaders are smart and skillful enough to come to and remain in power in what is always a contentious process, sometimes with fatal risks. The rise to leadership is, itself, proof of the political astuteness of incumbent leaders. Backwardness is likewise problematic as an explanation. This condition imposes a normative assumption on what is generally viewed as a positive process. It is not obviously backward for a leader to take actions that enhance his or her welfare. It does seem backward to assume that a leader will take actions contrary to his or her own interests.

Growth is likely to follow when the institutions of government and the incentives of leaders to stay in office coincide with the need to produce successful economic policies. When economic crises threaten the leadership's hold on power, leaders are motivated to find new institutional solutions. The difficulty is that many institutional environments insulate leaders from the need to find new institutional solutions and may provide leaders with incentives to avoid competition. In such instances, transparency and accountability are not valued. We make a mistake if we infer that politicians who rule through patronage-based systems are backward thinking, irrational, or malevolent. Likewise, we are mistaken if we believe that it takes good, civic-minded leaders to provide policies that enhance the welfare of their subjects. Having the right institutionalized incentives makes even the least civic-minded leader do what is good for society exactly because doing so is good for the leader's hold on office. In short, political institutions are a critical influence on whether rulers rule for performance or for patronage. The goal of development assistance should, therefore, be to enhance the ability of government to sustain itself in office through policy performance rather than through graft and corruption. Yet, obvious as this may seem, most development assistance today ignores the institutional incentives for corruption and assumes that development follows as a consequence of large-scale capital enrichment programs without performance-based criteria for renewal, extension, or new awards. Most development assistance programs, like most macroeconomic theories of growth, mistakenly assume that interest groups take governments off the course of development and that governments are benign or disinterested. The chapters in this book show clearly how political institutions can produce governments that ignore the general welfare and are anything but benign.

Advanced democratic societies often have good institutions and policies because leaders need these in order to be reelected. When majoritarian outcomes matter, leaders will invest in good institutions. To take credit for effective policy reforms, leaders want the outcomes of their policies to be transparent to voters. Asking politicians to rule on behalf of the common good or for the sake of civic-mindedness may feel good, but it is unlikely to persuade any dictator to change his or her ways. Governing for prosperity requires that leadership does not risk authority for the sake of civic virtue.

One way to evaluate how politicians rule is to assess their propensity to spend money that helps consolidate their hold on power, the repayment of which falls to others. That is, they contract debts in the name of the sovereign for their personal benefit. The result often is "debt overhang." Debt overhang, not surprisingly, diminishes the attractiveness of a society for investors. Many of the world's poorest countries have profitable investment opportunities that are not realized because they are burdened by debt. They do not have enough cash to pay current debt obligations; consequently, little is left to pursue profitable new investment. The problem is so widespread that the idea of a debt moratorium is gaining popularity to relieve these countries of the need to repay existing lenders for funds squandered by previous leadership. Annulling the debts, however, does not get to the source of the problem. Excessive debt, which prevents countries from financing profitable investment opportunities, exists because of the political incentive structure that protects leadership from the consequences of bad outcomes. For instance, there is a significant negative correlation between government expenditures as a proportion of government revenue and the size of the country's winning coalition. Those governments with small winning coalitions tend to have larger ratios of expenditures to revenue. The robustness of this observation is tested in an examination of data for forty-six countries from 1946–1993. Controlled for the significant impact of the previous year's inflation and growth rates on indebtedness, the results show that the size of the winning coalition affects the outcome so significantly that it could have occurred by chance only about two times in a hundred. Table 9.1 crystallizes the relationship between the size of winning coalitions and the efficient management of national resources.[1]

The regression analysis reported in Table 9.1 shows that an increase in the size of a country's winning coalition corresponds to a decrease in the ratio of the government's expenditures to revenues. That is, the government lives more fully within its means when there is a large winning coalition than when there is a small winning coalition. The more populous a country, the more likely it is to outspend its revenues. High inflation in the previous year also encourages a significant increase in expenditures relative to revenues, while

Table 9.1. *Winning Coalition Size and Government Expenditure,*
Revenue Ratios

Variable	Coefficient	Standard Error	t-Statistic	Significance
Winning coalition size	−0.122	0.053	−2.29	0.02
Population size	0.001	0.000	9.09	0.00
Inflation rate	0.430	0.083	5.21	0.00
Growth rate	−0.343	0.195	−1.76	0.08
Democraticness	0.001	0.001	0.61	0.55
Constant	1.243	0.036	35.02	0.00

Note: $N = 422$; $F = 24.99$; $p = 0.000$; $R^2 = 0.23$.

higher growth rates in the previous year modestly discourage such high expenditures. Therefore, multiparty elections are not sufficient to ensure that government lives within its means or that leaders have the proper incentives to provide efficient management.

Countries experience debt overhang because few pressures exist for leaders to provide good policies for their citizens. In many developing countries the banking system is used as a passive instrument for financing government deficits and allocating credit to cronies of the government. Unless the control systems are transformed so that citizens can monitor and dismiss leaders who abuse the public trust, long-term relief will not be gained from annulling the existing debt. The problem is not the existence of the debt but the lack of political incentives to inhibit leadership from squandering the nation's economic resources.

When the winning coalition is small, it has an interest in taking out bank loans for projects from which it draws benefits, knowing that the country at large is responsible for paying back the debt. When international donors are the source of funds, the incentive problem is exacerbated. International donors are not in a position to see whether their funds are well spent; they cannot effectively discipline governmental officials who do not perform according to expectation. They cannot discriminate against leaders who use donor funds to line their own pockets at the expense of the nation's citizens. Because of the fungibility of donor funds, leaders can cross-subsidize their poorly selected investments.

With donor-assisted projects, there is no owner—no one has a claim on the residual returns. Even if managers do not pocket the returns directly, they may select inappropriate investments or provide projects that are in turn managed by friends or relatives; they may allocate resources for their own consumption such as expensive residences or offices in central districts of major cities, avoiding cost-efficient sites. Plush offices, short hours, frequent vacations, and business trips throughout the world that are in fact paid vacations are luxuries commonly dispensed by project managers in developing countries. Donors cannot effectively monitor such abuses if competitive domestic political pressures cannot control the indulgences of leadership. Without ownership incentives for cost control, misappropriation of donor funds is not easily discernible among the statistics typically available to measure a country's economic performance.

One of the many ways the size of the winning coalition affects leadership incentives concerns the strategic management of a country's assets. Developing countries, like companies, require management structures designed to ensure that major investment decisions are consonant with the country's development strategy, that investments are financially well justified, that evaluation is not dominated by the private interests of the decision makers, and that the selection and implementation process draws upon the knowledge of those who are best informed and who have a stake in the outcome. Very few poor countries have such systems.

The absence of transparent decision making allows poor policies to proliferate, but failed management systems are less easily observed or addressed than failed monetary or trade policies.Poor policies are often easy to identify when they concern monetary policy or trade, but when the decision-making structures distort policy outcomes and reflect a failed pattern of control that weakens accountability for outcomes, donors rarely comment or act. Thus, donor reforms rarely get at the cause of policies that have failed to produce results.

When investments are risky and funding is available from outside, political leaders do not have to worry whether the project serves their own interests; they are not politically accountable to the donors from whom the funds were derived. This lack of accountability encourages leaders to undertake projects for which no resources have been set aside for maintenance. Consequently, many roads, factories, and buildings throughout the Third World deteriorate quickly after being built; they have been contracted to disburse kickbacks to political cronies rather than to produce benefits for citizens. Typically, capital is not allocated effectively because institutions designed to ensure that policies reflect broad citizen interests are lacking, thus allowing managers to risk capital-intensive projects with limited economic viability. To avoid such inappropriate outcomes, managerial incentives must be strengthened.

There is another reason misaligned incentives result in projects chosen on the basis of economically inappropriate criteria. When all investors face the same cost of capital, they select investments on the merits of the project. Then the identity of the investor does not matter, and those individuals with the most attractive investments invest the most. In developing countries, however, credit is typically available on the basis of personal connections. Funds go to friends of those in power—the goal being political loyalty, not economic profit. The economic merits of the project are secondary. Even when a country's leaders have high standards for allocating funds, as in Malaysia, they are unlikely to monitor prudentially the economic risk.

An additional source of moral hazard in development assistance is that the debts are sovereign, that is, they are in the name of the country and not in the name of the leaders who derive private benefits. Because the funds are likely to be repaid (countries are not allowed to go bankrupt) lenders do not have to worry about whether investments are sound; for the same reason, however, borrowers do not have to worry about how the money is used—they can always hope to borrow more. These soft borrowing constraints relax concerns over project quality, allowing leaders to select projects that provide private benefits to their supporters. The result is poor projects that require future rates of borrowing to be sustained. There is no direct correlation between those who benefit and those who pay the costs.

Donors are at a disadvantage because they cannot collect information from different interested groups. They are constrained by their charters to transact only with the existing government, often with a single ministry in that government so that an annual country assistance plan is discussed exclusively with the finance ministry. Opposition groups have virtually no link to international donors and therefore have no motivation to collect information about the abuse of donor-funded projects. Donors must depend for their information on those within a country who enjoy the greatest possibility of using donor funds for private benefit.

Donor organizations must directly consider the control problems and the motivations from which they arise if they are to provide effective assistance. More effective oversight by citizen groups is essential to determine whether assistance is effective and consistent with the agreements. The terms of reform agreements, however, are rarely public knowledge. Because donors do not provide that information in a timely fashion, citizens and investors cannot effectively monitor the agreements. Improved information will come with improved incentives—the issue is accountability. One way to insulate the provision of services from direct political interference is to develop an effective civil service which donors can insist upon before committing funds. Rarely does a donor condition the availability of funds upon a country's ability to perform routine administrative tasks effectively.

In the 1980s business organizations in the English-speaking world were transformed by a series of financing reforms that changed the incentives for managers. New managerial systems that increased accountability throughout the firm were essential in breaking barriers to technological adaptation. It is now standard knowledge in the field of industrial organization that the ability to transfer technology and knowledge is a component of organizational reform, coordination, and incentives: changes in organizational structure often prompt changes in the adoption of technology.

Just as innovations in ownership, financing, and control resulted in a dramatic transformation of industry, changes in the structure of international capital markets now offer countries new opportunities to change. The most important opportunity is that international capital since the mid-1990s has provided more than 80 percent of funding for international development, whereas only five years earlier it provided 20 percent. The new financing opportunities created by the emergence of international capital markets should alter the strategic and organizational opportunities to which leadership must learn to respond creatively.

The effective solution to economic development must be tied to effective institutional solutions that promote effective public policy. Leaders value accountability, predictability, and transparency when holding office depends on receiving credit for effective policies. Therefore, it is fundamental to the eradication of poverty that leaders are provided with solutions that simultaneously change their political incentives and maintain their prospects of remaining in office. Currently in much of the world, even policies that have a firm intellectual or popular consensus are not implemented because they do not help leaders and their cronies. Only when these countries face a severe problem in their balance of payments or a drastic collapse in their terms of trade do they introduce policies that improve those terms. As with greed, leaders are motivated to change terms of trade primarily when doing so is necessary to remain in office. The motivation, then, is based on the welfare not of the country, but of the politician.

Effective implementation of reform agreements is a question of aligning managerial incentives with desired policy outcomes, and this is where most donor approaches falter. The principal bottlenecks are not problems of capital shortage. The poorly performing nations require a new definition of ownership that will redistribute rights and duties among politicians and citizens alike. The accountability problems that government experiences are no different from the problems of control in large enterprises in the private sector. The principal bottlenecks to development resemble those faced by company managers of private U.S. firms during the 1980s: when management motivation is ignored, shareholders are in for trouble. Economic reform must be concerned with improving shareholder control over managers in the public sector.

A leader's hold on office may depend on access to external funds whose misdirection to cronies is not subject to domestic supervision or accountability.

The international donors who supply these funds are unwittingly shaping domestic institutions. They are sustaining institutions that might otherwise not be viable. The desire for political neutrality often leads international donors to overlook the use of their funds for political gains by corrupt leaders. Even in such seemingly humanitarian assistance as is provided when food or medicine is given to distressed areas, its politicization can prevent its effective utilization. When the distribution of medicine and food creates an opportunity for graft and favoritism, it can prolong a crisis by reducing the probability of institutional reform. Even in such urgent circumstances, there is no such thing as apolitical expertise or apolitical international assistance. Moreover, as this books shows, crises often motivate elites to put aside their differences and to agree on institutional innovations that make it possible to create future wealth.

Some suggest that the solution to the problems of poverty and corruption lies in creating a global governance structure to deal with development aid. For instance, all donor activity and responsibility might be centralized in the hands of the International Monetary Fund. Such a structure for international crisis management would only create incentives for mismanagement. A single international bureaucracy with vast resources is analogous to a small winning coalition drawn from a large selectorate—the world community of donors. This recreates the institutional arrangements that foster leadership by graft and corruption. The incentive problems this book identifies for governments apply equally to international agencies, including those mandated to resolve problems of economic growth.

Winning coalitions and selectorates, coordination and distribution issues, and incentives to remain or rise in office permeate all organizations, not just governments. If control over development assistance is too heavily concentrated in a few hands, the motives to reward cronies (read: fellow bureaucrats) and ensure longevity in office will be enhanced in lieu of the promotion of public welfare. International officials and bureaucrats are no less motivated by self-interest than are national leaders. Therefore, if international organizations are to foster growth they must face competition, and the organizational criteria for evaluating performance must be based on measures of success in altering growth rates.

Competing sources of donor funds, each responsive to its own coalition, is more likely to foster a performance orientation. The assistance environment should discourage the expectation that any one donor agency will be in place in perpetuity. The development of competitive, private international capital markets will do more to discipline governments than a centralized distribution structure controlled by the very governmental officials who need to be disciplined. Development assistance, conditioned by simultaneous demands for political institutional reform, provides the best opportunity donors have to create political incentives that ensure future prosperity.

Note

1. Growth-rate data are taken from Heston-Summers, as reported in Fischer (1993). Inflation-rate data are computed from the consumer price index series in International Financial Statistics with GDP deflator data from the World Bank for the Central African Republic, Malawi, and Chad. These are also reported in Fischer (1993). All other variables are from the Polity III data set. Winning coalition size is a composite index explained more fully in Chapter 3. Democraticness is measured according to the widely used eleven-point scale devised by Gurr.

References

Alagappa, Muthiah. 1995. "Contestation and Crisis," in Muthiah Alagappa, ed., *Political Legitimacy in Southeast Asia: The Quest for Moral Authority,* pp. 54–68. Stanford: Stanford University Press.

Alesina, Alberto, and Roberto Perotti. 1996. "Income Distribution, Political Instability, and Investment." *European Economic Review* 40: 1203–1228.

Alesina, Alberto, and Dani Rodrik. 1994. "Distributive Politics and Economic Growth," *Quarterly Journal of Economics* 109: 465–490.

Alesina, Alberto, Sule Özler, Nouriel Roubini, and Phillip Swagel. 1996. "Political Stability and Economic Growth," *Journal of Economic Growth* 1(2): 189–211.

Almond, Gabriel A., and Sidney Verba. 1963 [1989]. *The Civic Culture: Political Attitudes and Democracy in Five Nations*. Newbury Park: Sage Publications.

American Economics Association. *Readings in the Economics of Taxation.* R. Musgrave and Carl S. Shoup, selection committee. Homewood, IL: Irwin.

Anderson, Rodney D. 1976. *Outcasts in Their Own Land: Mexican Industrial Workers, 1906–1911.* De Kalb: Northern Illinois University Press.

Aristotle. 1932. *Politics,* translated by H. Rackham. Cambridge, MA: Harvard University Press.

Arnott, Richard, Bruce Greenwald, Joseph E. Stiglitz. 1994. "Information and Economic Efficiency," *Information Economics and Policy* 6: 77–88.

Arrow, Kenneth J. 1951. *Social Choice and Individual Values*. New York: Wiley.

———. 1964. "The Role of Securities in the Optimal Allocation of Risk Bearing," *Review of Economic Studies* 31: 91–96.

Arthur, W. Brian. 1997. "Beyond Rational Expectations: Indeterminacy in Economic and Financial Markets," in John N. Drobak and John V. C. Nye, eds., *The Frontiers of the New Institutional Economics,* pp. 291–304. San Diego, CA: Academic Press.

Atack, Jeremy. 1985. *Estimation of Economies of Scale in Nineteenth Century United States Manufacturing*. New York: Garland Press.

Azariadis, Costas. 1996. "The Economics of Poverty Traps: Part One: Complete Markets," *Journal of Economic Growth* 1(4): 449–496.

Balassa, Bela. 1991. *Economic Policies in the Pacific Area Developing Countries*. New York: New York University Press.

Banks, Arthur S. 1979. *Cross-National Time-Series Data Archive User's Manual.* Binghamton, NY: SUNY Binghamton.

———. 1996. *Cross-National Time-Series Data*. Binghamton, NY: SUNY Binghamton.

Banning, Lance. 1995. *Sacred Fire of Liberty. James Madison*. Ithaca: Cornell University Press.

Barman, Roderick J. 1988. *Brazil: The Forging of a Nation, 1798–1852*. Stanford: Stanford University Press.

Barrett, David B., ed. 1982. *World Christian Encyclopedia*. Oxford: Oxford University Press.

Barro, Robert J. 1991. "Economic Growth in a Cross-Section of Countries," *Quarterly Journal of Economics* 106(2): 408–443.

———. 1997. *Determinants of Economic Growth: A Cross-Country Empirical Study*. Cambridge, MA: MIT Press.

Barzel, Yoram. 1989. *The Economic Analysis of Property Rights*. New York: Cambridge University Press.

Beatty, Edward. 1996. "The Political Basis of Industrialization in Mexico before 1911," Ph.D. Dissertation, Stanford University.

Becker, Gary S. 1983. "A Theory of Competition among Pressure Groups for Political Influence," *Quarterly Journal of Economics* 98(3): 371–400.

Bello, Walden, and Stephanie Rosenfeld. 1990. *Dragons in Distress: Asia's Miracle Economies in Crisis*. San Francisco: Jabula Desktop.

Benjamin, Thomas, and Mark Wasserman, eds. 1990. *Provinces of the Revolution: Essays on Regional Mexican History, 1910–1929*. Albuquerque: University of New Mexico Press.

Bernard, A. B., and C. I. Jones. 1996. "Productivity across Industries and Countries: Time Series Theory and Evidence," *The Review of Economics and Statistics* 78(1): 35–146.

Bernstein, Marvin D. 1964. *The Mexican Mining Industry, 1850–1950: A Study of the Interaction of Politics, Economics, and Technology*. Albany: State University of New York, pp. 17–94.

Bhagwati, Jagdish. 1995. *India in Transition: Freeing the Economy*. Oxford: Clarendon Press.

Bollen, Kenneth A. 1990. "Political Democracy: Conceptual and Measurement Traps," *Studies in Comparative International Development* (spring): 7–24.

Bortz, Jeffrey. 1995. "The Genesis of the Mexican Labor Relations System: Federal Labor Policy and the Textile Industry, 1925–1940," *The Americas* 52(1): 43–69.

———. 1997. "'Without Any More Law Than Their Own Caprice': Cotton Textile Workers and the Challenge to Factory Authority during the Mexican Revolution," *International Review of Social History* 42: 253–288.

Breton, Albert, and Ronald Wintrobe. 1982. *The Logic of Bureaucratic Conduct*. Cambridge: Cambridge University Press.

Brown, Jonathan C. 1993. *Oil and Revolution in Mexico*. Berkeley: University of California Press.

Buchanan, Iain. 1972. *Singapore in Southeast Asia: An Economic and Political Appraisal*. London: G. Bell and Sons.

Bueno de Mesquita, Bruce. 1978. "Redistricting and Political Integration in India." *Comparative Political Studies* 11(2): 279–288.

Bueno de Mesquita, Bruce, David Newman, and Alvin Rabushka. 1985. *Forecasting Political Events*. New Haven and London: Yale University Press.

———. 1996. *Red Flag Over Hong Kong*. Chatham, NJ: Chatham House.

Bueno de Mesquita, Bruce, James D. Morrow, Randolph M. Siverson, and Alastair Smith. 1999a. "Endogenous Political Institutions and the Survival of Leaders," Working Paper, Hoover Institution, Stanford University.

———. 1999b. "Policy Failure and Political Survival: The Contribution of Political Institutions," *Journal of Conflict Resolution* 43:147–161.

Bueno de Mesquita, Bruce, and Randolph M. Siverson. 1997. "Nasty or Nice: Political Systems, Endogenous Norms, and the Treatment of Adversaries," *Journal of Conflict Resolution* 41: 175–199.

Burkholder, Mark A., and Lyman L. Johnson. 1990. *Colonial Latin America*. New York: Oxford University Press.

Calvert, Randall L. 1994. "Explaining Social Order: Internalization, External Enforcement, or Equilibrium?" Department of Political Science, University of Rochester.

Campos, Jose Edgardo, and Hilton L. Root. 1996. *The Key to the Asian Miracle: Making Shared Growth Credible*. Washington, DC: The Brookings Institution.

Cárdenas, Enrique. 1997. "A Macroeconomic Interpretation of Nineteenth-Century Mexico," in Stephen Haber, ed., *How Latin America Fell Behind: Essays on the Economic Histories of Brazil and Mexico, 1800–1914*, pp. 65–92. Stanford: Stanford University Press.

Case, William. 1995. "Malaysia: Aspects and Audiences of Legitimacy," in Muthiah Alagappa, ed., *Political Legitimacy in Southeast Asia*, pp. 69–107. Stanford: Stanford University Press.

Cass, David. 1965. "Optimum Growth in an Aggregative Model of Capital Accumulation," *Review of Economic Studies* 32: 223–240.

Chang, Mao-kui. 1993. "The Provincial Complex and Nationalism," in Chang Mao-kui et al., eds., *Ethnic Relationships and National Identification*, pp. 233–278. Taipei: Zhikucongshu.

Chen, Baizhu, and Yi Feng. 1996a. "Economic Development, Political Cost, and Democratic Transition: Theory, Statistical Testing and a Case Study." *Journal of Economic Development* 21: 185–220.

———. 1996b. "Some Political Determinants of Economic Growth." *European Journal of Political Economy* 12: 609–627.

———. 1999. "Economic Development and the Transition to Democracy—A Formal Model." *Social Choice and Welfare* 16(1): 1–16.

———. 1999. "Political Regime Change and Economic Development: A Formal Model." *Social Choice and Welfare* 16.

Chu, Yun-kan. 1996. "Taiwan's Unique Challenge," *Journal of Democracy* 7: 69–82.

Clark, Gregory. 1987. "Why Isn't the Whole World Developed? Lessons from the Cotton Mills," *Journal of Economic History* 47(1): 141–174.

Coatsworth, John H. 1978. "Obstacles to Economic Growth in Nineteenth Century Mexico," *American Historical Review* 83(1): 80–100.

———. 1981. *Growth Against Development: The Economic Impact of Railroads in Porfirian Mexico*. De Kalb: Northern Illinois University Press.

———. 1990. *Los Orígines del Atraso*. Mexico, D.F.: Alianza Editorial Mexicana.

Comptroller's Office, Government of Thailand. 1997. *The Income Summary of the Thai Public Enterprises*.

Crystal, David. 1990. *The Cambridge Encyclopedia*. Cambridge: Cambridge University Press.

Cukierman, Alex, Sebastian Edwards, and Guido Tabellini. 1992. "Seigniorage and Political Instability," *The American Economic Review* 82: 537–555.

Davis, Lance E. 1963. "Capital Immobilities and Finance Capitalism: A Study of Economic Evolution in the United States, 1820–1920," *Explorations in Entrepreneurial History*. Series 2, vol. 1, no. 1 (Fall).

de Allende Costa, Veronica, and Luis Felipe López Calva. 1991. "La economía mexicana durante el Porfiriato: analisis macroeconómico y interacción entre los sectores público y privado," Tesis de Licenciatura, Departamento de Economía, Universidad de las Américas-Puebla, pp. 198–203.

Debreu, G. 1959. *The Theory of Value*. New York: Wiley.

de Figueiredo, Rui, and Barry R. Weingast. 1999. "Rationality of Fear: Political Opportunism and Ethnic Conflict," in Jack Snyder and Barbara Walter, eds., *Civil Wars*. New York: Columbia University Press.

Deininger, Klaus, and Lyn Squire. 1996. "Measuring Income Inequality: A New Data Base," Working Paper, The World Bank.

Denzau, Arthur T., and Douglass C. North. 1994. "Shared Mental Models: Ideologies and Institutions," *Kyklos* 47: 3–31.

Department of Budget, Accounting and Statistics, Taiwan Provincial Government, Republic of China. 1996. *Statistical Yearbook of Taiwan Province* No. 55. Taipei: Taiwan Provincial Government, Republic of China.

Deutsch, Karl W. 1961. "Social Mobilization and Political Development," *American Political Science Review* 55: 493.

Diamond, Larry. 1997. "Prospects for Democratic Development in Africa," *Hoover Essays in Public Policy No. 74*. Stanford, CA: Hoover Institution Press.

———. 1999. "Democratization." Unpublished manuscript. Hoover Institution.

Dunne, John. 1972. *Modern Revolutions: An Introduction to the Analysis of a Political Phenomenon*. Cambridge, England: Cambridge University Press.

Easton, David. 1965. *A Systems Analysis of Political Life*. New York: Wiley.

Eggertsson, Thrainn. 1990. *Economic Behavior and Institutions*. New York: Cambridge University Press.

Engerman, Stanley L., and Kenneth L. Sokoloff. 1997. "Factor Endowments, Institutions, and Differential Paths of Growth among New World Economies: A

View from Economic Historians of the United States," in Stephen Haber, ed., *How Latin America Fell Behind*, pp. 269–304. Stanford, CA: Stanford University Press.

Evans, Peter B., Dietrich Rueschemeyer, and Theda Skocpol. 1985. *Bringing the State Back In*. New York: Cambridge University Press.

Falcón, Romana. 1977. *El agrarismo en Veracruz: La etapa radical, 1928–1935*. Mexico: El Colegio de México.

———. 1984. *Revolución y caciquismo: San Luis Potosí, 1910–1938*. Mexico: El Colegio de México.

Feng, Yi. 1995. "Regime, Polity and Economic Performance: The Latin American Experience," *Growth and Change* 26: 77–104.

———. 1997a. "Democracy, Political Stability and Economic Growth," *British Journal of Political Science* 27: 391–418.

———. 1997b. "Growth and Democracy: The Sub-Saharan African Case, 1960–1992," *The Review of Black Political Economy* 25: 93–124.

———. 1997c. *Democracy, Governance, and Economic Performance: Theory, Data Analysis, and Case Studies*. Manuscript.

Feng, Yi, and Baizhu Chen. 1996. "Political Environment and Economic Growth," *Social and Economic Studies* 45: 77–105.

———. 1997. "Government Capacity and Private Investment: A Study of Developing Countries," in Marina Arbetman and Jacek Kugler, eds., *Political Capacity and Economic Behavior*, pp. 101–114. Boulder, CO: Westview Press.

Feng, Yi, and Antonio Hsiang. 1997. "Developmental Experience and Issues in Latin America," in K. T. Liou, ed., *The Handbook of Economic Development*, pp. 523–549. New York: Marcel Dekker.

Feng, Yi, and Paul J. Zak. 1998. "Growth and the Transition to Democracy," Working Paper, Claremont Graduate University.

———. 1999. "The Determinant of Democratic Transitions," *Journal of Conflict Resolution* 43(2): 162–177.

Ficker, Sandra Kuntz. 1995. *Empresa extranjera y mercado interno: el Ferrocarril Central Mexicano, 1880–1907*. Mexico: El Colegio de México.

Ficker, Sandra Kuntz, and Paolo Riguzzi, eds. 1996. *Ferrocarriles y vida económica en México, 1850–1950: del surgimiento tardio al decaimiento precoz*. Mexico: El Colegio Mexiquense.

Finkelman, Paul. 1996. *Slavery and the Founders: Race and Liberty in the Age of Jefferson*. Armonk, NY: Sharpe.

Fischer, Stanley. 1993. "The Role of Macroeconomic Factors in Growth," *Journal of Monetary Economics* 32: 485–512.

Fletcher, Matthew, and Julian Gearing. 1996. "Now It's Up to Him: With Chavalit Poised to Take His Dream Job, the Economy Is the First Priority," *Asia Week* November 29, pp. 20–22.

Frank, Robert, H. Frank, and Philip J. Cook. 1995. *The Winner-Take-All Society: How More and More Americans Compete for Ever Fewer and Bigger Prizes, Encouraging*

Economic Waste, Income Inequality, and an Impoverished Cultural Life. New York: Free Press.

Freedom House. 1997. "Tables of Independent States: Comparative Measures of Freedom," *Freedom Review* 28: 12–13.

Friedman, Milton. 1961. "Capitalism and Freedom," *New Individualist Review* 1: 3–10.

———. 1962. *Capitalism and Freedom*. Chicago: University of Chicago Press.

Fukuyama, Francis. 1995. *Trust: The Social Virtues and the Creation of Prosperity*. New York: Free Press.

Galenson, David W. 1981. *White Servitude in Colonial America*. New York: Cambridge University Press.

Gastil, Raymond D. 1978–1989. *Freedom in the World*. Westport, CT: Greenwood Press.

Gayle, Dennis J. 1986. *The Small Developing State*. Aldershot, Hampshire: Gower.

Geddes, Barbara. 1991. "How the Cases You Choose Affect the Answers You Get: Selection Bias in Comparative Politics," in James A. Stimson, ed., *Political Analysis: An Annual Publication of the Methodology Section of the American Political Science Association, Volume 2*. Ann Arbor: University of Michigan Press.

George, Alexander L. 1979. "Case Studies and Theory Development: The Method of Structured, Focused Comparison," in Paul Gordon Lauren, ed., *Diplomacy: New Approaches in History, Theory, and Policy*, pp. 43–68. New York: Free Press.

Gerschenkron, Alexander. 1962. *Economic Backwardness in Historical Perspective*. Cambridge, MA: Belknap Press of Harvard University Press.

Gibbons, Robert. 1992. *Game Theory for Applied Economists*. Princeton, NJ: Princeton University Press.

Gilly, Adolfo. 1994. *La revolución interrumpida: edición corregida y aumentada*. Mexico: Ediciones Era.

Gochman, Charles S., and Zeev Maoz. 1984. "Serious Interstate Disputes, 1816–1976," *Journal of Conflict Resolution* 28: 585–616.

Goldstein, Steven M. 1993. *Mini-Dragons*. New York: St. Martin's Press.

Goldstone, Jack. 1991. *Revolution and Rebellion in the Early Modern World*. Berkeley: University of California Press.

Gootenberg, Paul. 1989. *Between Silver and Guano: Commercial Policy and the State in Post Independence Peru*. Princeton, NJ: Princeton University Press.

Graham-Clark, William A. 1909. "Cuba, Mexico, and Central America." Part 1. *Cotton Goods in Latin America*. Washington, DC: U.S. Government Printing Office.

Green, Jack P. 1986. *Peripheries and Center*. New York: Norton.

Greene, William H. 1993. *Econometric Analysis*. New York: Macmillan.

Greenwald, Bruce, and Joseph E. Stiglitz. 1986. "Externalities in Economies with Imperfect Information and Incomplete Markets," *Quarterly Journal of Economics* 101: 229–264.

Greenwood, Jeremy, and Boyan Jovanovic. 1992. "Financial Development, Growth and the Distribution of Income," *Journal of Political Economy* 99: 1076–1107.

Greif, Avner. 1997. "Microtheory and Recent Developments in the Study of Economic Institutions Through Economic History," in David M. Kreps and Kenneth F. Wallis, eds., *Advances in Economic Theory Vol. II,* pp. 79–113. Cambridge: Cambridge University Press.

———. 1998. *Genoa and the Maghribi Traders: Historical and Comparative Institutional Analysis.* New York: Cambridge University Press.

Greif, Avner, Paul Milgrom, and Barry R. Weingast. 1994. "Coordination, Commitment, and Enforcement: The Case of the Merchant Guild," *Journal of Political Economy* 102: 745–776.

Gwartney, James D., Robert Lawson, and Walter Block. 1996. *Economic Freedom of the World: 1975–1995.* Vancouver, BC: The Fraser Institute.

Haavelmo, Trygve. 1954. *A Study in the Theory of Economic Evolution.* Amsterdam: North-Holland.

Haber, Stephen H. 1989. *Industry and Underdevelopment: The Industrialization of Mexico, 1890–1940.* Stanford, CA: Stanford University Press.

———. 1991. "Industrial Concentration and the Capital Markets: A Comparative Study of Brazil, Mexico, and the United States, 1830–1930," *Journal of Economic History* 51(3): 559–580.

———. 1992. "Assessing the Obstacles to Industrialization: The Mexican Economy, 1830–1940," *Journal of Latin American Studies* 24(1): 1–32.

———, ed. 1997. *How Latin America Fell Behind: Essays on the Economic Histories of Brazil and Mexico, 1800–1914.* Stanford, CA: Stanford University Press.

Haber, Stephen, and Herbert Klein. 1993. "Consecuencias Económicas de la Independencia Brasileña," in Leandro Prados de la Escosura y Samuel Amaral, ed., *La Independencia Americana: Consecuencias Económicas,* pp. 147–163. Madrid: Alianza Editorial.

Haggard, Stephen, and R. R. Kaufman. 1993. *The Political Economy of Democratic Transitions.* New York: Cambridge University Press.

Hall, Linda B. 1995. *Oil, Banks, and Politics: The United States and Postrevolutionary Mexico, 1917–1924.* Austin: University of Texas Press.

Hart, John Mason. 1987. *Revolutionary Mexico: The Coming and Process of the Mexican Revolution.* Berkeley: University of California Press.

Hartz, Louis. 1955. *The Liberal Tradition in America.* New York: Harcourt, Brace and World.

Hayek, Friedrich A. von. 1944. *The Road to Serfdom.* Chicago: University of Chicago Press.

Higley, John, and Richard Gunther. 1991. *Elites and Democratic Consolidation in Latin America and Southern Europe.* New York: Cambridge University Press.

Holden, Robert H. 1994. *Mexico and the Survey of Public Lands: The Management of Modernization, 1876–1911.* De Kalb: Northern Illinois University Press.

Horowitz, Donald S. 1985. *Ethnic Groups in Conflict.* Berkeley: University of California Press.

Huntington, Samuel P. 1987. *Understanding Political Development.* Boston: Little, Brown.

———. 1991. *The Third Wave: Democratization in the Late Twentieth Century.* Norman: University of Oklahoma Press.

Hurwicz, Leonid. 1993. "Toward a Framework for Analyzing Institutions and Institutional Change," in Samuel Bowles, Herbert Gintis, and Bo Gustafsson, eds., *Markets and Democracy: Participation, Accountability, and Efficiency,* pp. 51–67. Cambridge: Cambridge University Press.

Inkeles, Alex. 1991. *On Measuring Democracy.* New Brunswick, NJ: Transaction.

Instituto Nacional de Estadística Geografía e Informática. 1994. *Estadísticas históricas de México.* Mexico: Instituto Nacional de Estadística Geografía e Informática.

Jaggers, Keith, and Ted R. Gurr. 1996. "Polity III: Regime Change and Political Authority, 1800–1994." Ann Arbor, MI: Inter-University Consortium for Political and Social Research.

Johnson, John W. 1964. *The Military and Society in Latin America.* Stanford, CA: Stanford University Press.

Johnson, Ronald N., and Allen Parkman. 1983. "Spatial Monopoly, Non-Zero Profits, and Entry Deterrence: The Case of Cement," *The Review of Economics and Statistics* 65(3): 431–439.

Kane, Nancy F. 1988. *Textiles in Transition: Technology, Wages, and Industry Relocation in the U.S. Textile Industry.* Westport, CT: Greenwood Press.

Karl, Terry. 1991. "Getting to Democracy," in Commission on Behavioral and Social Sciences and Education, National Research Council, ed., *The Transition to Democracy: Proceedings of a Workshop,* pp. 29–40. Washington, DC: National Academy Press.

Katz, Friedrich. 1981. *The Secret War in Mexico: Europe, the United States and the Mexican Revolution.* Chicago: University of Chicago Press.

———. 1986. "Mexico: Restored Republic and Porfiriato, 1867–1910," in Leslie Bethell, ed., *The Cambridge History of Latin America: Volume 5, 1870–1930,* pp. 3–78. Cambridge: Cambridge University Press.

Knack, Stephen, and Phillip Keefer. 1995. "Institutions and Economic Performance: Cross-Country Tests Using Alternative Institutional Measures." *Economics and Politics* 7: 207–227.

Knight, Alan. 1987. *The Mexican Revolution.* Cambridge: Cambridge University Press.

Knight, Frank. 1921. *Risk, Uncertainty and Profit.* Boston: Houghton Mifflin.

Kochanek, Stanley A. 1987. "Briefcase Politics in India: The Congress Party and the Business Elite." *Asian Survey* 27(12): 1278–1301.

Koh, B. C. 1996. "South Korea in 1995: Tremors of Transition," *Asian Survey* 36: 53–60.

Koopmans, Tjalling C. 1965. "On the Concept of Optimal Economic Growth," in Pontificia Accademia delle Scienze, ed., *The Econometric Approach to Development Planning.* Chicago: Rand McNally.

Kormendi, Roger C., and Philip G. Meguire. 1985. "Macroeconomic Determinants of Growth: Cross-Country Evidence," *Journal of Monetary Economics* 16: 141–163.

Krueger, Anne. 1974. "Political Economy of Rent-Seeking Society," *American Economic Review* 64: 291–303.

Kuznets, Simon. 1955. "Economic Growth and Income Inequality," *American Economic Review* 49: 1–28.

Langer, William L. 1972. *Encyclopedia of World History.* Boston: Houghton Mifflin.

Leng, Tse-kang. 1996. *The Taiwan-China Connection: Democracy and Development Across the Taiwan Straits.* Boulder, CO: Westview Press.

Levine, Ross, and David Renelt. 1992. "A Sensitivity Analysis of Cross-Country Growth Regressions," *American Economic Review* 82: 942–963.

Liebcap, Gary D. 1989. *Contracting for Property Rights.* Cambridge, England: Cambridge University Press.

Lijphart, Arend. 1975. *The Politics of Accommodation: Pluralism and Democracy in the Netherlands.* 2d ed. Berkeley: University of California Press.

Lim, Chong Yah. 1988. *Policy Options for the Singapore Economy.* London: McGraw-Hill.

Lin, Chung-cheng, and Lin He-ling. 1993. "Economic Difference among Different Ethnic Groups on Taiwan," in Chang Mao-kui et al. eds., *Ethnic Relationships and National Identification*, pp. 101–161. Taipei: Zhikucongshu.

Lipset, Seymour M. 1959. "Some Social Requisites of Democracy: Economic Development and Political Legitimacy," *American Political Science Review* 53: 69–105.

———. 1960. *Political Man.* Garden City, NY: Anchor Books.

———. 1963. *The First New Nation: The United States in Historical and Comparative Perspective.* New York: Basic Books.

Loayza, Norman V. 1996. "The Economics of the Informal Sector: A Simple Model and Some Empirical Evidence from Latin America," *Carnegie-Rochester Conference Series on Public Policy*, 129–162.

Lockhart, James, and Stuart B. Schwartz. 1983. *Early Latin America.* Cambridge, England: London, Saunders & Otley.

Londregan, John, and Keith Poole. 1990. "Poverty, the Coup Trap and Seizure of Executive Power," *World Politics* 42: 151–183.

———. 1992. "The Seizure of Executive Power and Economic Growth: Some Additional Evidence," in Alex Cukierman, Zvi Hercowitz, and Leonardo Leiderman, eds., *Political Economy, Growth, and Business Cycles*, pp. 51–80. Cambridge, MA: MIT Press.

Lucas, Robert E., Jr. 1988. "On the Mechanics of Economic Development," *Journal of Monetary Economics* 22: 3–42.

———. 1993. "Making a Miracle," *Econometrica* 61(2): 251–272.

Lynch, John. 1986. *Spanish American Revolutions, 1808–1826.* 2d ed. New York: Norton.

Marichal, Carlos. 1997. "Obstacles to the Development of Capital Markets in Nineteenth Century Mexico," in Stephen Haber, ed., *How Latin America Fell Behind: Essays on the Economic Histories of Brazil and Mexico, 1800–1914,* pp. 118–145. Stanford, CA: Stanford University Press.

Marshall, Alfred. 1890. *Principles of Economics.* London: Macmillan and Co.

Maurer, Noel. 1997. "Finance and Oligarchy: Banks, Politics, and Economic Growth in Mexico, 1876–1928," Ph.D. Dissertation, Stanford University.

Mauzy, Diane K. 1996."Singapore in 1995: Consolidating the Succession," *Asian Survey* 36: 117–122.

McKinlay, Robert D., and A. S. Cohan. 1975. "A Comparative Analysis of the Political and Economic Performance of Military and Civilian Regimes: A Cross-National Aggregate Study." *Comparative Politics* 8: 1–30.

Meyer, Jean. 1986. "Mexico: Revolution and Reconstruction in the 1920s," in Leslie Bethell, ed., *The Cambridge History of Latin America: Volume 5, 1870–1930,* pp. 155–196. Cambridge: Cambridge University Press.

Milgrom, Paul, and John Roberts. 1990. *Economics, Organization, and Management.* Englewood Cliffs, NJ: Prentice Hall.

Milken Institute. 1998. *The Milken Institute Global Conference.* Santa Monica, CA: The Milken Institute (March).

Mises, Ludwig von. 1981. *Socialism: An Economic and Sociological Analysis.* Indianapolis, IN: Liberty Classics.

Moore, Barrington, Jr. 1967. *Social Origins of Dictatorship and Democracy.* Boston: Little, Brown.

Morell, David, and Chai-anan Samudavanija. 1981. *Political Conflict in Thailand: Reform, Reaction, and Revolution.* Cambridge, MA: Oelgeschlager, Gunn, and Hain Publishers.

Moreno, Humberto Morales. 1996. "Economic Elites and Political Power in Mexico, 1898–1910," *Bulletin of Latin American Research* 15(1): 101–121.

Morgan, Edmund. 1992. *Birth of the New Nation: 1763–1787.* 3d ed. Chicago: University of Chicago Press.

Morrow, James D. 1994. "Modeling the Forms of Cooperation: Distribution versus Information," *International Organization* 48: 387–423.

Morse, Richard M. 1964. "The Heritage of Latin America," in Louis Hartz, ed., *The Founding of New Societies.* New York: Harcourt, Brace, and World.

Muscat, Robert. 1994. *The Fifth Tiger: A Study of Thai Development Policy.* New York: United Nations University Press.

Musgrave, R. 1959. *The Theory of Public Finance: A Study in Public Economy.* New York: McGraw-Hill.

Neher, Clark. 1992. "Political Succession in Thailand." *Asian Survey* 32: 585–605.

North, Douglass C. 1981. *Structure and Change in Economic History.* New York: Norton.

———. 1983. "Toward a Theory of Institutional Change," in William A. Barnett,

Melvin J. Hinich, and Norman J. Schofield, eds., *Political Economy: Institutions, Competition, and Representation*. Cambridge, England: Cambridge University Press.

———. 1988. "Institutions and Economic Growth: An Historical Introduction," in Michael A. Walker, ed., *Freedom, Democracy and Economic Welfare*, pp. 3–25. Canada: The Fraser Institute.

———. 1990. *Institutions, Institutional Change, and Economic Performance*. New York: Cambridge University Press.

North, Douglass C., and Andrew R. Rutten. 1987. "The Northwest Ordinance in Historical Perspective," in D. Klingaman and R. Vedder (eds.), *Essays on the Old Northwest*. Athens: Ohio University Press.

North, Douglass C., and Barry R. Weingast. 1989. "Constitutions and Commitment: The Institutions Governing Public Choice in Seventeenth Century England," *Journal of Economic History* 44: 803–832.

O'Donnell, Guillermo, and Philippe Schmitter. 1988. *Transitions from Authoritarian Rule: Tentative Conclusions about Uncertain Democracies*. Baltimore: Johns Hopkins University Press.

Ojeda, Leticia Gamboa. 1984. "La CROM en Puebla y el movimiento obrero textil en los Años 20," in *Memorias del encuentro sobre historia del movimiento obrero II*. Puebla, Mexico: Universidad Auto'noma de Puebla.

———. 1985. *Los Empresarios De Ayer: El Grupo Dominante En La Industria Textil De Puebla, 1906–1929*. Puebla: Editorial Universidad Autónoma de Puebla.

Olson, Mancur. 1982. *The Rise and Decline of Nations*. New Haven and London: Yale University Press.

Özler, Sule, and Dani Rodrik. 1992. "External Shocks, Politics and Private Investment," *Journal of Development Economics* 39: 141–162.

Paige, Jeffrey M. 1975. *Agrarian Revolution: Social Movements and Export Agriculture in the Underdeveloped World*. London: Free Press.

Pastor, Manuel Jr.; and Eric Hilt. 1993. "Private Investment and Democracy in Latin America," *World Development* 21(4): 489–507.

Perotti, Roberto. 1996. "Growth, Income Distribution, and Democracy: What the Data Say," *Journal of Economic Growth* 1(2): 149–187.

Perry, Laurens Ballard. 1978. *Juárez and Díaz: Machine Politics in Mexico*. De Kalb: Northern Illinois University Press.

Persson, Torsten, and Guido Tabellini. 1994. "Is Inequality Harmful for Growth? Theory and Evidence," *American Economic Review* 84: 600–621.

Potter, David C. 1986. *India's Political Administrators, 1919–1983*. Oxford: Clarendon Press.

Prasad, K. N. 1995. *India's Economic Problems: Regional Aspects*. New Delhi: MD Publications.

Primer Congreso Nacional de Industriales. 1918. *Reseña y memorias del primer congreso nacional de industriales reunido en la Ciudad de México bajo el patrocinio de la Secretaría de Industria, Comercio y Trabajo*. Mexico: Secretaría de Industria Comercio y Trabajo.

Przeworski, Adam. 1991. *Democracy and the Market*. New York: Cambridge University Press.

Przeworski, Adam, and Fernando Limongi. 1993. "Political Regimes and Economic Growth," *Journal of Economic Perspectives* 7(3): 51–69.

Putnam, Robert. 1993. *Making Democracy Work*. Princeton: Princeton University Press.

Pye, Lucian. 1966. *Aspects of Political Development*. Boston: Little, Brown.

Rae, Douglas. 1968. "A Note on the Fractionalization of Some European Party Systems," *Comparative Political Studies* 1: 413–418.

Rakove, Jack. 1979. *The Beginnings of National Politics*. Baltimore: Johns Hopkins University Press.

———. 1995. *Original Meanings*. New York: Knopf.

Rakove, Jack, Andrew Rutten, and Barry R. Weingast. 1999. "Ideas, Interests, and Credible Commitments in the American Revolution." Working Paper, Hoover Institution, Stanford University.

Rancaño, Mario Ramírez. 1987. *Burguesía Textil Y Política En La Revolución Mexicana*. Mexico: Universidad Nacional Autónoma de México.

Rebelo, Sergio. 1992. "Growth in Open Economies," *Carnegie-Rochester Conference Series on Public Policy*, 36: 5–46.

Reid, John Phillip. 1995. *Constitutional History of the American Revolution*, abridged ed. Madison: University of Wisconsin Press.

Reynolds, Clark W. 1970. *The Mexican Economy: Twentieth Century Structure and Growth*. New Haven and London: Yale University Press.

Riker, William H., and David L. Weimer. 1993. "The Economic and Political Liberalization of Socialism: The Fundamental Problem of Property Rights," *Social Philosophy and Policy* 10: 79–102.

Roemer, John. 1995. "On the Relationship between Economic Development and Political Democracy," in Amiya Kumar Bagchi, ed., *Democracy and Development*, pp. 28–55. New York: St. Martin's Press.

Romano, Roberta. 1985. "Law as a Product: Some Pieces of the Incorporation Puzzle," *Journal of Law, Economics, and Organization* 1: 225–283.

Romer, Paul M. 1986. "Increasing Returns and Long-run Growth," *Journal of Political Economy* 94: 1002–1037.

Root, Hilton L. 1994. *The Fountain of Privilege: Political Foundations of Markets in Old Regime France and England*. Berkeley: University of California Press.

———. 1996. *Small Countries: Big Lessons, Governance, and the Rise of East Asia*. New York: Oxford University Press.

———. 1997. "Transparency and China's Aspirations." *The Asian Wall Street Journal* January 13.

Safford, Frank. 1987. "Politics, Ideology, and Society," in Leslie Bethell, ed., *Spanish America after Independence, c. 1820—c. 1870*. New York: Cambridge University Press.

Salvucci, Richard J. 1997. "Mexican National Income in the Era of Independence, 1800–45," in Stephen Haber, ed., *How Latin America Fell Behind: Essays on the Economic Histories of Brazil and Mexico, 1800–1914*, pp. 216–242. Stanford, CA: Stanford University Press.

Samudavanija, Chai-Anan. 1982. "The Thai Young Turk," *Singapore Institute for Southeast Asian Studies* 17(3): 2–19.

Sanders, David. 1981. *Patterns of Political Instability*. New York: St. Martin's Press.

Schlossstein, Steven. 1991. *Asia's New Little Dragons: The Dynamic Emergence of Indonesia, Thailand, and Malaysia*. Chicago: Contemporary Books.

Sened, Itai. 1997. *The Political Institution of Private Property*. New York: Cambridge University Press.

Shirk, Susan L. 1993. *The Political Logic of Economic Reform in China*. Berkeley: University of California Press.

Sirowy, Larry, and Alex Inkeles. 1990. "The Effects of Democracy on Economic Growth and Inequality: A Review," *Studies in Comparative International Development* 25: 126–157.

Skidmore, Thomas E., and Peter H. Smith. 1992. *Modern Latin America*. 3d ed. New York: Oxford University Press.

Skocpol, Theda. 1979. *States and Social Revolutions*. New York: Cambridge University Press.

Skowronek, Stephen. 1982. *Building the New American State*. New York: Cambridge University Press.

Small, Melvin, and J. David Singer. 1982. *Resort to Arms: International and Civil Wars, 1816–1980*. Beverly Hills, CA: Sage.

Smith, Adam. 1937 [1776]. *An Inquiry into the Nature and Causes of the Wealth of Nations*. New York: Modern Library.

———. 1961. *An Inquiry into the Nature and Causes of the Wealth of Nations,* edited by Bruce Mazlish. Indianapolis: Bobbs-Merrill.

Sokoloff, Kenneth L. 1984. "Was the Transition from the Artisanal Shop to the Nonmechanized Factory Associated with Gains in Efficiency? Evidence from the U.S. Manufacturing Censuses of 1820 and 1850," *Explorations in Economic History* 21(4): 351–382.

Solow, Robert M. 1956. "A Contribution to the Theory of Economic Growth," *Quarterly Review of Economics* 70: 65–94.

Spuler, Bertold, C. G. Allen, and N. Saunders. 1977. *Rulers and Governments of the World*. New York: Bowker.

Stevens, Donald Fithian. 1991. *Origins of Instability in Early Republican Mexico*. Durham: Duke University Press.

Stiglitz, Joseph E. 1994. *Whither Socialism?* Cambridge, MA: MIT Press.

Straszheim, Donald. 1998. "The Realities of Global Competition," paper presented at the annual meeting of International Studies Association, West, in Claremont, October 9–10.

Summerhill, William. 1999. *Order Against Progress: Government, Foreign Investment, and Railroads in Brazil, 1852–1913.* Stanford, CA: Stanford University Press.

Summers, Robert, and Alan Heston. 1991. "The Penn World Table (Mark 5): An Expanded Set of International Comparisons," *Quarterly Journal of Economics* 106(2): 327–368.

———. 1995. *The Penn World Table (Mark 5.6).* Cambridge, MA: National Bureau of Economic Research.

Tai, Hung-chao. 1989. *Confucianism and Economic Development.* Washington, DC: Washington Institute Press.

Tenenbaum, Barbara. 1986. *The Politics of Penury: Debt and Taxes in Mexico, 1821–1856.* Albuquerque: University of New Mexico Press.

Tilly, Charles. 1978. *From Mobilization to Revolution.* New York: Random House.

———. 1993. *European Revolututions, 1492–1992.* Cambridge, MA: Blackwell.

Tocqueville, Alexis de. 1835. *Democracy in America,* translated by Henry Reeve. London: Saunders and Otley.

Tollison, Robert. 1981. "Rent-Seeking," *Kyklos.* 35: 575–602.

Trebilock, Michael J. 1995. "What Makes Poor Countries Poor? The Role of Institutional Capital in Economic Development," Working Paper No. WPS-38, University of Toronto Faculty of Law.

Tucker, Robert W., and David C. Hendrickson. 1982. *The Fall of the First British Empire: Origins of the War of American Independence.* Baltimore: Johns Hopkins University Press.

Tullock, Gordon. 1975. "The Transitional Gains Trap," *Bell Journal of Economics* 6: 671–678.

Venieris, Yiannis, and Dipak Gupta. 1985. "Sociopolitical and Economic Dimensions of Development: A Cross-Section Model," *Economic Development and Cultural Change* 31: 727–756.

———. 1986. "Income Distribution and Socio-Political Instability as Determinants of Savings: A Cross-Sectional Model," *Journal of Political Economy* 94(4): 873–883.

Venieris, Yiannis, and Douglas Stewart. 1987. "Sociopolitical Instability, Inequality and Consumption Behavior," *Journal of Economic Development* 12(2): 7–20.

Wade, Robert. 1985. "The Market for Public Office: Why the Indian State Is not Better at Development," *World Development* 13(4): 467–497.

Wasserman, Mark. 1993. *Persistent Oligarchs: Elites and Politics in Chihuahua, Mexico, 1910–1940.* Durham, NC: Duke University Press.

Weber, Max. 1978. "Patriarchalism and Patrimonialism," in Guenther Roth and Claus Wittich, eds., *Economy and Society: An Outline of Interpretive Sociology,* p. 236. Berkeley: University of California Press.

Weingast, Barry R. 1995. "The Economic Role of Political Institutions: Market-Preserving Federalism and Economic Development," *Journal of Law, Economics, and Organization* 11: 1–31.

———. 1997a. "The Political Foundations of Democracy and the Rule of Law," *American Political Science Review* 91: 245–263.

———. 1997b. "The Political Foundations of Limited Government: Parliament and Sovereign Debt in 17th- and 18th-Century England," in John N. Drobak and John V. C. Nye, eds. *The Frontiers of the New Institutional Economics,* pp. 213–246. San Diego, CA: Academic Press.

———. 1998. "Political Stability and Civil War: Institutions, Commitment, and American Democracy," in Robert Bates, Avner Greif, Margaret Levi, Jean-Laurent Rosenthal, and Barry R. Weingast, eds., *Analytic Narratives.* Princeton, NJ: Princeton University Press.

Wiarda, Howard J., and Harvey F. Kline. 1990. *Latin American Politics and Development.* 3d ed. Boulder, CO: Westview Press.

Womack, John Jr. 1969. *Zapata and the Mexican Revolution.* New York: Knopf.

———. 1978. "The Mexican Economy During the Revolution, 1910–1922: Historiography and Analysis," *Marxist Perspectives* 1(4): 80–123.

———. 1986. "The Mexican Revolution, 1910–1920," in Leslie Bethell, ed., *The Cambridge History of Latin America: Volume 5, 1870–1930,* pp. 79–154. Cambridge: Cambridge University Press.

Wood, Gordon S. 1969. *The Creation of the American Republic, 1776–1787.* New York: Norton.

———. 1991. *Radicalism and the American Revolution.* New York: Vintage Books.

World Bank, The. 1993a. *Sustaining Rapid Development in East Asia and the Pacific.* Washington, DC: The World Bank.

———. 1993b. *World Tables of Economic and Social Indicators, 1950–1992.* Ann Arbor, MI: Inter-university Consortium for Political and Social Research.

Wu, Nai-te. 1993. "The Provincial Complex, Political Support, and National Identification," in Chang Mao-kui et al., eds., *Ethnic Relationships and National Identification,* pp. 27–52. Taipei: Zhikucongshu.

Yang, Sung Chul. 1994. *The North and South Korean Political System: A Comparative Analysis.* Boulder, CO: Westview Press.

Zak, Paul J. 2000. "Institutions, Property Rights, and Growth," *Advances in Macroeconomic Theory* 1. Forthcoming.

———. 1997a. "Optimal Government Policy and Endogenous Growth," Working Paper, Claremont Graduate University.

———. 1997b. "Larceny," *Claremont Graduate University,* working paper.

Zak, Paul J., and Yi Feng. 1998. "A Dynamic Theory of the Transition to Democracy," Working Paper, Claremont Graduate University.

Zwart, Frank de. 1994. *The Bureaucratic Merry-go-round: Manipulating the Transfer of Indian Civil Servants.* Amsterdam: Amsterdam University Press.

Contributors

Robert J. Barro is Robert C. Waggoner Professor of Economics at Harvard University, a senior fellow at the Hoover Institution, Stanford University, and a viewpoint columnist for *Business Week*. Recent publications include *Determinants of Economic Growth* (1997), *Macroeconomics*, 5th edition (1997), and *Getting It Right* (1996).

Bruce Bueno de Mesquita is a senior fellow at the Hoover Institution, Stanford University. Recent books include *Principles of International Politics* (2000), *European Community Decision Making* (with Frans Stokman, 1994), and *War and Reason* (with David Lalman, 1992).

Yi Feng is associate professor of politics and policy at Claremont Graduate University. Along with fifty other publications, his recent ones include *Financial Market Reform in China: Progress, Problems and Prospects* (forthcoming), "Economic Development and the Transition to Democracy: A Formal Model," *Social Choice and Welfare* (1999), and "Determinants of Democratic Transitions," *Journal of Conflict Resolution* (1999).

Stephen Haber is professor of history and political science at Stanford University and Peter and Helen Bing Senior Fellow at the Hoover Institution, Stanford University. He is also director of Stanford's Social Science History Institute. Haber's recent publications include: *How Latin America Fell Behind: Essays on the Economic Histories of Brazil and Mexico, 1800–1914* (1997) and "The Efficiency Consequences of Institutional Change: Financial Market Regulation and Industrial Productivity Growth in Brazil, 1866–1934," in John Coatsworth and Alan Taylor, eds., *Latin America and the World Economy* (1998).

James D. Morrow is professor of political science at the University of Michigan. His recent publications include "How Could Trade Affect Conflict?" *Journal of Peace Research* (1999), "The Political Determinants of International Trade: The Major Powers, 1907–1990," *American Political Science Review* (with Randolph M. Siverson and Tressa Tabares, 1998), and "When Do 'Relative Gains' Impede Trade?" *Journal of Conflict Resolution* (1997).

Nahalel Nellis received a master's degree from Stanford University's international policy studies program and currently is studying law at Cornell University.

Douglass C. North, a Nobel laureate in economics, is a senior fellow at the Hoover Institution, Stanford University, and Luce Professor of Law and Liberty at Washington University, St. Louis. His most recent book is *Institutions, Institutional Change and Economic Performance* (1990).

Armando Razo is a graduate student in political science at Stanford University. His current research focuses on the regulation of telecommunications, federalism, and the political economy of growth. Recent publications include (cowritten with Stephen Haber) "Political Instability and Economic Growth: Evidence from Revolutionary Mexico," *World Politics* (October 1998), and "The Rate of Growth of Productivity in Mexico: Evidence from the Textile Industry," *Journal of Latin American Studies* (October 1998).

Hilton L. Root is a senior fellow and director of global studies at the Milken Institute, where his research focuses on the global economy. With expertise in Asia, and Southeast Asia in particular, Root has extensively studied developing countries and the relationship between their economies and political systems. Recent publications include *The Key to the Asian Miracle* (with Jose Edgardo Campos, 1996) and *Small Countries, Big Lessons* (1996).

Randolph M. Siverson is professor of political science at the University of California, Davis. His publications include "War and the Survival of Political Leaders" and "The Political Determinants of International Trade," both articles in the *American Political Science Review* and *Strategic Politicians, Institutions and Foreign Policy* (1999).

Alastair Smith is assistant professor of political science at Yale University. His recent publications include "International Crises and Domestic Politics" (*American Political Science Review,*1998) and "Fighting Battles, Winning Wars" (*Journal of Conflict Resolution,* 1998).

Paul J. Zak is assistant professor in the school of politics and economics at Claremont Graduate University. Recent publications include *Currency Crises, Monetary Union, and the Conduct of Monetary Policy: A Debate Among Leading Economists* (as volume editor) (1999), "The Determinants of Democratic Transitions" (with Yi Feng) (*Journal of Conflict Resolution,* 1999); "Larceny" (*Economics of Governance,* forthcoming).

William Summerhill is associate professor of history, University of California, Los Angeles. Publications include *Order Against Progress: Government, Foreign Investment, and Railroads in Brazil, 1852–1913* (1999).

Barry R. Weingast is senior fellow at the Hoover Institution, Ward C. Krebs Family Professor, and chair, department of political science, Stanford University. His recent book (with Bates, Greif, Levi, and Rosenthal) is *Analytical Narratives* (1998).

Index